Human Trafficking

Human Trafficking

Edited by Maggy Lee

WILLAN
PUBLISHING

Published by

Willan Publishing
Culmcott House
Mill Street, Uffculme
Cullompton, Devon
EX15 3AT, UK
Tel: +44(0)1884 840337
Fax: +44(0)1884 840251
e-mail: info@willanpublishing.co.uk
website: www.willanpublishing.co.uk

Published simultaneously in the USA and Canada by

Willan Publishing
c/o ISBS, 920 NE 58th Ave, Suite 300,
Portland, Oregon 97213-3786, USA
Tel: +001(0)503 287 3093
Fax: +001(0)503 280 8832
e-mail: info@isbs.com
website: www.isbs.com

First published 2007

Hardback
ISBN 978-1-84392-242-1

Paperback
ISBN 978-1-84392-241-4

British Library Cataloguing-in-Publication Data

A catalogue record for this book is available from the British Library

Project managed by Deer Park Productions, Tavistock, Devon
Typeset by GCS, Leighton Buzzard, Bedfordshire
Printed and bound by T.J. International Ltd, Padstow, Cornwall

Contents

Acknowledgements

This book was made possible by the help and support of a number of people. I would like to thank the reviewers who provided useful suggestions and encouraging remarks about the original proposal. I am also grateful to Brian Willan at Willan Publishing for guiding the manuscript through to publication with much enthusiasm and patience.

The idea for this edited book came about as a result of conversations with Marla Asis and Nicola Piper at the 'Migrations in Asia and Europe' conference organised by the Scalabrini Migration Centre in the Philippines in January 2005. The Department of Sociology at the Universities of Essex and Hong Kong have provided an intellectually stimulating and convivial environment in which to pursue the book project. Much of the work was facilitated by a grant from the British Academy and generous sabbatical leave from the University of Essex in the winter of 2005. Colleagues and friends have supported and advised me during the course of preparing this book. I am particularly grateful to Eugene McLaughlin, Loraine Gelsthorpe, Maurice Punch, Tim Newburn, Rob Stones, and Thomas Wong. This edited volume has been a truly international collaborative effort. New friendships have been forged and new joint scholarly endeavours developed in the process. I am deeply appreciative of the contributing authors for their commitment to the book project, for working to the deadlines, and for offering their outstanding contributions to this collection.

Maggy Lee
University of Essex and the University of Hong Kong
June 2007

Notes on contributors

Mary Bosworth is University Lecturer at the Centre for Criminology, University of Oxford. She works on punishment, incarceration and immigration detention with a particular focus on how matters of race, gender and citizenship shape the experience and nature of confinement. She is author of *Engendering Resistance: agency and power in women's prisons* (Ashgate, 1999); *The US Federal Prison System* (Sage, 2002); and *Explaining US Imprisonment* (Sage, forthcoming 2008), and has edited books and written numerous journal articles and book chapters on prisons, punishment, race, gender and qualitative research methods. She is currently book review editor of *Theoretical Criminology*.

Andrea Di Nicola is Researcher at the Faculty of Law, University of Trento and Research Coordinator (Trento office) of Transcrime, University of Trento/Catholic University of Milan in Italy. His main publications include: 'National Criminal Records and Organised Crime in Italy' (with Vettori) in *Financial Crime in the EU: Criminal records as effective tools or missed opportunities?* (Kluwer Law International, 2005); 'Trafficking in Human Beings and Smuggling of Migrants', in *Handbook of Transnational Crime and Justice* (Sage, 2005); *Measuring Organised Crime in Europe* (with Van der Beken *et al.*) (Maklu Publishers, 2004); 'Trafficking in Persons and Smuggling of Migrants into Italy' (with Savona *et al.*), *Transcrime Reports* (2004); 'Trafficking in Women for the Purpose of Sexual Exploitation: knowledge-based preventative strategies from Italy', in *Managing Security* (Perpetuity Press, 2003).

Michael Grewcock is a PhD candidate at the University of New South Wales, where he also teaches courses on state and transnational crime. He was previously the legal officer for the Howard League for Penal Reform in London and a solicitor in private practice. He has an MA in Refugee Studies from the University of East London, UK, and has written extensively on issues relating to teenage imprisonment and border controls.

Barbara Hudson is Professor of Law, University of Central Lancashire. Her teaching and research interests are in theories and philosophies of justice; criminal justice, race, gender and poverty. Her current research concerns the possibility of extending 'justice' to people who are in some way outside the boundaries of 'community', whether the moral, cognitive or geo-political community. Recent publications include: *Justice in the Risk Society* (Sage, 2003); *Understanding Justice* (2nd edition, Open University Press, 2003); 'Gender Issues in Penal Policy and Penal Theory', in *Women and Punishment: the struggle for justice* (P. Carlen [ed.], Willan Publishing, 2002); 'Beyond white man's justice: race, gender and justice in late modernity', *Theoretical Criminology* (2006), and 'Punishing Monsters, Judging Aliens: justice at the borders of community', *The Australian and New Zealand Journal of Criminology*, 39 (2).

Liz Kelly is Director of the Child and Woman Abuse Studies Unit and Roddick Chair on Violence Against Women at the London Metropolitan University. Her recent publications include: *Fertile Fields: trafficking in persons in Central Asia* (IOM, 2005); *Journeys of Jeopardy: a review of research on trafficking in women and children in Europe* (IOM, 2002), 'The wrong debate: reflections on why force is not the key issue with respect to trafficking in women for sexual exploitation', *Feminist Review* (2003); *Moving in the Same or Different Directions? Reflections on recent developments in domestic violence legislation in Europe* (Ashgate, 2005). She has extensive policy and consultancy experience both nationally and internationally and chaired the Group of Specialists for the Council of Europe (COE) on violence against women. She is a member of the European Women's Lobby think tank on Violence Against Women, and has responsibility of violence issues in the UK Women's National Commission.

Maggy Lee is Senior Lecturer in the Department of Sociology at the University of Essex and Associate Professor in the Department of Sociology at the University of Hong Kong. She has worked on research projects on Chinese migrant women in Britain (funded by the ESRC), human smuggling and the policing of migrant sex workers in Hong Kong (funded by the British Academy), and migrant workers in global cities (funded by the University of Hong Kong). Her publications include: *Youth, Crime and Police Work* (Macmillan, 1998); *Crime in Modern Britain* (with Carrabine *et al.*) (Oxford University Press, 2002); *Criminology: a sociology introduction* (with Carrabine *et al.*) (Routledge, 2004); 'Human trade and the criminalization of irregular migration', *International Journal of the Sociology of Law* (2005); 'Policing Chinese Migrant Sex Workers in Hong Kong', *International Migration* (forthcoming, 2007), and *Trafficking and Global Crime Control* (Sage, in preparation). She is currently Associate Editor of *Sociology* and *Crime, Media, Culture: an international journal*.

Johan Lindquist is Assistant Professor of Social Anthropology at Stockholm University. His book *The Anxieties of Mobility: emotional economies at the edge of the global city* is forthcoming from the University of Hawaii Press. His current work focuses on the emergence of 'human trafficking' as a problem in Indonesia and Southeast Asia.

Ewa Morawska is Professor of Sociology at the University of Essex in the UK. Her recent publications include: *International Migration Research: constructions, omissions, and the promises of interdisciplinarity* (ed. with M. Bommes), (Ashgate, 2005); 'Exploring Diversity in Immigrant Assimilation and Transnationalism', *International Migration Review* (2004); *Toward Assimilation and Citizenship in Liberal Nation-States* (ed. with C. Joppke), (Palgrave Macmillan, 2003); 'Structuring Migration: the case of Polish income-seeking travellers to the West', *Theory and Society* (2001); 'Immigrant-Black Dissensions in American Cities: an argument for multiple explanations' in *Problem of the Century: racial stratification in the United States* (Russel Sage, 2001); 'International Migration and the Consolidation of Democracy in Post-Communist Eastern Europe' in *Democratic Consolidation In Eastern Europe: domestic and international factors* (OUP, 2001).

John T. Picarelli is an expert in transnational threats and their impact on national and homeland security, specifically transnational organised crime, terrorism and trafficking in human beings. He will complete his PhD dissertation, entitled 'A Factoral Explanation of the Persistence of Trafficking in Persons', at the School of International Service at American University in 2007. He earned his MA in International Affairs from the Graduate School of Public and International Affairs at the University of Pittsburgh, and his BA in International Relations from the University of Delaware.

Nicola Piper is Senior Research Fellow at the Asia Research Institute, National University of Singapore, and soon to take up a new position at the University of Wales, Swansea (Geography). She holds a PhD in Sociology from the University of Sheffield in the UK and had previous appointments with the Nordic Institute of Asian Studies in Copenhagen, and the Australian National University in Canberra. Her research interests revolve around international economic migration, governance and policy networks, gender, non-governmental organisations and transnational political activism, the rights of migrants, with empirical focus of Southeast and East Asia as well as Europe. She is the author of the book *Racism, Nationalism and Citizenship* (Ashgate, 1998), the co-editor of the volumes *Women and Work in Globalising Asia* (Routledge, 2002), *Wife or Worker? Asians marriage and migration* (Rowman & Littlefield, 2003), *Transnational Activism in Asia – Problems of Power and Democracy* (Routledge, 2004), as well as the author of numerous journal articles and background papers for various international organisations such as IOM, UNESCAP, UNRISD and the Global Commission on International Migration.

Louise Shelley is Professor in the School of International Service and the founder and director of the Terrorism, Transnational Crime and Corruption Center at American University. Her current research focuses on human trafficking, nuclear smuggling, and the links between transnational crime and terrorism. She is the author and editor of several books on police, organised crime and trafficking. Professor Shelley is the recipient of Guggenheim, Fulbright, IREX fellowships and has established centres in Russia, Ukraine and Georgia to study questions of organised crime and corruption collaboratively since the mid-1990s.

Chapter 1

Introduction: Understanding human trafficking

Maggy Lee

Introduction

The trafficking of human beings has attracted considerable public and political concern in recent years. It is commonly understood to involve a variety of crimes and abuses associated with the recruitment, movement and sale of people (including body parts) into a range of exploitative conditions around the world. Media stories of international human trafficking typically conjure up images of all-pervasive organised crime networks, underworld mafias and unscrupulous snakeheads taking advantage of the illicit opportunities and unprecedented ease of communication and transportation offered by the new social and technical infrastructures in an increasingly globalised world.

Yet trafficking is nothing new. Trafficking and smuggling has been described as a diverse form of trade that is 'as old as trade itself', even though there is great diversity in what is trafficked, what trade is prohibited, and by whom over time. 'Depending on the political winds and dominant social norms of the day, what is an illegitimate trade in one era may be a legitimate trade in another'(Andreas 1998: 78).[1] Indeed, human trafficking has historical parallels with the traffic in and exploitation of black Africans in previous centuries, when the colonial slave trade was considered not only a lawful but desirable branch of commerce by European empires.

Today, human trafficking has become the subject for much empirical research, academic debate and advocacy in diverse disciplines and fields such as criminology, politics, law, human rights, sociologies of migration, gender, and public health. It has been variously understood as the new white slave trade, transnational organised crime, an illegal migration problem, a threat to national sovereignty and security, a labour issue, human rights violations, or a combination of the above. Global and regional responses to the problem have been phenomenal, so much so that trafficking has arguably been transformed from 'a poorly funded, NGO [non-governmental organisation] women's issue in the early 1980s', into 'the global agenda of high politics' of the United States Congress, the European Union (EU) and the United Nations (Wong 2005: 69).

Yet there remain considerable limitations in our knowledge and understanding of human trafficking. Indeed, the trafficking debate has been criticised by some for its 'shoddy research, anecdotal information, or strong moralistic positions' (Sanghera 2005) and emotive manipulation of 'wobbly' statistics (Murray 1998). Anti-trafficking programmes and the development of state policies also reflect conflicting agendas and strategic policy goals in the control of all those who cross borders illegally. Whilst there is obvious concern to protect victims and to prevent a range of trafficking harms, states also tend to conflate anti-trafficking with immigration and asylum controls. Many of the counter-trafficking initiatives, punitive sanctions and border controls that have emerged alongside the (re)discovery of the 'trafficking problem' have been contentious and paradoxical, arguably pushing a larger proportion of unauthorised and forced migrants into the hands of professional smugglers or traffickers, making limited impact on the social causes of trafficking, and generating troubling consequences for the irregular migrants.

This edited volume aims to inject some conceptual clarity and critical insights into our understanding of the complex social phenomenon of, and responses to, human trafficking. It does so by considering the debates and controversies around several key themes: trafficking as a historical phenomenon rather than a purely modern 'problem'; the nature, patterns and extent of global human trade; the social organisation and processes of trafficking and re-trafficking; the links between trafficking and other forms and dynamics of migration and exploitation; and state-sponsored responses to trafficked persons and all those considered as non-citizens. There are important reasons to examine the core concepts, definitions and diverse frameworks within which trafficking has been understood over time, as the approaches that are chosen will shape the strategies used to address the trafficking problem. For example, when the problem is defined as a moral, crime or public order issue, there is a tendency to opt for solutions that involve control or punishment; when the problem is defined as a social or human rights issue, strategies of empowerment may be preferred. Equally, it is important to reflect on areas of agreement and disagreement in the trafficking debate across disciplines and to unravel the many contradictions in the smugglers/traffickers discourse and attendant controls. Such an analysis enables a more balanced and nuanced understanding of the different dimensions and policies of trafficking as well as a more critical assessment of the role of the state in human trade.

What is human trafficking?

Human trafficking is an imprecise and highly contested term.[2] So what are the various conceptions of trafficking/traffickers/trafficked victims?

Slavery

First, human trafficking has been conceptualised as a form of 'slavery' (Bales 2005; Ould 2004). Slavery has been held up as the worst possible exploitation in human history. Although old forms of slavery, with kidnapping, auction blocks and chattel slaves forced to work in chains, may be rare incidences today, scholars have argued that there are parallels between traditional and modern forms of human trading in that desperate and vulnerable human beings are taken advantage of and treated as commodities in contemporary conditions akin to slavery. From this perspective, human trafficking as a contemporary form of slavery is marked not by legal ownership of one human being by another or long-term enslavement, but by temporary ownership, debt bondage, forced labour and hyper-exploitative contractual arrangements in the global economy (Bales 2000; Bales 2005). Miers (2003), for example, identifies the main forms of slavery that have persisted or emerged by the end of the twentieth century: bonded labour systems and forced labour in sweatshops, private households and on farms not only in poorer regions such as South Asia but also in Western Europe and the US; the exploitation of children as labourers in cottage industries or quarries on the Indian subcontinent, as camel jockeys in the Gulf States or as soldiers in Africa; and servile marriage in South Asia and Muslim societies. Scholars who insist on the value of using the term 'slavery', argue that it alerts us to the 'underlying and essential elements' of 'violence and its threat, absolute control, economic exploitation' (Bales 2000: 476) and that it 'guarantees a wider audience' in the fight against present injustice (Anker 2004: 19). Others, however, warn of the need to avoid sensationalism (Anderson 2004) and conceptual slippage, and advocate the term 'slavery-like practices' to 'signal the commonalities and distinctions between legal enslavement and forced, waged labour'(Kempadoo 2005: xx).

Prostitution

Second, definitions of human trafficking have coalesced around contested positions on issues of prostitution, individual agency, and consent. The notion that trafficking is synonymous with the traffic of women for commercial exploitation can be traced back to public concerns about the 'white slave trade' of women and young girls into prostitution at the end of the nineteenth century. Some scholars have suggested that the emergence of a social panic about white slavery was linked not only to welfarist concerns but also to broader anxieties about growing transatlantic migrations and fears directed at white, European or American women's mobility and sexual freedoms (Chapkis 2003; Doezema 2000; Keire 2001; Scully 2001). A series of international agreements adopted in the early part of the twentieth century on the 'traffic of women' include: the 1910 White Slavery Convention, the 1919 Covenant of the League of Nations, the 1921 Convention for the Suppression of the Traffic of Women and Children, the 1933 Convention for the Suppression of the Traffic of Women of Full Age and, notably, the 1949 Convention for the Suppression of the Traffic in Persons and of the Exploitation of the Prostitution of Others.[3] Then as now, trafficking narratives have relied heavily on the paradigmatic images of female powerlessness and childlike sexual vulnerability and the spectacle of transgressive bodies.[4]

Notwithstanding recent international instruments that recognise people can be trafficked into sectors and settings other than prostitution, trafficking of women and children for sexual exploitation has continued to be the dominant paradigm in the fields of research, enforcement and prevention (see Di Nicola, Piper and Lindquist, Chapters 3 and 7, this volume). Such conceptualisation of trafficking as exclusively linked to sexual exploitation meant that other forms of exploitation tend to be ignored in anti-trafficking initiatives even though there is increasing evidence that suggests global trafficking for labour exploitation is also prevalent in domestic labour, agriculture, construction and other 'dirty, dangerous, degrading' industries

(Anderson 2004; Anti-Slavery International 2006; Sharma 2006).[5] Children may be kidnapped, trafficked and sold not only into sex trade but also as casual labourers, soldiers or camel jockeys (Anti-Slavery International 2002; Dottridge 2002; Human Rights Watch 2002a; International Labour Organization 2001). Significantly, as Bastia (2005) suggests, child trafficking may be widely practiced but unrecognised as such because they are embedded in traditional forms of child patronage and cultural attitudes towards child labour. Ambiguities and tensions remain, as the feminist anti-trafficking agenda is split along ideological lines on their views of prostitution as 'work', women's agency in relation to prostitution, and the distinction between 'voluntary' migrant sex work and 'forced' trafficking (Doezema 2000; Doezema 2002; Kempadoo 2005; Murray 1998; Sullivan 2003). Critics have also pointed to the criminalising and moralising tendencies of the abolitionist discourse about sexual slavery, and argued that anti-trafficking measures have been used not so much to protect women from exploitation, but to police and punish female migrants and sex workers (Chapkis 2003; Kapur 2002).

Organised crime

Third, human trafficking has been conceptualised within a framework of organised crime. The role of criminally sophisticated, transnational organised crime groups as a driving force behind the highly profitable trade of smuggling and trafficking unauthorised migrants or asylum seekers has been commented upon widely (Bruinsma and Meershoek 1999; Budapest Group 1999; Shelley *et al* 2003; Williams 1998; Williams 2002). Indeed, an important aspect of the institutionalisation of the 'trafficking-as-organised crime' approach has taken place vis-à-vis the 2000 UN Convention Against Transnational Organised Crime (see below).[6] In the UK, the government regards the problem of 'illegal trade in people' as primarily instigated by 'organised crime groups', to be dealt with under the rubric of its overall organised crime strategy and as a priority of the new Serious Organised Crime Agency (Home Office and Scottish Executive 2006). Since the 1990s, the transnational criminal trafficker has also been the target of anti-trafficking legislations in the US (notably the Trafficking Victims' Protection Act of 2000) and a plethora of action-oriented programmes under the EU justice and home affairs policy, and multilateral initiatives around the world (Andreas and Snyder 2000; Goodey 2005; Green and Grewcock 2002).

The 'trafficking-as-transnational organised crime' approach has been premised on two contrasting views of the relationship between the state and the trafficking problem. The first view, epitomised by what Taylor and Jamieson (1999) have termed the use of 'the Mafia shorthand' and an alarmist interpretation of the threat posed by foreign gangsters and organised crime networks, takes border control as the basis of the state's sovereignty and as intrinsic to its logic of being. Indeed, the regulation and monitoring of cross-border flows has been central to the modern state's claims of territorial sovereignty and, in the European context, to 'the cultivation of a hegemonic European character built upon principles of exclusion' (Green and Grewcock 2002). From this perspective, trafficking is seen as a serious and unambiguous threat to the peace and security of the developed world, and hence legitimises state response of increased surveillance and tighter immigration controls. The blurring of issues of organised crime involvement in trafficking with the more symbolic issues of national security, sovereignty and the role of borders has been referred to as indicative of the 'militarising of social problems' (Beare 1997). As Andreas (1998: 86) suggests, using 'old security institutions and technologies' and intelligence services to fight against 'new' security targets of smugglers, traffickers, terrorists and unauthorised border crossers may be 'an awkward and expensive fit', but there are 'bureaucratic incentives and political pressures' which continue to push in this direction in the post-Cold War (and post-September 11) era.

An alternative view takes issue with the simplistic – even misleading – imagery of nation states fighting valiantly against global organised crime groups, and points to the symbiotic relationship between the state and transnational organised crime (Andreas 1998; Williams 2002). The extensiveness of organised crime and its penetration of the political sphere especially in Latin America and the former Soviet States have arguably led to a criminalisation of the political process and a weakening of the rule of law (Shelley 1999; 2003). Crucially, critics have argued that the illicit movement of people would not thrive as it does in particular regions without the complicity of public officials (Phongpaichit et al 1998; Ruggiero 1997). Others have questioned the dominance of transnational organised crime groups and have problematised their role in human trade. Indeed, there is a growing body of work that emphasises the diverse agents and beneficiaries of human trafficking and smuggling – for example, the more nebulous crime networks operating in particular locales; short-lived 'mom and pop' type operations; opportunistic freelance criminals; and intermediaries or employers otherwise engaged in legitimate businesses (Finckenauer2001; Kyle and Siracusa 2005; Richard 1999).

Related to this view, is the notion of human trafficking as a 'business'. Salt and Stein (1997: 468), for example, wrote of migrant trafficking as 'an international business', involving a 'system of institutionalised networks with complex profit and loss accounts, including a set of institutions, agents and individuals, each of which stands to make a commercial gain'. This system is arguably maintained by the performance of a variety of planning, information-gathering, financing, technical, and operational tasks. These tasks can be carried out by either larger or smaller trafficking organisations, in the form of a 'segmented business'(Aronowitz 2001) and involving a number of specific roles (for example, recruitment, transportation, management, debt-collection) for different individuals and organisations which may or may not be engaged in other forms of criminal activity (Budapest Group 1999; Finckenauer 2001; Schloenhardt 1999). In this way, organised crime is broken down into discrete, constituent parts, each of which can be the target of a law enforcement process.

Migration

Fourth, trafficking has been understood within the context of broader migration patterns, policies and politics of migration control. Sociologists, criminologists and political scientists working on migration research have pointed to the growth in regular, irregular and/or forced migratory movements in various regions, which in turn have been spurred on by economic crises, lack of sustainable livelihoods, political conflict, civil war, ethnic persecution, social inequalities, gender-blind macroeconomic policies, and wider processes of global social transformation (Asis 2004; Castles 2003; Kelly 2005; Koser 2000; Piper 1999; Sassen 2000).[7] For many trapped in dire poverty, displaced by political turmoil, and turned away by increasingly restrictive immigration and asylum policies in what Green and Grewcock (2002) have termed the 'broad zones of exclusion',[8] migration through irregular channels of smuggling and trafficking has become their only means of escape.

Various scholars have considered the 'migration-trafficking nexus' (Piper 2005), noting a 'continuum of facilitation' (Skeldon 2000) in both regular and irregular flows of male and female labourers. There are economic, cultural, social and legal factors that are conducive to the exploitation and abuse of migrant workers, especially irregular migrants in unprotected, informal and/or illegal labour markets

(Anderson 2004; Anderson and O'Connell Davidson 2003; Pearson 2005). Seen in this light, promoting transparent legal channels of labour migration, ending the use of trafficked labour by employers, and protecting workers' rights in the context of internal and cross-border migration, may be crucial to tackling the trafficking trade.

More specifically, there is a substantial body of literature that points to the structural conditions which are conducive to sex and labour trafficking of women, notably the feminisation of poverty, the secondary positioning of women within their families and societies, and the repressive regimes that constrain women's life chances in the context of rapid, globalised marketisation. The emergence of extensive sex markets, either as a state-sponsored strategy of economic development in South-east Asia (Lim 1998; Sassen 2000) or as a result of armed conflict and militarisation in areas such as Kosovo and the former Yugoslavia (Amnesty International 2004; Commission of Experts on the Former Yugoslavia 1994; Rehn and Sirleaf 2002), has generated and supported thriving 'markets in women'. The traffic of women from the former Soviet States, Central Asia and in Eastern Europe has also been well-documented (Hughes 2000; Kelly 2002; Shelley 2003). Women who are increasingly breadwinners but make up substantial proportions of the newly unemployed, are arguably hardest hit by the collapse of the communist system and what Taylor and Jamieson (1999) have termed the commodification of sex within the 'culture of marketised society'.

As Kelly (Chapter 4) and Morawska (Chapter 5) suggest in this volume, the desire to escape from chronic economic and social crises makes many of these women highly vulnerable to trafficking harms. To date, we know relatively little about the actual experiences of migrants in the trafficking and re-trafficking process. There is a limited amount of work on the experiences and agency (albeit severely constrained) of trafficked women (Ahmad 2005), children and their families (Kielland and Sanogo 2002), and asylum seekers (Koser 2000). Critics have argued that it is counter-productive for state authorities to 'rescue' trafficked persons out of their situation and simply return them to their home communities, often to the same conditions from which they originally left and back into the hands of the same recruiters or other traffickers. Indeed, we know very little about resettled victims' (or 'ex-captives', Brennan 2005) attempts to rebuild their lives, and how or why some become re-trafficked but not others.

Human rights

Fifth, trafficking has been conceptualised from a human rights perspective. The consolidation of human rights has gathered momentum in the later half of the twentieth century through the proliferation of human rights institutions and the rise in the international efficacy of human rights as principles of broad value to all people. Against this background, trafficking has been seen as a violation of basic human rights of a person under the 1948 Universal Declaration of Human Rights, including the right to be free from slavery or servitude; right to freedom of movement; right to life, liberty and security; right to health; and right to free choice of employment. The human rights discourse which posits the trafficked victim as a bearer of universal rights derived from personhood is most apparent in the work of various UN agencies such as UNICEF and UNOHCHR (United Nations High Commissioner for Human Rights 2002), in legal writings (Chuang 1998; Corrin 2005; Gallagher 2002; Macklin 2003), and in the advocacy work of non-government organisations such as Amnesty International and Human Rights Watch. Recent evidence of organised traffic of women for military and international peacekeeping and reconstruction personnel in conflict and post-conflict regions has brought the commercial sex trade onto political and human rights agendas, and placed the role of the state in the development and continuation of traffic in women under the spotlight (Corrin 2005; Rehn and Sirleaf 2002). A human rights approach arguably offers a conceptual and normative framework for understanding the broader causes and consequences of trafficking, for developing counter-trafficking legislation and policies, and for monitoring and evaluating state policies and practices against international human rights standards, including states' human rights obligations owed to non-citizens within their territory (Experts Group on Trafficking in Human Beings 2004; Kaye 2003; Patten 2004).

Notwithstanding the development of international instruments in recent years, critics have noted the competing concerns of human rights protection of trafficking victims and the interests of states in immigration controls and border integrity. Whilst the 1991 UN International Convention on the Protection of the Rights of all Migrant Workers and Members of their Families provides significant rights to victims of international trafficking under the rubric of rights accorded to undocumented migrant workers (such as the right not to be subjected to torture or degrading treatment or punishment; the right not to be held in slavery or servitude; the right to effective protection by the states against violence, physical injury, threats and intimidation), the Convention has limited authority in international law, much less the domestic laws of most destination (non-signatory) countries (Bosniak 1991). Clearly, there remains a rights deficit in the treatment of non-citizens under the dominant political constructions of legitimate/illegitimate citizens and migrants. In her analysis of the UN Trafficking and Smuggling Protocols, Gallagher (2001: 976) argues that even though 'human rights concerns may have provided some impetus (or cover) for collective action, it is the sovereignty/ security issues surrounding trafficking and migrant smuggling which are the true driving force behind such efforts'. Similarly, Sullivan (2003) suggests that although the Trafficking Protocol establishes some 'new' (and confirms existing) rights of trafficking victims, the rights and protections offered to victims remain 'meagre'. Green and Grewcock (2002: 99) went further to suggest that legitimate concerns about protecting the human rights of trafficking victims have been co-opted into wider state policies of control and surveillance and the political project of cultivating 'a hegemonic European (identity) built upon principles of exclusion.'

Trafficking versus smuggling

By advancing the first definition of trafficking in international law, the UN Convention Against Transnational Organised Crime Trafficking Protocol (2000) has gone some way towards creating an international consensus in our understanding of human trafficking. The UN definition of trafficking in persons identifies several key elements of trafficking: recruitment and facilitated movement of a person within or across national frontiers by means of coercion, threats or deception for the purpose of exploitation. 'Exploitation' is conceived to include not only prostitution or other forms of sexual exploitation, but also forced labour or services, slavery, servitude or the removal of organs.[9] There is evidence to suggest that the range of trafficking harms may also include high risks to personal safety, loss of all legal rights and personal dignity, physical abuse and, in the case of sexual abuse, exposure to sexually transmitted diseases and reproductive illnesses (Kelly and Regan 2000). In contrast, smuggling of migrants is defined as the illegal movement of person across international borders in order to obtain a financial benefit under the UN Smuggling Protocol (2000).[10] Whilst trafficking entails subsequent exploitation of people, the services of smugglers are assumed to end when migrants reach their destination. Further, whilst a key distinguishing criterion of trafficking under the UN Protocols is the existence of a victim whose individual rights have been violated, smuggling is seen as a violation of the political interest of the state (Experts Group on Trafficking in Human Beings 2004).

Although the UN definitions mark an important international consensus on the definition of human trade, many commentators have pointed to the continued difficulties of drawing clear and consistent boundaries between human trafficking and migrant smuggling, or between criminal accomplice and victim, on the basis of consent (Gallagher 2001; Lee 2005; Morrison 1998; Munro 2006). It is often unclear whether a person is trafficked or smuggled at the beginning of his or her journey, as deception, exploitation and human rights abuses may not be apparent until later stages. Equally, smuggled persons may fall victims to abuses and human rights violation during or after they reach their destination, as there have been many harrowing accounts of migrants being abandoned at various transit points, physically or sexually abused, suffocated in containers or drowned crossing the sea, killed by their smugglers to avoid police action, or subjected to exploitation as they become indebted to their smugglers. As Liz Kelly in this volume points out (in Chapter 4), there are both overlaps and transitions from smuggling to trafficking, and that trafficking is best understood as a 'continuum' which involves various degrees of force, exploitation, and positions of vulnerability. All this suggests that a discrete categorisation of 'trafficking' and 'smuggling' may be artificial and unhelpful, and may draw attention away from the broader context of exploitation and complex causes of irregular migration.

The criminalisation of migrants

The artificial distinction between trafficking and smuggling also extends to the state's distinction between 'deserving' and 'undeserving' victims of human trade, with varying degrees of blame being attributed to various categories of unauthorised migrants. For example, smuggled migrants tend to be regarded as willing violators of immigration laws and undeserving of protection, as any harm or exploitation they experience is considered to be their own fault.[11] Those who were previously engaged in prostitution may also be perceived to lack the 'real' victim status, as they have consented to illegal border crossing and to working in the sex trade.

In crime discourse, this hierarchy of victimisation is apparent when some victims enjoy a higher status than others and where their experiences of victimisation are taken more seriously accordingly. The distinction between 'innocent' and 'blameworthy' victims (Christie 1986) and the impact of 'victim blaming' on particular social groups has been highlighted in studies on sexual and domestic violence (Edwards 1989; Lees 1996). In the context of trafficking, although trafficked persons are designated victims under various policies and laws and may be given some form of protection and temporary residency if they agree to testify against their traffickers, many are arrested and detained as illegal migrants rather than as legitimate victims of crime.

More broadly, the current dominance of discourses that identify unauthorised, unwanted and forced migrants as lawbreakers, a public order risk, a menace to national sovereignty, an existential threat to our way of life, or a combination of all of the above, has been well-documented in criminological literature. In what Welch (2003) and Melossi (2003; 2005) have referred to as the 'criminalisation of migrants', migrants (especially undocumented migrants) have become the archetypal 'problem populations' and subjected to an 'amplified process of penalisation'. In the process, the scope for anti-smuggling and anti-trafficking laws and state practices that marginalise and stigmatise through heightened surveillance, harassment, ethnic profiling and so on, has been expanded. New 'control filters' have emerged whereby 'phenotypical criteria like skin pigmentation, speech, "alien" behaviour and other visible signs of foreign origin' become 'markers' for surveillance, monitoring and investigation (Morrison 1998: 56).[12] As Welch and Schuster (2005) argue, the state's power to punish illegal aliens and the growing prison populations and longer periods of confinement in the West exemplify 'a globalising culture of control' driven by 'perceptions of difference and putative threats'. Indeed, undocumented or irregular migrants make up a large and increasing proportion of prisoners within the EU (Melossi 2005: 345–7); they constitute what Christie (2000) referred to as 'suitable enemies' in society. In this respect, the prison complex underpins the very boundaries of our notions about the Others and illustrates the state's power to exclude the unwanted. As Bosworth (Chapter 8) and Grewcock (Chapter 9) point out in this volume, current migration control measures ranging from militarised border policing to privatised or offshore detention and processing of unwanted aliens have been highly contentious. Critics have argued that an ever-increasing emphasis on border restrictions and enforcement measures may have the unintended side effects of expanding the business of human trade and pushing greater numbers of unauthorised migrants into the hands of exploitative organised crime networks. Others have highlighted the politics and human cost of such measures.

Overview of the book

This volume brings together a number of key scholars in the fields of Sociology, Social Anthropology, Criminology, Political Science and International Relations, to provide a mix of conceptual analysis and empirical discussion on human trafficking, with a view to pushing back the boundaries of existing knowledge and creating critical dialogues about trafficking abuses, unauthorised migration, the treatment of non-citizens, and global state control.

While many scholars approach the trade in human beings as it is presently constituted, adopting a historical perspective provides important insights into the continuities and discontinuities in the forms and practices of human trade. Sophisticated slave trading systems existed in much of Africa, Asia and the Ottoman Empire, with Britain as the leading slave-trading nation dominating the highly profitable trade of transporting Africans to the colonies and the plantations and mines of the Americas in the eighteenth century (Miers 2003; Walvin 1996). It was an important branch of British commerce and regarded as vital for the prosperity of the slaving ports and a large number of slave-holding colonies.

Notwithstanding the apparent success of the global antislavery movement in the nineteenth century, John Picarelli (Chapter 2 in this volume) argues that 'slavery' and trade in human beings have continued to evolve into new and more complex forms of unfree labour. Trafficking in persons is best understood as a phenomenon that has retained some of the core aspects of previous forms of servitude and human trade whilst also adapting to meet changing economic, cultural and political realities. Then as now, the role of the state in human trade has been double-edged. Initially through mercantilist policies and subsequently through the benefits of colonial economies and trade, European states had a vested interest in maintaining chattel slavery and the trade in slaves; the trade was taxed and regulated much like other forms of commerce. The eventual British-led campaign to outlaw slavery and the traffic in slaves within the empire and beyond has been described as one of the first 'global prohibition regimes' directed at activities which were seen as threats to 'the safety, welfare, and moral sensibilities of international society' (Nadelmann 1990: 526). Yet even in the face of such prohibition, states either retained or allowed some elements of the trade and of servitude to continue in order to advance their colonial interests. State policy and control practices were, and still remain, inextricably tied with competing interests and geopolitical considerations. Taking a longer and wider view of human trafficking and the states' own actions in creating and/or maintaining it, helps to illuminate the ways in which present experiences of trafficking are invariably connected to those of the past.

Despite continuous media reports and the consensus at a mainstream policy level that human trafficking is widespread and on the rise, there is an absence of reliable statistical data. Criminologists have noted the partial and problematic nature of crime statistics in general; they reveal just as much if not more about reporting, policing and prosecution patterns than about patterns of actual criminal activity. In Chapter 3, Andrea Di Nicola assesses the various types of data and knowledge base in scholarly, official and grey literature on global human trade and argues there is an urgent need to improve how and what we research. In particular, he considers the strengths and weaknesses of many estimates of the scale of human trafficking; the advantages and disadvantages of using strict legal definitions to guide research in this area; and the methodological challenges, risks and ethical dilemmas associated with researching into this politically sensitive, hidden problem and 'hard-to-reach' populations (including trafficking victims, organised criminals, corrupt officials). Di Nicola warns that official data on human trafficking is often unverifiable and skewed (for example, focusing on sex trafficking and neglecting other forms of exploitation), and may be shaped by institutional exigencies and particular conceptualisations of the trafficking problem. Consequently, there is a danger that anti-trafficking policies and interventions based on such findings will be ineffective and self-serving.

In the first of two case studies of human trade in regions where migratory patterns reflect legacies of the Soviet past, Liz Kelly (Chapter 4) considers the patterns, social organisation and conducive contexts of trafficking in five Central Asian Republics. Although the UN protocol provides definitions of trafficking and smuggling, the debates continue as to whether it is feasible and desirable to draw such boundaries. At a definitional level, Kelly's study highlights the difficulties of drawing clear and consistent boundaries between trafficking, smuggling and various forms of irregular migration, and raises the question of whether the concept of a continuum might more accurately reflect the human rights abuses involved. Whilst previous studies found that most trafficking in persons was for sexual exploitation, Kelly's study reveals that intraregional trafficking for labour exploitation is also widespread. This pattern is especially evident in, but not confined to, states in transition where a set of interlocking social, political and economic conditions create fertile grounds on which trafficking in men and women can emerge and flourish. The case study of Central Asia poignantly demonstrates the links between trafficking, cultural traditions and existing inequalities as well as the relevance of histories of forced labour and migration to contemporary patterns and social dynamics of human traffic. Clearly, adopting a wider definition of trafficking to capture a diversity of contexts in which human beings are exploited as commodities has important implications for identifying trafficked persons, agents/ intermediaries, and estimating the scale of trafficking. Perhaps more significantly, Kelly's chapter provides a compelling case for addressing the connections (or lack of connections) between official policy and the multiple realities of trafficking, and for tackling the structural aspects of migration as part of any integrated counter-trafficking initiative.

Unlike the pattern in previous decades where trafficked women came mainly from Asia and South America, the strongest trafficking flows are taking place within Europe. In Chapter 5, Ewa Morawska draws on the insights from the sociology of international migration and outlines some of the main 'push/pull' factors and mechanisms behind human trafficking – especially for sexual exploitation – in and from Eastern Europe. Indeed, the emergence of extensive sex markets in the poorest countries in Europe has taken place in the nexus between the poverty of transition, gender inequality, and human trafficking routes. The collapse of Soviet communist regimes and the subsequent incorporation of Eastern Europe into global capitalism, and a more recent eastward enlargement of the EU, have arguably turned this region into 'a perfect hub for international human trafficking'. Morawska's chapter provides an overview of the volume, socio-demographic profile, routes and flows of trafficked migrants in this region. Her account draws attention to the macro-, mezzo- and micro-level factors that generate this movement, the socio-economic asymmetries that fuel the globalisation of the sex trade, and the trafficked migrants' own motivations and purposes in illicit border crossing. Notwithstanding the recent regional and multilateral efforts in tackling trafficking, Morawska argues that human trade will not disappear as long as the structural forces and mechanisms generating it – economic (core-periphery structural imbalances), political (lack of coordination of law enforcement, corruption of officials), cultural (secondary positioning of women) and social organisational (effective transnational criminal networks) – remain in force.

This last point is particularly pertinent to Louise Shelley's (Chapter 6) analysis of human trafficking as a problem of transnational crime. Here, she documents the macro- and micro-level factors behind the emergence of human trafficking as a 'crime of choice' for transnational organised groups, including the high profits, low risk, and their ability to capitalise on the demand to leave transitional/conflict-ridden/less developed states, the demand for cheap physical and sexual labour in developed countries, and the complicity from the legitimate community and corrupt officials. Shelley challenges the notion of a homogeneous model of trafficking/trafficker, and notes their diverse profile (including women as traffickers), motivations (economic, political), organisational forms (clan or family-based versus individual-based structures; integrated versus less integrated groups), routes (inter- and intraregional), trafficking methods, exploitative and dehumanising practices, and the differences and overlaps between the business of human and other forms of commodity trafficking and smuggling. Whether trafficked persons are treated just like any other 'commodity' is debatable, and may in part depend on the organisational features of the organised crime groups. In trafficking businesses where trafficked women are passed from one set of owners to others repeatedly, the scope for abuse is greater. Violations are more frequent when the recruitment of future victims does not depend on the treatment of previous victims of trafficking. The trade in human beings also operates differently across regions depending on the cultural, historical and political contexts and traditions of trade. Thus, the contemporary trade in people out of Africa resembles the historical slave trade. In the case of post-socialist countries, traffickers in China use trade in people as a means of generating revenue for development at home whereas traffickers from the former USSR sell off human beings as if they were a natural resource with little consideration of investment of the profits in the domestic economy.

In principle, non-governmental organisations (NGOs) are well placed to capture and interpret the detail and nuances of issues surrounding trafficked persons, and to advocate for them as a result of the practical and front line aspects of their work. The extent to which NGOs have been able to realise this potential in the face of political influence and the dictates of the market remains an open question, however. In Chapter 7, Johan Lindquist and Nicola Piper examine the institutional and discursive links between HIV/AIDS prevention and counter-trafficking through a case study of the Indonesian island of Batam. Batam, part of the so-called Indonesia-Malaysia-Singapore Growth Triangle, was first identified as a high-risk area for the spread of HIV in the 1990s and more recently as a potential hub for trafficking. For many local NGOs, the shift of attention from HIV/AIDS to trafficking has not led to a radical break in practice. As Lindquist and Piper argue, HIV prevention and counter-trafficking work depend on a common infrastructure of information, funding, and intervention, and, in both cases, female sexuality is of central concern. By examining these commonalities, the authors offer us important insights into the power of trafficking discourse and the way in which particular state interests and institutional histories help to shape local interventions, thereby excluding other concerns about irregular migration from the policy agenda.

To Mary Bosworth (Chapter 8), there are actual and metaphorical overlaps between the use of criminal justice confinement as a means of excluding the 'undeserving poor' from society and the use of immigration detention as a 'sorting mechanism' for managing different types of non-citizens (including trafficked persons, asylum seekers, and foreigners found in violation of immigration rules). Symbolically, immigration detention identifies foreign nationals, 'bogus' asylum seekers and criminals as threats to the economic well-being and safety of the British community; practically, immigration detention and removal centres are being run and often experienced 'like prisons'. The emergence of the 'immigration complex' (involving not only the Immigration and Nationality Directorate and the Prison Service but also private security companies) therefore raises important questions about the complex role played by detention in maintaining borders of the British nation state. As Bosworth argues, prisons and detention centres are singularly useful in the management of non-citizens because they provide both a physical and a symbolic exclusion zone.

Michael Grewcock extends these arguments in his chapter (Chapter 9) on the 'war' on illicit migrants and addresses three key themes with particular reference to Australia: the role played by the war on human trafficking and smuggling in the exclusion and criminalisation of unauthorised migrants; the fusion of migration control and national security agendas; and the implications of border policing practices for forced and unauthorised migrants. In the Australian context, the so-called 'War on People Smugglers' has been central to the government's border protection policy and the construction of Western exclusion zones. It has provided justifications for the use of militarised policing methods, notably during the Tampa events of 2001, and an increasing reliance on detention measures to control non-citizens. The war on human trade also reflects particular notions of transnational criminal threats which have been, especially in the aftermath of Australian intervention in East Timor and the Bali and Jakarta bombings.

In principle, the war on human trafficking and smuggling is justified as an exercise in defending the human rights of forced and unauthorised migrants. In practice, Australia's border controls have been driven by its military and regional security rationales and the 'Pacific Solution' and a desire to stop unwanted migrants entering the Australia's border zone. The exclusionary impact of the 'war' against human smuggling and trafficking on forced and unauthorised migrants highlights a fundamental disjuncture between border policing and human rights at a global level. The Australian case study is particularly pertinent, as Grewcock reminds us that the migration control regime developed in Australia is being embraced as a model by other Western States – including the UK's proposals for EU buffer zones and offshore processing – and underpin practices that undermine the already limited protections offered by human rights instruments. What, then, are the limits and possibilities of challenging the enforcement priorities of dominant national and international policy makers and constructing an alternative approach to human trafficking that seeks to develop a more broadly formulated rights-based framework for non-citizens?

The volume ends with Barbara Hudson's examination (Chapter 10) of current European law and policy towards 'strangers', looking in particular at the way in which the figure of the 'illegal immigrant' has been constructed in law and in politics. Long-standing and generalised hostility towards strangers has, she argues, been given new focus by political-populist construction of this figure who comes to northern European countries, drawn by welfare benefits, and by the prospect of well-paid (by the standards of the countries of origin) work. Despite revelations of work conditions in cases such as the deaths of the Morecambe Bay cockle-pickers, and media stories about an influx of 'Polish plumbers', the migrant labourer is generally cast in terms of taking British jobs rather than filling gaps in the provision of goods and services. The response has been to try to reinforce barriers against illegal immigrants, and to create categories of semi-legal, second-class European citizenship which reduce the right of work throughout the EU for people from the new membership states of Eastern Europe. The chapter draws on criminological and social theory to look at the criminalisation of migration, especially the most recent work of Zygmunt Bauman and Dario Melossi. These writers analyse the relationships of modernisation and globalisation to migration, and look at the category of 'illegal immigrant' as a way of labelling and disposing of 'human waste' (in Bauman's terms). Hudson also considers recent debates in political philosophy which aim to find new approaches to the rights of strangers, notably the work of Jacques Derrida, Jurgen Habermas and Seyla Benhabib, and concludes that basing principles of cosmopolitan justice on an 'ethics of hospitality' may offer a more secure foundation for the rights of strangers.

Notes

1 Contrast, for example, China's efforts to prohibit American and British opium exports in the nineteenth century and America's current efforts to prohibit Chinese alien smuggling.
2 Salt and Hogarth (2000), for example, identified over 20 definitions of the concept of trafficking in their review of literature.
3 According to Chiang (1999) and Chuang (1998), most of these international agreements failed to provide explicit definitions of 'trafficking' and forced prostitution and tended to attract limited political support and resources.
4 For a critique of the white slavery discourse as 'moral panic' and its parallels with contemporary discourses of sex trafficking, see Doezema (2000).
5 In the UK, although specific offences of trafficking for sexual exploitation and trafficking for 'slavery or forced labour, human organ transplant or other forms of exploitation' now exist, 'there have been fourteen successful convictions for trafficking for sexual exploitation under the Sexual Offences Act 2003', but no cases have been brought in relation to trafficking for labour exploitation (Home Office and Scottish Executive 2006).
6 The UN Convention seeks to promote cooperation among states parties to combat transnational organised crime more effectively through criminalising a number of activities, improving information flows, enhancing cross-border coordination between relevant authorities, and eliminating 'safe havens' where organised criminal activities or the concealment of evidence or profits can take place by promoting the adoption of basic minimum measures.

7 According to Taylor and Jamieson (1999: 263), there were over 12 million forced migrants in all regions of the world in 1994; since then, genocidal and civil conflicts meant some 700,000 people have been displaced from the former Yugoslavia, 2 million people uprooted in Bosnia-Herzegovina, and several million people living in camps and shanty towns in Rwanda, Uganda, Burundi, Congo, Sudan and Ethiopia. They form what Kevin Bales (2000) has termed 'disposable people' – that is, 'a vast reservoir of human beings living without rights, security, and, usually, any hope of a return home'.

8 As Green and Grewcock (2002: 99) suggest, the construction of 'broad zones of exclusion' ('Fortress Europe'; the US/Mexico border; and the Australasian/South-east Asian Rim) represents 'a common strategic response to instability and crisis and a means by which to identify, control and exclude those who are deemed to be a threat to social order or economic prosperity'.

9 UN Convention against Transnational Organized Crime, Protocol to Prevent, Suppress and Punish Trafficking in Persons, especially Women and Children 2000, Article 3, paragraph (a).

10 UN Convention against Transnational Organized Crime, Protocol against the Smuggling of Migrants by Land, Sea and Air 2000, Article 3.

11 For a discussion of the differential protection provisions stipulated under the Smuggling Protocol and Trafficking Protocol and policy implications for temporary residence, safe repatriation and so on, see Gallagher (2001).

12 Some states have set up special police units to follow and search for overstayers, undocumented migrants who have gone underground, and asylum seekers who have received a deportation decision (Brochmann and Hammar 1999). In Malaysia, a nationwide crackdown on undocumented migrants in 2005 involving almost half-a-million police officers, immigration officials and civilian volunteers (who were paid for every undocumented migrant they caught) in the mass arrest and detention operations, attracted widespread criticisms from human rights organisations and international migrant groups.

References

Ahmad, N. (2005) 'Trafficked Persons or Economic Migrants? Bangladeshis in India', in K. Kempadoo (ed.) *Trafficking and Prostitution Reconsidered: New Perspectives on Migration, Sex Work, and Human Rights*. Boulder, CO: Paradigm Publishers.

Amnesty International (2004) 'So does that mean I have Rights?' Protecting the Human Rights of Women and Girls Trafficked for Forced Prostitution in Kosovo'. Amnesty International.

Anderson, B. (2004) 'Migrant Domestic Workers and Slavery', in Christien van den Anker (ed.) *The Political Economy of New Slavery*. Basingstoke: Palgrave Macmillan.

Anderson, B. and O'Connell Davidson, J. (2003) 'Is Trafficking in Human Beings Demand Driven? A Multi-Country Pilot Study'. Geneva: International Organization for Migration.

Andreas, P. (1998) 'Smuggling Wars: Law Enforcement and Law Evasion in a Changing World', *Transnational Organized Crime*, 4: 75–90.

Andreas, P. and Snyder, T. (2000) *The Wall Around the West: State Borders and Immigration Controls in North America and Europe*. Maryland: Rowman & Littlefield Publishers, Inc.

Anker, C. van den (2004) *The Political Economy of New Slavery*. Basingstoke: Palgrave Macmillan.

Anti-Slavery International (2002) *'The Trafficking of Child Camel Jockeys to the United Arab Emirates. Report to the UN Working Group on Contemporary Forms of Slavery'*. London: Anti-Slavery International.

Anti-Slavery International (2006) *'Trafficking for Forced Labour UK Country Report'*. London: Anti-Slavery International.

Aronowitz, A. (2001) 'Smuggling and Trafficking in Human Beings: The Phenomenon, the Markets that Drive it and the Organizations that Promote it', *European Journal on Criminal Policy and Research*, 9: 163–195.

Asis, M. (2004) 'Borders, Globalization and Irregular Migration in Southeast Asia', in A. Ananta and E.N. Arifin (eds) *International Migration in Southeast Asia*. Singapore: Institute of Southeast Asian Studies.

Bales, K. (2000) 'Expendable People: Slavery in the Age of Globalization', *Journal of International Affairs*, 53: 461–485.

Bales, K. (2005) *Understanding Global Slavery*. Berkeley: University of California Press.

Bastia, T. (2005) 'Child Trafficking or Teenage Migration? Bolivian Migrants in Argentina', *International Migration* 43: 57–89.

Beare, M. (1997) 'Illegal Migration: Personal Tragedies, Social Problems, or National Security Threats', *Transnational Organized Crime*, 3: 11–41.

Bosniak, L. (1991) 'Human Rights, State Sovereignty and the Protection of Undocumented Migrants Under the International Migrant Workers Convention'. *International Migration Review*, 25: 737-770.

Brochmann, G. and Hammar, T. (1999) (eds) *Mechanisms of Immigration Control: A Comparative Analysis of European Regulation Policies*. Oxford: Berg.

Bruinsma, G.J.N. and Meershoek, G. (1999) 'Organized Crime and Trafficking Women from Eastern Europe in the Netherlands', *Transnational Organized Crime*, 4: 105–118.

Budapest Group (1999) *'The Relationship Between Organized Crime and Trafficking in Aliens'*. Vienna: International Centre for Migration Policy Development.

Castles, S. (2003) 'Towards a Sociology of Forced Migration and Social Transformation', *Sociology*, 37: 13–34.

Chapkis, W. (2003) 'Trafficking, Migration and the Law: Protecting Innocents, Punishing Immigrants', *Gender and Society*, 17: 923–37.

Chiang, L. (1999) 'Trafficking in Women', in K.D. Askin and D.M. Koening (eds) *Women and International Human Rights Law*. Ardsley, NY: Transnational Publishers.

Christie, N. (1986) 'The Ideal Victim', in E.A. Fattah (ed.) *From Crime Policy to Victim Policy*. Basingstoke: Macmillan.

Christie, N. (2000) *Crime Control as Industry*. London: Routledge.

Chuang, J. (1998) 'Redirecting the Debate over Trafficking in Women: Definitions, Paradigms, and Contexts', *Harvard Human Rights Journal*, 11: 65–108.

Commission of Experts on the Former Yugoslavia (1994) *'Final Report of the Commission of Experts on the Former Yugoslavia'*. New York: UN Security Council S/1994/674-27 May 1994.

Corrin, C. (2005) 'Transitional Road for Traffic: Analysing Trafficking in Women From and Through Central and Eastern Europe', *Europe-Asia Studies*, 57: 543-560.

Doezema, J. (2000) 'Loose Women or Lost Women? The Re-emergence of the Myth of White Slavery in Contemporary Discourses of Trafficking in Women', *Gender Issues*, 18: 23–50.

Doezema, J. (2002) 'Who Gets to Choose? Coercion, Consent, and the UN Trafficking Protocol', *Gender and Development*, 10: 20–27.

Dottridge, M. (2002) 'Trafficking in Children in West and Central Africa', *Gender and Development*, 10: 38–42.

Edwards, S. (1989) *Policing Domestic Violence*. London: Sage.

Experts Group on Trafficking in Human Beings (2004) *'Report of the Experts Group on Trafficking in Human Beings'*. Brussels: European Commission Directorate-General Justice, Freedom and Security.

Finckenauer, J.O. (2001) 'Russian Transnational Organized Crime and Human Trafficking', in D. Kyle and R. Koslowski (eds) *Global Human Smuggling – Comparative Perspectives*. Baltimore: The Johns Hopkins University Press.

Gallagher, A. (2001) 'Human Rights and the New UN Protocols on Trafficking and Migrant Smuggling: A Preliminary Analysis', *Human Rights Quarterly*, 23: 975–1004.

Gallagher, A. (2002) 'Trafficking, Smuggling and Human Rights: Tricks and Treaties', *Forced Migration Review*, 12: 25–28.

Goodey, J. (2005) 'Sex Trafficking in the European Union', in J. Sheptycki and A. Wardak (eds) *Transnational and Comparative Criminology*. London: Glasshouse.

Green, P. and Grewcock, M. (2002) 'The War against Illegal Immigration: State Crime and the Construction of a European Identity', *Current Issues in Criminal Justice*, 14: 87–101.

Home Office and Scottish Executive (2006) *'Tackling Human Trafficking – Consultation on Proposals for a UK Action Plan'*. London: Home Office.

Hughes, D. (2000) 'The "Natasha" Trade: The Transnational Shadow Market of Trafficking in Women', *Journal of International Affairs*, 53: 625–51.

Human Rights Watch (2002) *'Key Findings of the Global Report on Child Soldiers 2001'*. New York: Human Rights Watch.

International Labour Organization (2001) *'Combating Trafficking in Children for Labour Exploitation in West and Central Africa'*. Geneva: ILO.

Kapur, R. (2002) 'The Tragedy of Victimization Rhetoric: Resurrecting the "Native" Subject in International/Postcolonial Feminist Legal Politics', *Harvard Law Review*, 15: 1–37.

Kaye, M. (2003) *'The Migration-Trafficking Nexus: Combating Trafficking Through the Protection of Migrants' Human Rights'*. London: Anti-Slavery International.

Keire, M. (2001) 'The Vice Trust: A Reinterpretation of the White Slavery Scare in the United States, 1907–1917', *Journal of Social History*, 35: 5–41.

Kelly, L. (2002) *'Journeys of Jeopardy: A Review of Research on Trafficking in Women and Children in Europe'*, *IOM Migration Research Series No. 11*. Geneva: IOM.

Kelly, L. (2005) *'Fertile Fields: Trafficking in Persons in Central Asia'*. Vienna: IOM.

Kelly, L. and Regan, L. (2000) *'Stopping Traffic: Exploring the Extent of, and Responses to, Trafficking in Women for Sexual Exploitation in the UK'*. London: Home Office.

Kempadoo, K. (2005) (ed.) *'Trafficking and Prostitution Reconsidered: New Perspectives on Migration, Sex Work, and Human Rights'*. Boulder, CO: Paradigm Publishers.

Kielland, A. and Sanogo, I. (2002) *'Burkina Faso: Child Labour Migration from Rural Areas'*. Terre des Hommes: World Bank.

Koser, K. (2000) 'Asylum Policies, Trafficking and Vulnerability', *International Migration* 38, 3: 91–112.

Kyle, D. and Siracusa, C. (2005) 'Seeing the State Like a Migrant – Why So Many Non-criminals Break Immigration Laws', in I.A. W. van Schendel and I. Abraham (eds) *Illicit Flows and Criminal Things – State, Borders, and the Other Side of Globalization*. Bloomington: Indiana University Press.

Lee, M. (2005) 'Human Trade and the Criminalization of Irregular Migration', *International Journal of the Sociology of Law*, 33: 1–15.

Lees, S. (1996) *Carnal Knowledge: Rape on Trial*. London: Penguin.

Lim, L. (1998) *'The Sex Sector: The Economic and Social Bases of Prostitution in Southeast Asia'*. Geneva: ILO.

Macklin, A. (2003) 'Dancing Across Borders: "Exotic Dancers", Trafficking, and Canadian Immigration Policy', *International Migration Review*, 37: 464–500.

Melossi, D. (2003) 'In a Peaceful Life – Migration and the Crime of Modernity in Europe/Italy', *Punishment and Society*, 5: 371–97.

Melossi, D. (2005) 'Security, Social Control, Democracy and Migration within the "Constitution" of the EU', *European Law Journal*, 11: 5–21.

Miers, S. (2003) *Slavery in the Twentieth Century: The Evolution of a Global Problem*. Walnut Creek, CA: Alta Mira Press.

Morrison, J. (1998) *'The Cost of Survival: The Trafficking of Refugees to the UK'*. London: The Refugee Council.

Munro, J. (2006) 'Stopping Traffic? A Comparative Study of Responses to the Trafficking in Women for Prostitution', *British Journal of Criminology*, 46: 318–33.

Murray, A. (1998) 'Debt-bondage and Trafficking: Don't Believe the Hype', in K. Kempadoo and J. Doezema (*eds*) *Global Sex Workers*. London: Routledge.

Nadelmann, E. (1990) 'Global Prohibition Regimes: The Evolution of Norms in International Society', *International Organization*, 44: 479–526.

Ould, D. (2004) 'Trafficking and International Law', in C. van den Anker (ed.) *The Political Economy of New Slavery*. Basingstoke: Palgrave Macmillan.

Patten, W. (2004) '*U.S.: Efforts to Combat Human Trafficking and Slavery. Human Rights Watch Testimony Before the U.S. Senate Judiciary Committee'*. Human Rights Watch.

Pearson, E. (2005) *The Mekong Challenge. Human Trafficking: Redefining Demand.* Bangkok: International Labour Organization.

Phongpaichit, P., Piriyarangsan, S. and Treeat, N. (1998) *Guns, Girls, Gambling and Ganja: Thailand's Illegal Economy and Public Policy*. Chang Mai: Silkworm Books.

Piper, N. (1999) 'Labour Migration, Trafficking and International Marriage: Female Cross-Border Movements into Japan', *Asian Journal of Women's Studies*, 5: 69–99.

Piper, N. (2005) 'A Problem by a Different Name? A Review of Research on Trafficking in South-East Asia and Oceania', *International Migration*, 43: 203–33.

Rehn, E. and Sirleaf, E. (2002) 'Women, War and Peace: The Independent Experts' Assessment on the Impact of Armed Conflict on Women and Women's Role in Peace-Building'. New York: UNIFEM.

Richard, A.O.N. (1999) 'International Trafficking in Women to the United States: A Contemporary Manifestation of Slavery and Organized Crime'. Centre for the Study of Intelligence, State Department Bureau of Intelligence, US State Department.

Ruggiero, V. (1997) 'Trafficking in Human Beings: Slaves in Contemporary Europe', *International Journal of the Sociology of Law*, 25: 231–44.

Salt, J. and Stein, J. (1997) 'Migration as a Business: The Case of Trafficking', *International Migration*, 35: 467–91.

Sanghera, J. (2005) 'Unpacking the Trafficking Discourse', in K. Kempadoo (ed.) *Trafficking and Prostitution Reconsidered: New Perspectives on Migration, Sex Work, and Human Rights*. Boulder, CO: Paradigm Publishers.

Sassen, S. (2000) 'Women's Burden: Counter-geographies of Globalization and the Feminization of Survival', *Journal of International Affairs*, 53: 503.

Schloenhardt, A. (1999) 'Organized Crime and the Business of Migrant Trafficking', *Crime, Law and Social Change*, 32: 203–333.

Scully, E. (2001) 'Pre-Cold War Traffic in Sexual Labour and its Foes: Some Contemporary Lessons', in D. Kyle, and R. Koslowski (eds) *Global Smuggling – Comparative Perspectives*. Baltimore: The Johns Hopkins University Press.

Sharma, B. (2006) *'Contemporary Forms of Slavery in Brazil'*. London: Anti-Slavery International.

Shelley, L. (1999) 'Transnational Organized Crime: The New Authoritarianism', in H. Friman and P. Andreas (eds) *Illicit Global Economy and State Power*. Maryland: Rowman & Littlefield Publishers, Inc.

Shelley, L. (2003) 'The Trade in People in and from the Former Soviet Union', *Crime, Law and Social Change*, 40: 231–49.

Shelley, L., Picarelli, J. and Corpora, C. (2003) 'Global Crime Inc.', in M. Love (*ed.*) *Beyond Sovereignty: Issues for a Global Agenda*. California: Wadsworth.

Skeldon, R. (2000) 'Trafficking: A Perspective from Asia', *International Migration*, 38: 7–29.

Sullivan, B. (2003) 'Trafficking in Women: Feminism and New International Law', *International Feminist Journal of Politics*, 5: 67–91.

Taylor, I. and Jamieson, R. (1999) 'Sex Trafficking and the Mainstream of Market Culture', *Crime, Law and Social Change*, 32: 257–78.

UN High Commissioner for Human Rights (2002) *'Recommended Principles and Guidelines on Human Rights and Human Trafficking: Report of the UN High Commissioner for Human Rights to the Economic and Social Council'*. Geneva: UNHCHR.

Walvin, J. (1996) *Questioning Slavery*. London: Routledge.

Welch, M. (2003) 'Ironies of Social Control and the Criminalization of Immigrants', *Crime, Law and Social Change*, 39: 319–37.

Welch, M. and Schuster, L. (2005) 'Detention of Asylum Seekers in the US, UK, France, Germany, and Italy: A critical view of the Globalizing Culture of Control', *Criminal Justice*, 5: 331–55.

Williams, P. (1998) 'Organizing Transnational Crime: Networks, Markets and Hierarchies', *Transnational Organized Crime*, 4: 57–87.

Williams, P. (2002) 'Transnational Organized Crime and the State', in R.B. Hall (*ed.*) *Emergence of Private Authority in Global Governance*. West Nyack, NY: Cambridge University Press.

Wong, D. (2005) 'The Rumor of Trafficking', in W. van Schendel and I. Abraham (eds) *Illicit Flows and Criminal Things – States, Borders, and the Other Side of Globalization*. Bloomington: Indiana University Press.

Chapter 2

Historical approaches to the trade in human beings

John T. Picarelli

Introduction

> Nearly two centuries after the abolition of the transatlantic slave trade, and more than a century after slavery was officially ended in its last strongholds, the trade in human beings for any purpose must not be allowed to thrive in our time. (President George W. Bush in a speech to the United Nations on 23 September 2003)

History is often invoked when identifying the significance of fighting the trade in human beings. State leaders use history as a mechanism to frame their arguments, often casting themselves in the legacy of forebears like Abraham Lincoln in fighting the modern-day traders in human beings. Non-governmental organisations (NGOs) fashion themselves as carrying forward the legacies of famous activists like William Wilberforce, William Lloyd Garrison or Josephine Butler. Academics and other scholars write about the fight against 'modern-day' forms of the slave trade of yore. As the above quote attests, experts from all aspects of the fight against the trade use history to give trafficking the gravitas it deserves.

The irony here lies in the fact that experts have rarely engaged history to inform our present-day understanding of trafficking. Far too many approach trafficking ahistorically, pointing to globalising forces unleashed at the end of the Cold War as the root causes of trafficking. A rich literature probes the economic, social, political and cultural aspects of the history of slavery and slave trading, but rarely is this literature cited in works addressing contemporary trafficking in persons. That history can and should inform our understanding of trafficking in human beings is beyond doubt. However, we need to challenge the received wisdom about trafficking by using a historical approach to the trade in human beings and the forms of servitude it supports.

Focusing solely on the European experience with chattel slavery and other forms of labour servitude, three broad observations with implications for the present are apparent. First, contrary to the aforementioned quote, 'slavery' did not end in the 1800s and continued to evolve in new forms that an international trade in human beings supplied. Second, state policy vis-à-vis the trade of human beings was and remains a derivative of national interests and is not solely altruistic or idealistic. Most important, however, is the observation that traders in human beings historically were small entrepreneurial organisations that had significant ties to legitimate business and political interests and often operated both legally and illegally, with the latter sector of the market becoming more prominent over time. The ramifications of these observations for scholars and policymakers alike are explored at the conclusion of the chapter.

Servitude, unfree labour and the 'end of slavery'

One of the first lessons that we can draw from history is that our imprecise terminology has produced a skewed historical understanding of how slavery came to an end. The problem lies with the use of the term 'slavery' as synonymous with all labour practices wherein adults and/or children are employed against their will, often utilise threats of violence or other harm in order to obtain compliance from victims, withhold payment or make payments that fail to meet even subsistence levels, use debt or barter to maintain control and limit free movement of labourers.

Slavery (specifically chattel slavery) is but one form of this phenomenon that scholars refer to as unfree labour. Chattel slavery describes a condition whereby labourers are legally owned as property and therefore their owners can buy, sell or transfer them much like any other good. Once the legal sanction for chattel slavery is removed, this form of unfree labour no longer exists. Another form of unfree labour is indentured servitude, wherein a subject agrees to work for a specified term in return for passage and boarding. Closely related to this is peonage or debt bondage in which a person is not paid for labour in lieu of cancellation of a debt. Both forms of unfree labour place the labourer in a highly vulnerable situation, since the holder of the bond or indenture can often arbitrarily change the terms of the agreement and leave the labourer with no outlet for redress. Some scholars include other labour practices like penal labour and the truck system as forms of unfree labour.

In other words, while chattel slavery by and large came to an end in the 1800s, unfree labour did not. The conventional wisdom is that, during the 1800s, a combination of pressure from international abolitionist groups, alterations in state policies and changes in international economics brought slavery to an end. Indeed it is true that by the end of the 19th century, only a handful of states still legally supported slavery, and none in Europe or the Americas (Miers 2003). But unfree labour did not come to an end; instead, new forms of unfree labour evolved to take the place of chattel slavery. One of the few experts to recognise this change is Bales (2000), who posits a difference between 'old' slavery, wherein slaves were held as property and thus deemed valuable, and 'new' slavery, wherein slaves are no longer property but are seen as a disposable commodity. Before discussion of the ramifications of this historical understanding on current anti-trafficking policy, let us examine a brief history of the evolution of unfree labour.

Early form of slavery

The earliest form of unfree labour, slavery, is ancient – the Code of Hammurabi contains some of the earliest references. Greenidge (1958) notes that the early periods of chattel slavery in Europe were closely tied to war fighting. The history of chattel slavery in the Greco-Roman era was rooted in conquest and booty. The ancient Greek experience with chattel slavery is well documented, with some scholars tracing the origins of abolitionist movements to the Greek philosophers Antisthenes and Epictetus (Sawyer 1986). The Romans, meanwhile, wrote chattel slavery into the *Jus Gentium* or 'law of nations' that applied to Roman dealings with foreigners and thus spread legal sanction for slavery throughout the Roman Empire. Throughout the Middle Ages, with the breakdown of legal codes and the promotion of Feudal estates rooted in serfdom, chattel slavery disappeared in the northern regions of Europe but survived in Mediterranean Europe.

European explorers mapping the coasts of Africa and the Americas set into motion the return of chattel slavery, which was itself the result of three overlapping forces. The first was the establishment of colonies that adopted a plantation economy rooted in slavery.

Starting in the 1500s, the European powers followed in the explorers' footsteps and established colonies on the African coast and in the Americas. The staples of the colonial economy were agriculture and extracted commodities. Colonies increasingly adopted a plantation system as the most efficient method of production. But labour was not plentiful in the colonies since it was difficult to recruit labour from the home countries and attempts to press indigenous peoples into service failed miserably. Drescher (1986) summarises this evolution and the centrality of the plantation system:

> Historians have carefully detailed the movement of slave-grown sugar and the plantation system from the Levant through Cyprus, Crete, Sicily, Italy, Spain and the African-Atlantic Islands. The Iberian pioneers drew on both their Roman Law traditions and Mediterranean technology and capital in transporting the institution of slavery to the New World. As the center of sugar production moved westwards the source of slaves also shifted. (Drescher 1986)

Grafting the slave-dependent plantation system onto colonial economies in the Americas starved for indigenous labour created the economic demand for a trade in human beings.

A second factor was European labelling or 'othering' of Africans as 'natural slaves,' establishing the supply for the transatlantic trade. Aristotle is often credited with the first expression of natural slaves, which one expert summarised as 'a barbarian whose inclination was to defer and who was distinguished by brawn, not brain,' and thus required 'the direction of those who were gifted with ... intelligence and civilisation' (Blackburn 1997). The justification of natural slavery remained a constant in Europe throughout the Middle Ages, though in northern Europe the serfdom replaced slavery. Thus while Eltis (2000) notes that the social forces unleashed during the Renaissance, Reformation and Enlightenment led Europeans to craft for themselves a new identity that rejected slavery in northern Europe, such beliefs did not extend to non-Europeans. Both intellectual stances combined on the shores of Africa as Mediterraneans first undertook the slave trade based on their notions of natural slavery, while northern Europeans followed suit later with their views of the peoples of Africa as non-Europeans. The importance of this process is the creation of outsiders who are eligible (or natural) for slavery, or 'who is to be considered an outsider and therefore enslavable and who is an insider and thus unenslavable' (Eltis 2000).

29

Lastly, changes in technology and economic conditions fundamentally altered the capital-labour equation and fostered conditions favourable to the trade in chattel slaves. Europeans had by this time acquired the naval technology to enslave large numbers of Africans, transport them across the Atlantic and then return to the continent with the fruits of their labours. Combined with advances in powder-based armaments and cannon, Europeans were able to sail into African and American waters with relative impunity. Europe also developed capital markets necessary to underwrite such journeys and the plantation system in general. Rawley (1981) notes that 'the relaxation of the medieval ban on money-lending' meant that 'the banking enterprise that financed the slave trade flourished successively at Genoa, Amsterdam and London.'

The result was a trade in human beings that expanded for 300 years in terms of absolute numbers and geographical scope. Between 1660 and 1867, a total of 10 million slaves left Africa for the Americas, with 65 per cent of this trade occurring in the century prior to the age of abolition (Richardson 1998). While Portugal and Spain initially served as the largest traders in slaves, by the 1700s the British had overtaken and well eclipsed their combined trade. Between 1700 and 1810, British traders brought some 3 million slaves away from the African continent (Richardson 1998). The trade in slaves would eventually engulf the entire Atlantic coast of the African continent past the Horn of Africa, and few regions of the Americas were left unstained by the practice.

Indentured servitude

Indentured servitude never achieved the level of prominence of chattel slavery in the seventeenth and eighteenth centuries. Borne of the high costs of transporting labourers from Britain and Europe, indentured servants agreed to provide labour for a fixed term in return for free passage to the Americas. First appearing in the Jamestown colony in 1620, where it served as the initial labour source, indentured servitude provided at least 50 per cent of all white immigrants to the American colonies between 1633 and 1776 and roughly 75 per cent of Virginia settlers in the seventeenth century (Smith 1947; Craven 1971). Indentured servitude concentrated in Virginia and Barbados in the seventeenth century and expanded into Maryland and Barbados in the eighteenth century. The combination of high transport costs and low labour output placed indentured servitude at a distinct disadvantage to other forms of unfree labour (Galenson 1984), and by the nineteenth century it was a minor and decreasing form of unfree labour.

Abolition

In the 1800s, abolitionist groups in Great Britain, the US, France and elsewhere began to make strides into abolishing slavery. By the middle part of the century, the trade in slaves was almost universally recognised as illegal, and states were implementing measures to emancipate slaves in their colonies. Great Britain criminalised the trade in slaves in 1807, and later put more teeth into this law's enforcement by equating slave trading with piracy – the latter an offence punishable by death. Great Britain also took the lead in abolishing slavery altogether, emancipating all slaves within its colonies on 1 August 1834. By the year 1870, all of the major slave holding states in the Americas had emancipated their slaves and criminalised the trade in human beings.

Unfree labour continued after 1870, with indentured servitude and to a lesser degree debt bondage as the primary forms of unfree labour in the Americas and a robust trade in human beings supporting them. While many felt that emancipated slaves would enter a free labour market that would prove more profitable and less costly than chattel slavery, in reality labour was sparse and less productive after emancipation. Many slaves chose to leave the plantations in search of their own plots of land rather than re-enter the labour market as wage earners. The result was a significant labour shortage that drove up prices for former slave holders already deep in debt. Further complicating this labour shortage was the economic expansion of colonial economies during the 1800s, which strengthened the economic incentives to perpetuate the trade in human beings to provide unfree labour. Finally, changes in the prices of staple crops and extracted ores created incentives for colonial economies to lower already low labour costs.

A few examples from many highlight how this evolution played out. A rapidly industrialising US economy led to the use of indentured and indebted Chinese labourers in the expansion of America's infrastructure, like the transcontinental railroad. American labour recruiters in Mexico acquired seasonal labour for railroads, mines and farms agricultural industries whose owners often used debt bondage schemes to force these labourers to stay on permanently (McWilliams 1949). In the Caribbean, sugar plantations proliferated in the latter half of the nineteenth century, leading to increased competition that resulted in a steady decline in the price of this staple between 1846 and 1896. The falling prices further drove the sugar producers to search for ever cheaper sources of labour, naturally, thus driving a significant demand for indentured servants in the Caribbean (Northrup 1995).

A number of unsavoury aspects of indentured servitude and debt bondage from this era demonstrate that they evolved more out of chattel slavery than were resurrections of earlier forms of unfree labour by the same name. Indians and Chinese rarely volunteered willingly or with full knowledge of what awaited them, and the contracts these labourers signed contained provisions that allowed masters to dock pay and time accrued for even the smallest of infractions. Galenson (1984) notes that:

> immigrants normally worked for fixed terms of years, without the power to change employers, under legal obligation of specific performance of their contracts with penalties including imprisonment, and they were therefore bound under genuine contracts of servitude rather than simply service contracts of debt that could be terminated by repayment of a stated principal sum.

Thus it was not uncommon for labourers to make far less than they were promised, and to have to work well beyond the time their term of service should have expired (Kloosterboer 1960).

One well-documented episode of debt bondage was the recruitment of Asian labourers for projects in the western US. Signed to debt contracts, these labourers agreed to repay their transportation costs from wages earned in the US. While debt bondage was presented as voluntary, short-term wage labour, Bush (2000) notes that it often drifted into unfree labour:

> ... in being unsupervised by official authority and in lacking legal warranty. It was more of an informal, private and even secret arrangement: in the case of Indian labor, between a broker who recruited it and then hired it out to planters; in the case of Chinese labor, between the person who, having bought it from a broker, had full use of it until the purchase price had been recovered from the wages earned. Neither employer nor worker could call upon the law to enforce their respective rights. The condition of work therefore depended upon the benevolence of the owner and the opportunities for workers to desert. (Bush 2000)

The abuses of employers and the vulnerability of workers away from the eyes of government officials led to the substitution of debt bondsmen for labour expected of chattel slaves in the past.

Demography and geopolitics played a significant role in the transformation of the trade in human beings that supported these new forms of unfree labour. On the one hand, centuries of African slave trading left it inhospitable to locating indentured servants on numerous levels. On the other hand, the domestic labour migration patterns of China and India facilitated the recruitment of labourers for overseas assignments. In these states, centuries of isolation led to labourers who left rural areas for either domestic work in urban areas or overseas work in the colonies. Both migration patterns created populations ripe for recruitment into indentured servitude or debt bondage. As a result, between 1831 and 1920 some 58,832 indentured migrants left Africa for the Americas while 380,651 Chinese and 552,605 Indians made the same journey (Northrup 1995).

What made this form of indentured servitude different from that found prior to 1800 was not just the vast increase in the scale of migration of indentures, but the emphasis on recruiting non-Europeans from other colonial territories to serve as indentured servants. The recruitment and importation of Indian and, to a lesser degree, Chinese indentured servants, serves as the defining characteristic of the drastic shift in indentured servitude that occurred in the 1800s. By 1844, numerous Indians began coming to the British Caribbean colonies on five year indentures in return for passage, wages and basic health care. Kloosterboer (1960) estimates that some 200,000 Indians and 16,000 Chinese emigrated to British Guiana while 150,000 Indians were sent to Trinidad as well. Another historian notes that between 1834 and 1922, some 2.5 million indentured servants passed through this second phase of the system (Bush 2000).

Most telling is that former slaveholders did not see indentured servitude or debt bondage anything more than chattel slavery under a different name. In the minds of many planters, this was simply one outside group of labourers replacing another:

Despite ... government efforts to protect indentured laborers and distinguish them from slaves, the inescapable fact was that their lives were controlled by employers who had recently been slave owners and protected by local officials who were closely allied to this class. Slavery has been ended over the protests of sugar planters, who in many cases were neither inclined nor capable of changing their labor practices. Associations with slavery were

> reinforced by the fact that in many early locations indentured laborers took over not merely the jobs but also the dwellings of the emancipated slaves. (Northrup 1995)

The isolation of plantations from the metropolitan centre, and their strong ties to local politicians and global business interests, insulated the culture of slavery from changing with the times. Indentured servitude thus emerged rooted in the cultural aspects of slavery and evolved as a new form of unfree labour.

Hence 1870 did not mark the end of all forms unfree labour. Chattel slavery, based on a system of legal codes to enforce the bondage, was wiped away at the stroke of a pen as state after state criminalised and emancipated its slaves. What did not disappear were the economic incentives and ideological beliefs of those who sought to benefit from unfree labour. The demand for servitude remained in place, as traders merely adopted new forms and tactics to maintain control while avoiding the eyes of government regulators and non-governmental abolitionists. And it was this demand that maintained a sturdy trade in human beings that evolved and remains with us today.

States and the trade in human beings

A second lesson from history that one can apply to the modern era is that the behaviour of nation-states vis-à-vis the trade in human beings is rooted in their interests. As such, the history of states concerning the trade is an uneven one, with states at first establishing and running the trade and later abolishing and working to end it. Examining selected portions of this history shows how state interests concerning the trade have evolved.

States began with a strong interest in seeing the growth and continuation of the trade in African slaves. First, through mercantilist policies, and later through the benefits of colonial economies and trade, European states had a solid economic interest in maintaining both chattel slavery and the trade in slaves. Between 1650 and 1850, the value of Atlantic commerce between Europe, Africa and North America associated with slavery and the trade in African slaves increased from £15 million to £77.5 million (Inikori 1998). This connection between mercantilism and slavery did not go unnoticed by observers of the time. Malachy Postlethwayt wrote in *The African Trade: The Great Pillar and Support of the British Plantation Trade in*

America (1745) that the 'Negro-Trade and the natural consequences resulting from it, may be justly esteemed an inexhaustible Fund of Wealth and Naval Power to this Nation' and that slavery was 'the first principle and foundation of all the rest, the mainspring of the machine which sets every wheel in motion.'

The actions of individual European states reflect this connection between mercantilism, trade and slavery. The Portuguese established a *feitoria* (factory) on Arguim Island off the coast of Mauritania in 1445 to provide some 800 to 1,000 slaves annually – the first organised effort to collect and transport slaves from Africa overseas. By the end of the fifteenth century, the Portuguese had established forts and trading posts along the West African coast from Mauritania to Angola and even around the horn of Africa in Mozambique. The Portuguese colony of São Tomé served as a critical source of sugar after using slave labour to clear forests and operate the sugar industry. By the end of the 1500s, São Tomé alone had imported some 76,000 slaves (Rawley 1981). During the sixteenth and the first half of the seventeenth century, Portugal owned a virtual monopoly on the African slave trade. After Columbian contact, Portuguese slave traders were called upon to supply slaves to Portuguese and Spanish colonies, and the ever increasing need for slaves in Brazil served as a constant driver of Portuguese slave trading.

Other European powers rose to prominent positions in the slave trade in order to improve their international position. During the Hundred Years War, Dutch forces conquered various Portuguese possessions in the Americas, but none proved as important as the island of Curacao in the Caribbean. Curacao became a critical slave-trading centre for South America as well as a major entrepôt for traders coming from West African slave factories. From 1640 to the end of the decade, owing largely to the number and technical sophistication of their ships as well as to the strength of their banking sector, the Dutch became the second most powerful slave trading state in the Atlantic market (Rawley 1981). The British, seeking to improve their international position through colonial wealth, conquered Spanish possessions throughout the Caribbean and slave trading centres along the African coast. The treaties ending the wars of Spanish Succession in 1711 and Austrian Succession in 1748 effectively ended Dutch and Spanish prominence in the slave trade, though the Netherlands retained their slave factories in Africa. Britain also expanded its colonial possessions on the North American continent throughout this period, and in so doing expanded slavery through the introduction of the plantation system to these colonies.

France followed a similar course to Britain in North America, starting plantations in the Louisiana territories that would lead to a growing trade in slaves in the western American colonies in the eighteenth and nineteenth centuries.

In sum, the trade in human beings and chattel slavery paralleled the growth of mercantilist trading systems. Chattel slavery formed the backbone of a triangular trade that connected European consumers to raw materials that African slaves produced and North American colonial producers refined. A parallel trade formed in South America, connecting European consumers with products drawn from agricultural plantations and mines that relied on chattel slavery to provide labour. European states created quasi-public monopolies to oversee the trade, while privately-held trading vessels worked the coast of Africa to acquire slaves, sailed across the Atlantic to deposit their cargoes and returned laden with goods and staples from the colonies.

The rapid growth of a truly international abolitionist movement began to change this in the 1800s. Abolitionism started as separate movements in Great Britain, France and the US in the late 1700s, and soon began to coordinate their efforts. The abolitionists first targeted the slave trade and later slavery itself. By the mid-nineteenth century, the movement held its first multilateral summit and delegates attended from Great Britain, the US, France, Spain, Switzerland and elsewhere, and by the 1900s abolitionists worked through new multilateral institutions like the League of Nations and the UN to achieve their goals. Throughout their existence, abolitionists have sought to inform societies about slavery and servitude in order to bring pressure on states to end their participation and the participation of other states. Abolitionists first sought for states to end their participation in the slave trade, then emancipate their slaves and finally bring their power to bear in order to convince other states to do likewise.

On the surface, the abolitionist movement met with great success. Most European states had emancipated their slaves by the mid-1800s, and some of the largest powers committed naval forces to halt the trade in slaves. However, national interests continued to guide the policies of states as well, making for a more complex picture. For example, Great Britain's decisions to ban the slave trade in 1807 and slave holding altogether in 1833 were neither purely humanitarian nor guided entirely by self-interests, but rather reflect a combination of the two:

The actual reasons for this volte-face by the leading slave-trading nation at the height of its power, when it controlled the largest number of slave-using colonies, have been the subject of academic debate. It has been portrayed on the one hand as the triumph of humanitarianism over vested interests, and on the other as the result of changing economic interests unleashed by the industrial revolution. Clearly ideology, economics, and politics were intertwined, but scholars have reached no consensus as to how they interacted or why the movement gained such popular support. (Miers 2003)

Likewise, unfree labour did not end during this period, known as 'the age of abolition'. For indeed states overlooked abuses of new labour systems that abolitionists only later recognised as forms of servitude. Emmer's (1985) examination of female indentured servants brought from India to Surinam between 1873 and 1916 details the industrial organisation of indentured servitude and the state's role in it. The British colonial office in India would license an agent in Calcutta, who in turn oversaw recruiting. The agent operated as part of a network, with assistant recruiters, recruiters, sub-recruiters and head recruiters all reporting to him. Recruiters in India supplied a specified number of indentureds to each British colony, and were tasked with the additional requirement that women constitute 40 per cent of the recruits (Emmer 1985). The distributed nature of recruiting practices for indentured servants were wide open to abuse and illegal acts, so long as they remained hidden from any state regulators. Discussing the arkatia, Indian recruiters of indentureds, Tinker (1974) notes:

> The arkatia was regarded as playing the most villainous part in the whole operation. Usually the arkatia worked within a local radius; he relied upon his local knowledge and local contacts. He knew who was in trouble, who had fallen out with his family, who was in disgrace, who was wild or wanton. If a big man wanted to get rid of a troublemaker, the arkatia was in contact ... He would then tell a story calculated to appeal to the individual prospect. (Tinker 1974)

Having secured a recruit, the arkatia turned him over to a licensed recruiter to get the local authorities (ie agents) to sanction the recruit as ready for debarkation. While licensed, many recruiters used illicit and clandestine methods like coercion, oftentimes debt bondage, in order to obtain control over and compel the migrant into the indentured state (Tinker 1974).

Whether through ignorance or benign neglect, states allowed unfree labour practices to continue in order to reap the benefits from colonial economies. As late as the 1920s, for example, NGOs were accusing the Compagnie Forestiere Sangha-Oubangui in French Equatorial Africa of using imprisonment and violence to press local labourers into slave-like conditions in the collection of rubber. Likewise, male and female labourers were pressed into service for British farmers in Kenya after the First World War, resulting in conditions akin to plantations. States also showed a significant lack of will when confronted with charges of unfree labour continuing in their colonial territories. In 1905, an anti-slavery group published evidence that the Peruvian Amazon Company, a British rubber company operating in Putumayo, not only held labourers from Barbados in debt bondage but that the company had also enslaved indigenous labourers. While British law clearly allowed for Britons associated with the company to be tried in Britain, the investigator assigned to the case found it difficult to collect evidence and the case was never brought to trial. Likewise, the atrocities that befell indigenous populations in the Belgian Congo during the boom years of the 1920s were well-documented but rarely acted upon (Hochschild 1998).

Thus, when European states did set out to 'combat slavery' through naval patrols or other active measures, they did not act entirely out of altruism. Indeed, these states used the arguments and evidence collected from abolitionist NGOs to improve their hold over colonial territories. A number of scholars have made a convincing argument that anti-slavery was an element of state policy that succumbed to national interests and therefore can be clearly interpreted through the lens of state power (Miers 2003). French and Italian representatives to the League of Nations' Temporary Slavery Commission highlighted slave raiding near the Sahara in part to justify the presence of their troops in their African possessions, and states used the trade in human beings to further tighten passport controls (Miers 2003; Salter 2002). Italy also used anti-slavery to try to obtain a moral basis for its October 1935 invasion of Ethiopia, providing evidence to the League of Nations and associated bodies of its success in freeing slaves in occupied territory.

In conclusion, states approached the trade in human beings and servitude through the lens of self interest. Where the state benefited from chattel slavery or the trade in human beings, it was taxed and regulated much like other forms of commerce. After abolitionists crafted a devastating argument detailing the immorality of the trade and built an impressive movement behind them, states criminalised the trade and on the surface sought to take measures to end the trade. But even in the face of this effort, states either retained or allowed some elements of the trade and of servitude to continue in order to maintain their colonial interests.

The traders in human beings

There are three observations we can draw from a historicised examination of human trafficking that lend themselves to improving our understanding of today's traders. The first lesson is that traders in human beings were entrepreneurial and small in size. In the 1600s and 1700s, while state-owned and quasi-public companies monopolised the trade in slaves, it was individuals and small private traders that conducted the bulk of the trade. Akinjogbin (1966) provides a detailed examination of one of these entrepreneurs, the British slave trader Archibald Dalzel. During the middle eighteenth century, Dalzel made the decision to enter the slave trade due to the lack of gainful employment coupled with a need to save his family from debt and ruin. Operating from the British fort at Whydah, Dalzel earned some £1,000 annually trading slaves with the French and Portuguese. Dalzel would parlay these gains into the sole ownership of three vessels, each of which earned him profits from the triangular trade between England, Africa and the New World. Thus, in the span of a decade, Dalzel had legally created a small slaving and trading company from the trade in chattel slaves.

A second conclusion is that traders in human beings maintained ties to commercial and government interests. While small, these traders were able to generate significant revenues that provided a platform for expansion into other forms of commerce. Profits of £7,000 for an individual voyage and some £12,000 for three voyages were possible. Likewise, African slaves were viewed as a special form of cargo for merchantment, and thus the ships that traded in slaves were also used for other forms of commerce. Consider this description of the early Spanish trade in African slaves:

> Sevillian Genoese and their capital resources played a significant role in the early Spanish slave trade. These Genoese enterprisers in Seville purchased licenses from the Crown. Their activities widened to a detailed organisation of slave trading. They

financed slaving voyages; in the New World they exchanged slaves for sugar and invested in sugar production. While their business interest expanded, they established agents in America to supervise their affairs, usually under powers of attorney with a short term to discourage fraud. (Rawley 1981)

Hyde *et al* (1953) also notes that slave traders did not just transport slaves during the middle passage, but also hauled European goods to barter for slaves and ivory. Finally, the slave traders of Bordeaux and La Rochelle were largely concentrated in 40 family-owned companies that formed a merchant elite. The traders combined their own capital with investors from major French cities to sponsor voyages, and in the eighteenth century were subsidised by the French state up to 60 per cent for each slave delivered to French colonies, cementing both commercial and governmental ties in the process.

The last conclusion to draw is that slave trading always contained an element of black marketeering, one that became more prominent as countries criminalised the trade in human beings and unfree labour. Smuggling slaves from Africa goes back to the 1600s. In the 1640s the Dutch exploited the Spanish revocation of Portuguese rights to sell slaves on Spanish territory by smuggling slaves into Spanish colonies. States were generally tolerant of the illicit trade in slaves as it met the exploding demand for slaves on the plantations, as black market traders were more efficient and cost-effective than the monopoly-controlled trading systems. Indeed, the Spanish tolerated the illicit trade in slaves to its colonies in the 1640s and 1650s for this reason (Rawley 1981). The slave trade in Bermuda is another example of how these forces combined to form a black market for slaves. By the 1670s, Bermuda served as a black market transhipment station, where slaves were offloaded from ships transiting to other markets rather than remaining on the island as their manifests would note. Private individuals thereby short-circuited the top-down approach of the large companies, using smuggling and off-the-record trades of slaves to accomplish these ends.

During the 1800s, the balance of the trade in human beings steadily tilted towards the illicit side as the British first banned the slave trade and then used naval patrols to try to bring it to a definitive end. One estimate, based on detailed archival research, identified some 3,033 French traders in slaves operating in the black market, which delivered some 25 per cent of the trade in slaves (Daget 1979). This high number of slave traders is also evidence of the continued domination of small, entrepreneurial traders in slaves in the 1800s.

Eltis (1979) notes that some 338 black market French slave traders brought some 105,000 African slaves into the French West Indies between 1821 and 1833. The illicit slave trade during this time was also far more multilateral than other forms of the trade. In 1820, the slave trade to Cuba was criminalised, but Spanish ships continued to carry slaves to the island until 1835, when Spain signed a treaty with Great Britain that allowed the latter to board Spanish-flagged ships looking for slaves on board. After this date, Portuguese and American flagged vessels continued to bring slaves to Cuba.

The trade in human beings after 1836 in Brazil is an excellent illustration of how all three observations about the traders in human beings come together. Black marketeering served as a natural outlet for the trade in human beings after abolition. After Brazil's 1826 treaty to end the importation of slaves in 1829, the tempo of the slave trade doubled and then tripled annually. Indeed, some 370,000 slaves had been smuggled into Brazil between 1840 and 1849 (Lloyd 1968). Likewise, slave trading remained strictly small in scope and entrepreneurial:

> On the whole, the later slave trade drew its participants from the Portuguese commercial class in Rio de Janeiro. In 1849, the Portuguese immigrants formed approximately 10 per cent of the population of Rio de Janeiro and its suburbs. Although of all economic levels, most of them shared two common characteristics: They had once been impoverished immigrants from Portugal or the islands off Africa; and most were engaged in trade or small business ... Most slave-traders had originally immigrated as young boys from Portugal, the Azores, or Madeira. Usually, they came as indentured servants to work in gin shops, petty dry-goods stores, and on slave ships as common seamen. When they became free of their 'masters', many joined the jobless poor whites of the cities. Others participated in the slave trade because no other way of earning a living was open to them. (Karasch 1967)

Over time, the risks associated with the illegal slave trade drove out the occasional traders and thus consolidated the trade in slaves into the hands of 'a small minority of merchants of Portuguese extraction, who had always controlled the nominally independent government' (Lloyd 1968). The trade in slaves therefore integrated itself into the governance of Brazil through corruption, as bribes were paid to those in control of the ports, to customs officials, to judges and other political agents. Corruption acquired clearances from port inspectors and papers for the ships to evade British patrols (Rodrigues 1965).

Karasch (1967) profiled Brazilian slave traders of this age and demonstrates their entrepreneurial nature, links to legitimate business and governments and black marketeering. Manoel Pinto da Fonesca, one of the wealthiest men in Rio estimated to hold £1.2 million in 1851, worked fastidiously in the late 1830s and 1840s to construct a trading house that operated on four continents and had the power to squeeze out many smaller slave traders from the market. His profits from the slave trade, estimated at one point to be roughly £150,000 per annum, allowed him to make substantial loans to the Brazilian government. Another trader, José Bernardino de Sá, was rumoured to have even more economic clout than Fonesca. Sá owned slave stations in southern Africa, used Portuguese-flagged ships to transport slaves and held a trading house in Rio, he like many other traders shifted to charter American ships to transport his slaves on their return legs from Africa. One legacy of Sá was 'his use of American-built steamers capable of transporting 1,000 to 1,500 slaves each trip' and having 'the Cacique especially built in New York and fitted [for] the reception of 1,500 slaves' (Karasch 1967).

The combination of entrepreneurship, embeddedness and black marketeering during this era also gave rise to some of the first transnational criminal organisations. Until 1821, for example, Florida provided an ideal location for smuggling, and was so well organised that a slave ferry operated between Havana and Florida starting in 1818. Richard Drake (1972), in his memoir of slave trading, notes that 'Florida was a sort of nursery for slave-breeders, and many American citizens grew rich by trafficking in Guinea negroes, and smuggling them continually, in small parties, through the southern United States'. Backed by capital obtained from American and Spanish mercantile houses, Drake was also responsible for the creation of a slave trading station off the coast of Honduras in 1940 that traded slaves to cities throughout the US. Corruption followed the trade, either through the active involvement of public officials in the slave trade or through bribery of port officials and the like.

In the end, these trends regarding traders in human beings helped perpetuate the trade to serve new forms of unfree labour. Recruiters of indentured servants and bonded labour are a good example of these trends continuing. By and large a function of private enterprise, recruiters were supposed to inform labourers of the conditions of work, the location of the work and the length of their contract. However, recruiters either obfuscated or ignored these conditions, and indeed engaged in illegal practices in order to meet their quotas:

> Often the recruiting was done in such a manner that there was hardly any question of a free choice on the part of the laborers. This became particularly known of China. The poverty-stricken Chinese were tempted with loans, after receipt of which they were immediately in the power of the recruiting agents because of the Chinese laws pertaining to debt slavery. Naturally they were also tempted with false promises of a glorious future in the foreign countries. (Kloosterboer 1960)

> The trade [in indentureds from China] was largely in the hands of two British firms, Tait and Company and Syme, Muir and Company. 'The latter built a special barracoon or "pig pen" (chu-tsai kuan), as the Chinese called it, in front of their firm' where the potential emigrants were stripped naked, examined for defects, and, if approved, made to put their mark on labor contracts then stamped or painted with the letter of their destination. (Northrup 1995)

Examples of recruiters engaging in illegal and clandestine behaviour were so common that the 'paragraphs on recruiters' licenses in the annual reports to the Protector of Emigrants provide ample evidence of this', including theft of money and valuables, illegal detention and rape (Emmer 1985). Furthermore, it was not out of the ordinary for the use of force to come into the recruiting process. In 1930, a League of Nations investigative committee led by Cuthbert Christy of Great Britain published its first report on unfree labour that accused Liberian officials of establishing a front company that used military units to forcibly recruit workers for Spanish cocoa plantation and the American Firestone rubber company (Christy 1930).

The trade in indentured servants, like the slave trade, relied on a large base of entrepreneurs and individuals that had a vested stake in seeing it continue. Individual recruiters were drawn from indigenous peoples and would bring their recruits to the firms located in the major port cities. Since recruiters were paid by the head and fees steadily increased during the 1800s as demand for indentured servants rose, the tactics that recruiters employed became steadily more illegal. It became common practice for black market Indian recruiters called arkatia to canvass markets, railway stations, temples and urban squares for potential recruits, whom they handed over to official recruiters for a fee. A story titled 'An Indian Slave

Trade' in the London Standard of 5 April 1871 described an Indian recruiter named Buldeo Jemadar who used deceptive recruiting and force to coerce young women into indentured servitude in Jamaica (Tinker 1974). Jemadar employed at least eight men to locate men and women, especially those coming to the city on pilgrimage, and delivered 'recruits' to a sub-agent, John Manasseh, who served as a go-between for Bird & Co, a firm that provided funds and other logistical support in order to aid recruiters in establishing relations with agents in Calcutta.

Overlap between the black market for indentured servants, legitimate business and government was as widespread as during the slave era. A number of corporations, such as the aforementioned Firestone rubber company, benefited from the employment of indentures. Some local government officials fostered an environment conducive to indentured servitude and debt bondage. Miers (2003) captures their mindset perfectly when she states that 'the colonial rulers need to extract labour led to ad hoc experiments, some of which resulted in atrocities causing scandals on an unprecedented scale'. Such experiments most often involved the trade in humans from other colonies and held under contract or debt bondage – such as the transfer of Indian indentured to South Africa. Indeed, some colonial officials experimented in multiple forms of unfree labour. In 1926, a French enquiry into high mortality rates amongst workers building a railroad from Brazzaville to the Atlantic Coast found the workers were in fact trafficked from Sudan and elsewhere and that trafficked women were supplied the labourers for sex on a regular basis.

The trade in Chinese debt bondsmen offers an additional facet to this overlap – the connection to the opium trade. The systematic bribery of Chinese officials overseeing the Opium ports of Whampoa, Macau and elsewhere shaped an environment conducive to trading in human beings (Meagher 1975). In 1861, the US Consul in Swatow, a Chinese opium port, noted at least 50,000 labourers that had been illegally recruited into indentured servitude and debt bondage. The British firms Syme, Muir & Co and Tait & Co, established barracoons at the Fukien Province port of Amoy and filled them using a series of recruiters quite similar in organisation to that found in India. Describing the conditions found in these locales, a British correspondence from 1853 notes that:

I have myself seen the arrangement for the shipment of coolies at Amoy: hundreds of them gathered together in barracoons, stripped naked, and stamped or painted with the letter C (California), P (Peru), or S (Sandwich Islands), on their breasts, according to the destination for which they are intended. (Meagher 1975)

Recruiters sold Chinese recruits to the companies at a varying per person rate, and periods of strong demand often drove recruiters to use deception, fraud and even kidnapping to attain the requested supply.

Conclusion

Trafficking in persons is a phenomenon that one cannot reduce to 'root causes' that culminated in the past few decades to give rise to a return of slavery. Rather, this chapter has demonstrated that trafficking in persons retains the legacies of prior forms of servitude and the trade in human beings, and that understanding these legacies is an additional source of comprehending contemporary trafficking in the local, regional, national and international settings. Evolving from chattel slavery, trafficking retains some of the core aspects of these historical forms while also adapting to meet new realities. Targeting vulnerable populations for profit or power remains relatively constant throughout history, but traders in human beings moved away from the use of legal codes to enslave chattels after abolition to focus more on debt contracts and other means to enslave trafficking victims. Policymakers would do well to try to anticipate how this evolutionary bent will impact new policy measures before they are implemented.

The evolution of the trade in human beings is not reducible to either economic or ideological forces. Indeed, the two remain at odds with one another throughout the history of servitude, reflected in how abolitionist groups matched wits with traders in human beings. When abolitionists lobbied on moral grounds for the end of the slave trade, traders appealed to the economic hardship they faced in ending slavery. When emancipation included remuneration for slave holders, traders returned to common arguments rooted in the 'natural slave' thesis to bring indentured servants from other parts of the globe into former slave-holding regions. Concurrently, traders shifted to an increasingly clandestine or illegal trade that retained markets and opened the way for new opportunities such as sexual slavery. Experts could garner much from this bottom-up approach to understanding how criminal markets continue to flourish.

The role of the state has predictably changed over time, but its importance to the continuation of the trade in human beings has changed little. As a reflection of the soft power of the abolitionist movements, states by and large adopted anti-slavery policies and allocated resources to enforce them both at home and abroad throughout the nineteenth and twentieth centuries. But states also aided and abetted the evolution of the trade in human beings, even after its abolition. Some states have done so wittingly, as is the case of some African and Middle East countries (Miers 2003). Perhaps more significantly, the competing interests of states meant they adopted an anti-slavery stance to serve other ends. The chapter notes numerous examples where colonial power, economic gain or geopolitical positions were enhanced through a selective use of anti-slavery policy. Scholars like Andreas (2000), Nadelmann (1990) and Grewcock (this volume) have laid the groundwork for furthering our understanding of how history exposes the more subtle shifts in state policy and their relation to the growth of trafficking in persons.

In the end, this chapter is not a Santayanan call to recall the past for fear of repeating it. Rather, the chapter is best understood in the tradition of Neustadt and May (1986) as a call for experts, decision-makers and scholars to use history to improve their work. In agreement with Bales, there is plenty of room for exploratory studies of trafficking in persons. This chapter serves as a call for more studies and reports that historicise trafficking. Doing so will not only close a significant gap in our understanding of how contemporary trafficking operates, but will build bridges to other rich literatures that have already debated the contemporary meanings of slavery's past.

References

Akinjogbin, I.A. (1966) 'Archibald Dalzel: Slave Trader and Historian of Dahomey', *Journal of African History*, 7: 67–78.

Andreas, P. (2000) *Border Games: Policing the U.S.–Mexico divide*. Ithaca: Cornell University Press.

Bales, K. (2000) *Disposable People: New Slavery in the Global Economy*. Berkeley: University of California Press.

Blackburn, R. (1997) *The Making of New World Slavery: From the Baroque to the Modern, 1492–1800*. London: Verso.

Bush, M.L. (2000) *Servitude In Modern Times*. Cambridge: Polity Press.

Christy, C. (1930) Report of the International Commission of Inquiry into the Existence of Slavery and Forced Labour in the Republic of Liberia. League of Nations.

Craven, W. (1971) *White, Red and Black: The Seventeenth-century Virginian.* Charlottesville: University Press of Virginia.

Daget, S. (1979) 'British Repression of the Illegal French Slave Trade: Some Considerations', in H. Gemery and J. Hogendorn (eds) *The Uncommon Market: Essays in the Economic History of the Atlantic Slave Trade.* New York: Academic Press.

Drake, P. (1972) *Revelations of a Slave Smuggler.* Northbrook: Metro Books.

Drescher, S. (1986) *Capitalism and Antislavery: British Mobilization in Comparative Perspective.* New York: Oxford University Press.

Eltis, D. (1979) 'The Direction and Fluctuation of the Transatlantic Slave Trade, 1821–1843: A Revision of the 1845 Parliamentary Paper', in H. Gemery and J. Hogendorn (eds) *The Uncommon Market: Essays in the Economic History of the Atlantic Slave Trade.* New York: Academic Press.

Eltis, D. (2000) *The Rise of African Slavery in the Americas.* Cambridge: Cambridge University Press.

Emmer, P.C. (1985) 'The Great Escape: The Migration of Female Indentured Servants from British India to Surinam, 1873–1916', in D. Richardson (ed.) *Abolition and its Aftermath: The Historical Context, 1790–1916.* London: Frank Cass and Company Limited.

Galenson, D. (1984) 'The Rise and Fall of Indentured Servitude in the Americas', *Journal of Economic History*, 44: 1–26.

Greenidge, C.W.W. (1958) *Slavery.* London: Ruskin House.

Hochschild, A. (1998) *King Leopold's Ghost.* Boston: Houghton Mifflin Company.

Hyde, F., Parkinson, B. and Marriner, S. (1953) 'The Nature and Profitability of the Liverpool Slave Trade', *Economic History Review*, 5: 368–77.

Inikori, J. (1998) 'Capitalism and Slavery', in S. Drescher and S.L. Engerman (eds) *A Historical Guide to World Slavery.* New York: Oxford University Press.

Karasch, M. (1967) *The Brazilian Slavers and the Illegal Slave Trade, 1836–1851,* unpublished MA thesis, University of Wisconsin.

Kloosterboer, W. (1960) *Involuntary Labour Since the Abolition of Slavery: A Survey of Compulsory Labour Throughout the World.* Westport: Greenwood Press.

Lloyd, C. (1968) *The Navy and the Slave Trade.* London: Frank Cass.

McWilliams, C. (1949) *North from Mexico: The Spanish-speaking People of the United States.* New York: Greenwood Press.

Meagher, A. (1975) *The Introduction of Chinese labourers to Latin America: The 'Coolie Trade', 1847–1874. History.* University of California: Davis.

Miers, S. (2003) *Slavery in the Twentieth Century: The Evolution of a Global Problem.* Walnut Creek: AltaMira.

Nadelmann, E. (1990) 'Global Prohibition Regimes: The Evolution of Norms in International Society', *International Organization*, 44: 479–526.

Neustadt, R. and May, E. (1986) *Thinking in Time: The Uses of History for Decisionmakers.* New York: Free Press.

Northrup, D. (1995) *Indentured Labour in the Age of Imperialism, 1834–1922.* New York: Cambridge University Press.

Rawley, J.A. (1981) *The Transatlantic Slave Trade: A History.* New York: W.W. Norton & Company.

Richardson, D. (1998) 'Volume of Trade', in S. Drescher and S.L. Engerman (eds) *A Historical Guide to World Slavery.* New York: Oxford University Press.

Rodrigues, J. (1965) *Brazil and Africa.* Berkeley: University of California Press.

Salter, M. (2002) 'The Appearance and Disappearance of the Passport in International Relations', *International Studies Association Annual Convention.* New Orleans.

Sawyer, R. (1986) *Slavery in the Twentieth Century.* London: Routledge & Kegan Paul.

Smith, A. (1947) *Colonists in Bondage: White Servitude and Convict Labour in America, 1607–1776.* Chapel Hill: University of North Carolina Press.

Tinker, H. (1974) *A New System of Slavery: The Export of Indian Labour Overseas, 1830–1920.* London: Oxford University Press.

Chapter 3

Researching into human trafficking: Issues and problems

Andrea Di Nicola

Introduction

Knowledge achieved through research develops progressively and sometimes slowly. People's ideas follow on from each other, they influence each other, they may be mutually contradictory or mutually confirmatory. The ultimate purpose of this process is always to understand phenomena and their causes, and to solve problems, thereby satisfying concrete societal needs. It is a fascinating process, which has its own rules. And the greater the value of the knowledge achieved through research, the greater the impact of that research on the solution of societal problems. This is also the case in the field of human trafficking: an area which in the last decade has attracted a great deal of attention, and in which there have also been numerous policy interventions to curb traffickers, to facilitate international cooperation, to prevent these criminal activities, and to assist victims. However, for a series of reasons, research in this area seems to languish. The knowledge achieved through research seems to be weak or piecemeal; and policies, as a consequence, are sometimes based more on emotions, political or dogmatic bias than on strong and substantiated research work.

Yet the value of good research on human trafficking is self-evident. To give one example, research on methods to estimate the number of trafficked persons in different countries of the world would not merely be an intellectual undertaking. It would enable the better allocation of law enforcement and preventative (limited) resources, and more accurate appraisal of the effectiveness of anti-human trafficking policies. It is only if research is able to provide an objective picture of the real world that policies would be tailor-made and more likely to succeed.

This chapter will also examine the area of research on human trafficking which seeks to measure the magnitude of the phenomenon. More specifically, its focus will be on the current state of worldwide research on human trafficking and its evaluation. It will review research on trafficking and endeavour to answer the following questions:

- Do all researchers speak a common language when they investigate trafficking in human beings? And are all researchers investigating the same phenomenon? Can they base their research on existing legal definitions or should they develop new ones? Does the definitional debate/distinction between 'smuggling' and 'trafficking' in current human trade discourse and policy discussions influence the way in which research is conducted?

- Why is it so difficult to conduct research on human trafficking? What are the main challenges?

- Do researchers on human trafficking know their jobs, or do they tend to forget the elementary rules of social research methodology while conducting their studies? Can we conceive of better research as far as methods are concerned?

- What are some of the problems associated with research which seeks to measure the magnitude of human trafficking? To what extent is this debate scientific, and to what extent is it influenced by the need of national and international governmental organisations to justify a 'war on trafficking'?

- Is what we know enough? Are the directions taken by current research the relevant ones, or can we imagine subjects or sectors that could be investigated to yield more significant help to policy-makers?

What are we researching? The never-ending story of a definition

Whatever the topic a researcher is working on, it is essential that s/he defines the phenomenon under scrutiny. Trafficking in human beings is no exception. The majority of current research documents on human trafficking contain a paragraph devoted to the definitional debate or which itself defines concepts (see for instance Carling 2006: 9–12; UNODC 2006: 49–52; UNICEF, UNOHCHR and OSCE-ODIHR 2002: 2–4). Whilst in the past there was much less consensus, the definitions now accepted and used are those of the United Nations (UN) (Laczko and Gramegna 2003: 180). Nevertheless, general agreement on these definitions has only recently been reached. The debate on the definition of human trafficking is, in fact, a 'never-ending story', and not only for researchers. 'Until recently, one of the fundamental problems in responding to trafficking in human beings has been the lack of international consensus on the definition of trafficking. Moreover, there has been a persistent confusion about the distinction between trafficking, smuggling and illegal migration' (Experts Group on Trafficking in Human Beings 2004: 47). In particular, during the 1990s, the distinction between trafficking in human beings and smuggling of migrants became consolidated *de facto*, and then definitively formalised in a legal text, in 2000, with the two Protocols Supplementing the UN Convention against Transnational Organized Crime. From a legal point of view, four elements must be present for behaviour to constitute trafficking in persons: (a) recruitment; (b) movement/receipt; (c) deception, abuse of power or of a position of vulnerability; (d) purpose of exploitation, which may take place in sex markets, forced labour or services, slavery or practices similar to slavery, servitude or the removal of organs. Smuggling is defined differently by the Protocol against the Smuggling of Migrants by Land, Air and Sea, supplementing the UN Convention against Transnational Organized Crime, where its main elements are: (a) the procurement of the illegal entry of a person into a State Party of which the person is not a national or a permanent resident; and (b) the obtaining, directly or indirectly, of a benefit (not necessarily financial).

Can we base our research on these existing legal definitions? Or should we go further? Does the definitional debate/distinction between smuggling and trafficking in current human trade discourse and policy discussions influence the way in which research is conducted? There are two aspects that require discussion here: using 'strict legal definitions' to define research concepts may be both an added value and a burden for research. The added value resides in the fact that if common legal definitions were used throughout the world, it would be easier to collect, share and compare data, thereby facilitating secondary research. 'One reason it has been difficult to measure trafficking is because, until fairly recently, there has been little agreement on how to precisely define human trafficking' (Laczko and Gramegna 2003: 180). The use of different (national) legal definitions of trafficking makes the statistical data incomparable, so that any international comparative research based on such data becomes difficult, if not impossible. In Europe and beyond, efforts by the European Union (EU) and other international organisations to approximate or to harmonise national legislation on the matter are producing results, but there is still considerable work to be done. Minor divergences in the field of criminal offences may impair the collection and comparability of data on trafficking for sexual exploitation. Action should be taken to close all the existing gaps. In some countries where specific offences of human trafficking exist, for instance, there are still some minor, separate, offences which the criminal courts can use to punish such behaviour. This may also hamper the collection of information on this type of criminal phenomenon (Di Nicola 2004: 44–45).

Using 'strict legal definitions' to guide research regarding trafficking in human beings may also place a burden on researchers by narrowing their horizons. As several contributors to this volume have pointed out, while it is possible to distinguish between human smuggling and trafficking in human beings in law, 'in reality the two categories often overlap' and 'the boundaries between help, facilitation, smuggling, trafficking and exploitation are not so clear as many conceptualisations suggest' (Kelly 2002: 9; see also Lee and Kelly, Chapters 1 and 4 in this volume). In other words, legal definitions may have a constraining effect. They may inculcate preconceptions in researchers so that their research is restricted. For example, again to quote Kelly (2005: 238), adhering too closely to the Palermo Convention's definition may deflect research attention from 'how service providers and state agents define trafficking, and especially the extent to which they introduce additional requirements which do not appear in the protocol in order to construct a category of "deserving" victims'.

Legal definitions may limit research directions and prevent the research community from producing new and helpful knowledge. For instance, although human beings, including men or young boys, can certainly be trafficked for many purposes, it is above all trafficking in women and girls for sexual exploitation that has caught the interest of academia. This may be because international and national political debate and the media concentrate on this sector. As a result, less is known about human trafficking for other purposes such as forced labour and street begging (Piper 2004: 210 and 221; Andrees and van der Linden 2005: 55–56). In this regard, Kelly (2005: 237) suggests that 'a wider framing' – that is, a broader approach to the definitional issue – 'might change what we think we know about the prevalence and patterns involved in trafficking'.

If we accept that the lack of agreement on what constitutes human trafficking is an obstacle for those who want to study and address the problem, researchers should be able, when and if necessary, to go beyond official definitions, though still bearing them in mind as essential initial bases. But once the problem of definition has been overcome, or almost overcome, new challenges arise.

Every piece of research has its own challenges ...

Any researcher concerned with trafficking in human beings would say that this is not an easy subject to tackle, for several reasons.

A problem 'unseen' and denied

Out of sight, out of mind: traffickers, victims (such as women forced into prostitution, children compelled to beg, men induced to work on illegal construction sites), and the clients of trafficked victims belong to so-called 'hidden populations'. A hidden population is difficult for researchers to access because its members are neither easily identifiable nor easily found. Statistically speaking, it is not possible to define a sampling frame for a hidden population.

Put simply, we cannot see and we cannot count a hidden population; we cannot know its size or its exact characteristics. What we see or know is only a part of the entire population, probably just the tip of the iceberg. Furthermore, membership of a hidden population often involves stigmatisation or the commission of illegal acts. As a consequence, these individuals are often unwilling to cooperate, or their replies to research questions may be misleading because they want to protect themselves (Tyldum and Brunovskis 2005: 18).

The fact that victims, traffickers, and clients are hidden not only implies that it is more difficult to research them – which entails methodological approaches different from those commonly used with more easily observable populations (for instance, snowball sampling techniques) – it also implies that sometimes 'a problem unseen does not exist' (Kelly and Regan 2000: 29). In other words, limited knowledge of a problem may result in limited action by police forces, and sometimes even in a lack of recognition or denial of the problem itself (see, for instance, Anti-Human Trafficking Unit Global Programme against Trafficking in Human Beings 2003: 10). In many parts of the world, government bureaucrats may fail to recognise this problem or may be reluctant to take concrete action (Adepoju 2005: 90). This non-recognition of the problem can also be linked to 'unsympathetic attitudes on the part of government officials towards trafficking victims' in some areas of the world (Piper 2005: 224–225). And a problem not recognised or denied is a problem even more difficult to investigate.

Limited validity and quality of data, lack of a good baseline

Secondary research – as opposed to empirical or primary research, in which data are collected specifically for the study at hand – relies on already-existing sources (previous research reports, newspaper, magazine and journal articles, government and NGO (non-governmental organisation) statistics, for example). Research on human trafficking has often been secondary. In North America, for instance, most researchers have long used 'information from newspaper reports and media investigations to compile a picture of trafficking' (Gozdziak and Collett 2005: 116). The same applies to other areas in which research has been conducted (Lee 2005: 168). Although there are many positive examples of research based on secondary sources (for recent research based on secondary source analysis, see UNICEF Innocenti Research Centre 2003; UN Office on Drugs and Crime 2006), the quality of such research depends on the quality of the sources. Especially when information is taken from the media, research may be anecdotal or based on stereotypes, and the validity of sources may be difficult to control.

The same problem arises even when the sources are official statistics. Despite improvements in recent years, the statistics on human trafficking are still highly unsatisfactory in the EU and elsewhere. Very little is known about the numbers of people who may have used the services of traffickers, or about the numbers of individuals working for the criminal groups involved in those trafficking activities. The problem becomes even more serious when the researcher sets out to obtain statistics on the numbers and characteristics of the trafficked persons, and if s/he wants to compare statistics across countries (Di Nicola 2004).

It is almost axiomatic for papers reviewing trafficking/smuggling to lament the statistical void and to call for research to fill the many lacunae. Often the statistics produced by countries experiencing trafficking are held by numerous different services and organisations there, collected in different ways at different times use diverse technologies and so are not comparable within the country let alone from one country to another (Salt 2000: 37).

The most serious shortcomings of the available data are: '(1) lack of concise data on offender characteristics and offender structures; (2) lack of data on the financial aspects, including the whereabouts of the profits; (3) lack of time series data and cross-nationally compatible data. Additional data do exist in the non-public domain, namely in the hands of customs and police, but these data is difficult to approach' (van Dijck 2005: 2). The shortage of quantitative information has often prompted researchers to resort to data-gathering strategies such as participant observation and interviews, but these pose other types of problems.

A business that can become risky for researchers

Crime research is sometimes risky. Although the dangers are not as common as one might imagine, they may arise when researchers apply particular techniques, such as ethnographic methods, and when the focus is on organised criminals and their activities. Risks may be particularly high in research on human traffickers because organised groups involved are prone to violence and ready to use it to defend their businesses. 'Interacting with and interviewing pimps, traffickers and other criminals has to be approached with care', hence researchers must be aware of such risks and seek to control them (Regional Working Group on Child Labour in Asia 2002: 16 and 22). A possible area of danger involves research into corrupt officials and other highly paid facilitators implicated in the trafficking process. Organised trafficking requires systematic and high level corruption.

> While there is a perception of wide-spread corruption in relation to trafficking and while there are reports on specific corruption cases, there are very few reports on investigations into corruption offences related to trafficking, and virtually no reports on cases going to court and leading to convictions; [...] The inconsistent enforcement of laws and regulations against traffickers and sexual exploitation is believed to be due to corruption. (PACO 2002: 9–10)

New research strategies are needed to delve deeper into these matters, but they may carry risks for those who implement them.

Inaccessibility of traffickers and victims

Even if a researcher is unconcerned about risks, it is easier to administer a questionnaire to, or interview, an expert on human trafficking than it is to do the same with a trafficker and/or a victim. Finding a trafficker and gaining his/her trust is a complex and time-consuming task, and even when contact has been established, the information given must be weighed carefully, considering that the informant is divulging his or her criminal activity. The fact that even those studies which deal with trafficking organisations are always based on sources other than the traffickers themselves – such as the victims (Human Rights Watch 2003), or NGOs, investigative and prosecution case files (Savona *et al* 2003; Vandekerckhove *et al* 2003), or investigators/prosecutors and other experts – highlights how complex accessing offenders may be.

Finding a victim willing to provide information may be less difficult if the person is no longer under the control of the criminals. However, should he or she still be under such control, matters are different. The control strategies adopted by traffickers and exploiters make their victims much less accessible to researchers. Unfortunately, the least accessible victims, ie those under the control of criminals, are also those able to furnish better insights into the phenomenon. The majority of studies which use victims as their sources of information instead rely on ex-victims in protection programmes or those who have been repatriated. Yet, whoever the victim may be, the problems persist: will s/he be willing to talk? Will s/he trust the researcher? How far can the researcher go? And the ethical implications, too, must be considered.

A research field with several ethical implications

Researchers may put the trafficking victims who cooperate with them at risk. Consequently, besides taking constant care to respect the principle of informed consent by participants (Zimmerman and Watts 2003), researchers must bear the vulnerability of their interviewees in mind and, as far as possible, ensure their safety, together with that of the third persons involved. They should also consider that involvement in the research may be stressful for the victims and do their best to mitigate any distress caused to participants. 'It is important to respect the subjectivity of the victim instead of trying to find the "ideal victim". As we know from numerous accounts of exploited/trafficked sex workers, they may not perceive their situation in the same way as the researcher' (Andrees and van der Linden 2005: 66). Another relevant issue is the protection of informants' privacy and dignity.

A politically sensitive area

Prostitution, labour market and management of migration flows are all politically sensitive areas pertaining to the trafficking of human beings. This further complicates the situation. Researchers, especially when their research is funded, may lose their objectivity and become caught up in the political debate. Consider prostitution policies and their impact on the trafficking in human beings: this is an interesting subject of study but, given the intense debate on prostitution in several countries and the lack of hard data with which to assess the impact of policies, there is the risk that researchers will conduct this assessment on subjective bases and be influenced by the current debate. Researchers may take the view that a prostitution policy is good according to ethical principles or to a human rights' approach, or because it encourages outdoor prostitution and thus facilitates contacts between NGO personnel and victims. The evaluation may thus be based on arguments which are not empirically grounded but are based on personal beliefs (Di Nicola *et al* 2005).

Are we sure we are doing our best? Methodological limitations

Studies on human trafficking are often rather methodologically weak or poor. Rarely does one find a paragraph in existing studies devoted to the research's strengths and weaknesses, including possible limitations and biases. This is a clear indicator of their methodological state of health. The following are the main methodological limitations of current research.

Research which describes

In general, only a small percentage of the overwhelming amount of world research on human trafficking goes beyond mere description of the phenomenon and its trends to become analytical by seeking to explain relations among variables, among causes and effects. Research in the field tends to be descriptive, or at most exploratory. Descriptive research aims at defining and describing social phenomena, while exploratory research aims at exploring the nature and frequency of a problem about which almost nothing is presently known. With regard to the latter, although exploration is undoubtedly a possible and valuable form of research, it is common in cases where researchers know almost nothing about the matters they are investigating, when there is insufficient information available on the research subjects, and when the researchers cannot count on past research to guide them. Most research on trafficking seeks 'to explore the topic and to provide some familiarity with, or understanding of, the topic', its purpose being 'to provide input to project/policy interventions' (Derks, Henke and Ly 2006: 10). Can we base our interventions on research which is mainly descriptive and exploratory and which has not been able to test or falsify hypotheses, that is, obtain scientifically verified results? Why do researchers on human trafficking tend to forget the existence of explanatory research, which endeavours to identify cause–effect relations and to foresee how a phenomenon will change in response to variation in another phenomenon?

Research which does not evaluate

As said, explanatory research is relatively rare, and this assertion holds true when we move to the type of explanatory research which is evaluative and whose aim is to determine the effects of social programmes, policies or other interventions. Although evaluation of the impact of projects for prevention and assistance, of legal reform and policy change in the field of human trafficking would be particularly useful, it is still in its early stages (Kelly 2002). Evaluating the effectiveness of these actions is certainly not easy, mainly because of deficiencies in the data available. One would nevertheless expect there to be much more thorough debate within the research community on alternative methodological strategies with which to remedy those deficiencies. How can we measure the inputs, outputs and outcomes of interventions? On what data can we rely? If official statistics are unavailable or unreliable or not comparable, can we resort to alternative data collection strategies? Evaluation research may be long-drawn-out and expensive but, besides being challenging, it would help construct a body of positively evaluated interventions, together with the conditions in which they would work. As the UN High Commissioner for Human Rights put it some years ago (UNHCHR 2002: 7–8) there is a need for 'monitoring and evaluating the relationship between the intention of anti-trafficking laws, policies and interventions, and their real impact. In particular, ensuring that distinctions are made between measures which actually reduce trafficking and measures which may have the effect of transferring the problem from one place or group to another'. Although there are some tentative signals of change (Huntington 2003; UNICEF 2006), a lot of work still remains to be done.

Research with problems of sampling and representativeness of results

The main problems with primary research on human trafficking are sampling and the representativeness of results. As we have seen, primary research may gather information from victims, who are by definition a hidden population. It is therefore well-nigh impossible to establish a sample frame and to select a random sample from it. What therefore happens in almost all research is that statements true for the group of victims subject to the research (the sample) cannot be generalised to the entire population of trafficked victims. For instance, the samples of several surveys suffer from a severe selection bias which reflects more institutional activity than the actual distribution of trafficked victims. If the sample is selected from, say, victims who come into contact with the judicial system during the prosecution of their traffickers, these victims will have specific characteristics reflecting the institutional view of the problem. The likely result is that almost all the victims interviewed will be female and trafficked for sexual exploitation, and that the trafficking of persons for labour is non-existent.

Researchers should pay closer attention to this drawback: they should, that is to say, do their best to deal with selection bias by taking it into account rather than pretending that it does not exist. They should consider – given the impossibility of random sampling – the possibility of sampling key informants with the snowball technique, or triangulating methods, in order to achieve greater representativeness. Another option is the random sampling of more general populations which comprise trafficking victims.

Research with little imagination in regard to data collection techniques

Research which uses primary sources on trafficking suffers from a certain flatness in its data collection techniques: surveys (questionnaires and interviews), life history and case studies are the most widely used, and perhaps abused, while one rather rarely encounters other techniques. Why do researchers adhere so closely to these methods?

Why do they not exploit more the potential of ethnographic techniques like participant observation? A recent study by Scheper-Hughes (2004), for instance, has shed light on organ-trafficking by using an ethnographic-anthropological approach. Posing as a prospective buyer, Scheper-Hughes established contact with kidney sellers and organs brokers, and ultimately with kidney buyers, and collected additional information via email or on the internet (so-called 'virtual ethnography'). This technique is one possibility; many others could be devised with a little imagination.

A focus on research measuring the magnitude of the problem

Measuring the magnitude of the problem has been a field in which many of the above-discussed research challenges and methodological limitations can be encountered. It is an area where world-wide research has been openly criticised for lacking a scientific basis. However, more scientific approaches have recently been adopted, and I shall now focus on several examples.

In 2004 the US government estimated that each year between 600,000 and 800,000 people are trafficked across transnational borders worldwide. Eighty per cent of these people are females, and 70 per cent of these females are trafficked for sexual exploitation. Those trafficked into the US range in number from 14,500 to 17,500. Again according to the US government, the yearly estimate of global intra-country trafficking in persons varies from 2 to 4 million (US Department of State 2004: 23). These figures represent an improvement – in the sense that an improved methodology was used to estimate trafficking flows – on those issued the year before, again by the US government, which indicated that about 800,000–900,000 people were annually trafficked across international borders in the world, with 18,000–20,000 bound for the US as their final destination (US Department of State 2003: 7). No information, however, is given on this improved methodology. The 2006 US Trafficking in Persons report states that 'according to the US Federal Bureau of Investigation, human trafficking generates an estimated $9.5 billion in annual revenue' (US Department of State 2004: 13). It says nothing about the scope of this estimate, whether it is US or world-wide. Moreover, no information is forthcoming on how this figure was obtained. O'Neill (2000: 3) from the US Department of State states that government and non-governmental experts in trafficking in human beings estimate the women and children trafficked globally each year at between 700,000 and 2 million. Who these experts are and how they calculated this amount, nobody knows.

At the EU level, in 2001 the European Commission (2001) reported that '120,000 women and children brought illegally into Western Europe seems to be a realistic figure', and that 'it is principally women that are trafficked for prostitution purposes' (EU Commission 2001). This figure has travelled around the world and is quoted by researchers in numerous studies. Of course, no one knows how it was produced. Also in 2001, IOM (International Organization for Migration) (2001) stated that until recently an estimated 500,000 women had been trafficked from Bangladesh to India to work in the sex industry, and that every year 5,000 women and girls from Nepal were forced into prostitution in India.

If we continued with this exercise at the national level, the result would be even more obvious: a wide and contradictory range of figures can be found in research reports around the world, and they have been quoted and disseminated by researchers with no regard to the estimation criteria used (for a review, see van Dijck 2005: 33–38). If these are the estimates, a legitimate doubt arises: could it not be possible that the main goal of those presenting these numbers is to feed figures to the press or to provide politicians with 'inflated' figures, the purpose being to induce them to divert resources and to increase their efforts in the 'war on trafficking'? The answer is left to the reader. Here suffice it to say that, fortunately, and notwithstanding many research difficulties, well-grounded attempts have also been made to measure the size of the phenomenon (see below). Indeed, we have seen the problems surrounding the study of trafficking. We have seen how trafficking victims form a hidden population and are therefore very difficult to estimate. This is not to imply that some attempts should not be made, but researchers and the international community should avoid issuing statistics without specifying the methods used to produce them. To date, only a handful of studies have estimated the number of persons trafficked for the purpose of sexual exploitation and explained the methodology used to produce their data. These few studies have tried to remedy the situation and to recover the credibility that this area of research has almost entirely lost.

For example, Kelly and Regan (2000) developed a well thought-out methodology to estimate the scale of trafficking in human beings into the UK. First, a total of 271 women were found to have been trafficked into the UK over a five-year period. This figure was based on official data (ie prostitution-related crimes reported to the police), known trafficking cases identified in off-street locations and known cases reported by the media (newspapers, etc). From these known cases and incorporating additional data sources, hypotheses, and minimum and maximum estimated multipliers into the calculations, the researchers reached the conclusion that 'the real scale of trafficking [in the UK] may be between two and twenty times that which has been confirmed'. 'It may be estimated that the scale of trafficking in women into and within the UK lies within the range of 142 and 1,420 women a year' (Kelly and Regan 2000: 21–22).

In Italy, research studies by Parsec-University of Florence (Carchedi *et al* 2000) have shown that the number of trafficked women can be estimated by extrapolating a sub-set of the population of foreign prostitutes calculated on the basis of empirical research. The numbers of trafficked women estimated by Parsec-University ranged from 1,453–1,858 (minimum) to 1,942–2,216 (maximum) for 1996, and from 1,103 (minimum) to 1,446 (maximum) for 1998.

A logical method with which to estimate trafficking can also be based on official information on the number of trafficking victims who come into contact with NGOs or with the police/judicial authorities (victims in judicial proceedings). If these data are used, it is necessary to determine the ratio between victims who contact the police/judicial authorities or NGOs and those who do not (ie the 'dark' figure of victims). This method has already been used by an IOM study of trafficking in women in Austria (IOM – Migration Information Programme (MIP) 1996), a country in which: (a) the crime of trafficking in women is envisaged by the criminal code, and (b) data are collected on the offence and on victims. This research reported that in the period considered (1990–94) the victims trafficked and then induced into prostitution and recorded by official statistics amounted to 751, but the researchers added that the real number therefore may be many times higher than shown in the statistics (MIP 1996: 32). That is to say, the officially recorded number of victims is only the tip of the iceberg, but it is certainly a useful starting point for calculating the part of the iceberg which remains submerged.

A first study by Transcrime (2002) applied this method[1] and produced the following for Spain and Italy: estimates of the yearly number of victims; estimates of the yearly maximum monetary turnover from the sale of trafficked people to exploiters (ie, the profits of criminals who transfer foreign persons from one country to another in order to procure prostitutes for exploiters in the destination countries) (TT); estimates of the yearly maximum turnover from the sexual exploitation of trafficked people (TE). In Spain, the estimate was based on victims who entered into contact with the law enforcement system, and the estimated total population of victims trafficked for sexual exploitation ranged from 4,120 (minimum) to 8,240 (maximum) for 1999, and from 3,920 (minimum) to 7,840 (maximum) for 2000. The estimated TT for 1999 ranged from €29,664,000–59,328,000 to €123,600,000–247,200,000 and, for 2000, from €28,224,000–56,448,000 to €117,600,000–235,200,000. The estimated TE for 1999 ranged from €380,160,000–760,320,000 to €475,200,000–950,400,000 and, for 2000, from €380,160,000–760,320,000 to €475,200,000–950,400,000.

In Italy, the estimate was elaborated on the basis of victims issued with a stay permit for social reasons. The estimated total population of victims trafficked for sexual exploitation in the period between 6 March 1998 and 31 December 2000 ranged from 7,260 (minimum) to 14,520 (maximum). The yearly estimated average of victims (for 1999 and 2000) ranged from 2,640 (minimum) to 5,280 (maximum). The yearly estimated TT for 1999 and for 2000 ranged from €2,640,000–5,280,000 to €36,960,000–73,920,000, and the estimated TE for 1999 and for 2000 from €380,160,000–760,320,000 to €475,200,000–950,400,000. This method has also been used for more recent studies by Transcrime (Savona *et al* 2003: 138–140) where the estimate was based on the number of victims who entered into contact with judicial authorities and were registered in judicial proceedings. The results were robust and based on a mapping of the judicial activities of all the Italian prosecutors' offices. Between June 1996 and June 2001, the real number of victims of trafficking was quantified at between a minimum of 27,410 and a maximum of 54,820. This estimate confirms the previous one. Again relying on this method, a recent study for the EU Parliament (Di Nicola *et al* 2005) estimated that in 2000, in 11 selected countries (namely Austria, Belgium, Czech Republic, France, Germany, Italy, Lithuania, Poland, Spain, Sweden and The Netherlands), between a minimum of about 44,000 and a maximum of about 88,000 women and children were trafficked for sexual exploitation. The estimate rose in 2002 to a minimum of about 50,000 and a maximum of 100,000. In 2003, the trend still seemed to be on the rise.

Of course, although this method probably yields a picture closer to the reality, it still suffers from severe limitations. 'Since the ratio of cases identified by law enforcement or non-governmental organisations (NGOs) to the total number of trafficking cases in an area is seldom known, it is difficult to determine to what extent the identified cases are representative of the universe of trafficking cases, and which biases they introduce to our data' (Tyldum and

Brunovskis 2005: 24). There may be a problem of institutional bias with these victims, precisely because they are those who have come into contact with the system. Hence, trying to estimate the entire population from them may be problematic, especially if the intention is to produce data relative to specific characteristics of the entire population (gender, origin, purpose of trafficking, etc).

Recently, a new method to perform this measurement has come to the attention of researchers. ILO (International Labour Organization) has estimated that the world minimum number of persons in forced labour at a given time as a result of trafficking is 2.45 million. Forty-three per cent of all these victims are trafficked into forced labour for commercial sexual exploitation, and 32 per cent for economic exploitation. The remaining 25 per cent are trafficked for mixed or undetermined reasons (Belser *et al* 2005: 4–6; ILO 2005: 14). The sources of this estimate were reported cases and reported victims of forced labour in the world media. First, the total number of cases of forced labour in the media from 1995 to 2004 was estimated. For this purpose, as an alternative to random sampling from sampling frames, it was decided to use a method called 'capture recapture'.[2] This method was employed for the world reports, achieving an estimated number of reported cases and victims over 1995–2004 in the world. Second, the total estimated reported victims over this period were used to develop estimates of the actual number of victims in forced labour (reported and unreported) in each of the three forms of forced labour mentioned above. To do this it was necessary to make certain assumptions on the ratio between reported and unreported victims.

The ILO study is well grounded, and it is very clear on the limitations of the approach taken. The use of the capture/recapture techniques is promising, especially because it can also be directly employed to estimate the number of victims of trafficking for sexual exploitation working outdoors in a spatially limited area (a town, for instance). It has also been used by Brunovskis and Tyldum (2004) to estimate the number of women selling sexual services in Oslo, including the distribution of different nationalities. The limitations of the ILO study are similar to those indicated for the Transcrime studies mentioned above. The analysis is entirely based on reports (in this case, press reports), while the Transcrime studies used the number of reported victims who came into contact with NGOs or with the police/judicial authorities. Possible problems may arise because some parts of the world and some forms of exploitation are more closely covered by the press than others, because researchers cannot read the languages in which news are written, and because the ratio between reported and unreported victims has to be calculated with a logical criterion. But all research has its limitations – and in this case they were not concealed by the authors – as well as its strengths. It should also be pointed out that those estimates produced by ILO are minimum estimates. Nevertheless, studies like this move in the right direction, representing cornerstones in an area which in the past has not been very satisfactory.

Are we sure that we know all we need to know?

Notwithstanding the many limitations described above, we now know a great deal about trafficking in human beings. Numerous studies have furnished interesting and useful information on causes, the characteristics of victims, the features and *modi operandi* of traffickers and exploiters, and trafficking flows and routes around the world. Those who take the time to read some or all of this literature will reach the same conclusion: that current research on trafficking invariably concentrates on the same topics, puts forward the same ideas, repeats similar thoughts and depicts problems in an uncritical manner.

This is not the place to attempt a synthesis of the enormous amount of world literature, especially because in-depth surveys have been published on the topic (Kelly 2002; van Dijck 2005; IOM 2005). Instead, it may be more appropriate to consider what remains to be done, especially with a view to facilitating more effective counter-trafficking interventions. As said, what is often lacking from research is thorough analysis. Numerous questions (which extend beyond description) still remain unanswered, such as:

- What are the variables that influence more, and those that influence less, the selection of victims to traffic and exploit? What are the relative weights of these variables? Is it possible to measure their relative influences? Are there factors that influence the risk of becoming a victim of trafficking, and how do they vary across geographical areas?

- What is the impact of regulation in the field of immigration, and of other kinds (eg work regulation), on the 'production' of trafficking in human beings?

- What factors induce traffickers to choose one organisational structure rather than another? Or more specifically, what is the impact of the environment, including law enforcement efforts, on the organisation of trafficking?

- What factors, in order of importance, influence the choice of trafficking route?

These questions spring directly from the current literature. They provide a good base for departure in that they can be transformed into as many hypotheses to be confirmed or falsified. Many other questions, with their respective hypotheses, could be envisaged in order for the work to become less descriptive and more analytical.

Moreover, there are numerous other aspects that have not been covered or fully covered by research. The main gaps are the following:

- The organisational models adopted by traffickers and exploiters have not been carefully studied (see as a positive example, Shelley 2003).

- In-depth research on the role of facilitators and intermediaries is still lacking.

- Research on trafficking for labour purposes (for instance, in the construction industry for men, or as home workers or nurses for women) and for purposes other than sexual exploitation (begging, the sale of human organs) has attracted much less attention in the international research community, probably because of some sort of institutional bias. The governmental bodies which fund research have always been more concerned with the victims of sexual exploitation.

- There has been little analysis of the relationship between trafficking and corruption. It is likely that some states, or some areas of certain states or individual nations in federal states, may attract or generate larger trafficking flows according to their respective levels of corruption. Is there a positive correlation between corruption and trafficking? If so, how do different forms of corruption (for example, law enforcement, judiciary, bureaucratic) operate and how do they facilitate trafficking?

Scant attention, too, has been paid to the demand for trafficking victims, and to the factors influencing that demand. Clients, final consumers, and also intermediate demand by, for instance, club owners or entrepreneurs looking for cheap labour, have been almost entirely neglected (see Anderson and O'Connell Davidson 2003). Hence, while in the general field of prostitution studies on clients are already rather rare (see Brooks-Gordon 2006), investigations into the clients of victims trafficked for sexual exploitation are almost non-existent (Hughes 2005). Who are the clients? What are their characteristics? What individual, network or environmental factors influence their choice of victims? Can they be influenced by criminal sanctions or do other forces direct their behaviours?

I have already touched on the issue of evaluating policies, and I have emphasised that the skills deployed in this area are rather weak. Once some tactical and methodological improvements in the sector have been achieved, researchers should concentrate on the impact of prostitution policies on trafficking for sexual exploitation (Di Nicola *et al* 2006), or assess the effectiveness of law enforcement measures and also of assistance projects. One area warranting attention is the use of stay permits issued for reasons of justice to persuade victims to testify against their traffickers. Likewise, requiring attention are stay permits issued for social reasons, as in Italy, which have been introduced without prior evaluation of their (positive or negative) effects.

Despite the abundance of data on victims, estimates of victims and the profits of their traffickers and exploiters are still an area which would repay research effort. Institutional actors and the media want figures. There is an evident need to base institutional interventions on a good understanding of the magnitude and geographical distribution of the problem. Perhaps also to please governments and the media, the research community (and others) has sometimes produced results of which it should not be proud. As we have seen, some progress has recently been achieved. The issue is certainly an important one, and more can be done.

Conclusions: time to grow up!

We have needed and still need 'rough and ready' research. It often happens that research is too slow, when quick interventions are imperative. In the past this 'rough and ready' research has been extremely useful, providing valuable information when it was scarce and institutions had to act.

Though sometimes prone to sensationalism, this approach has been an instrument, especially in emergencies, with which to speak louder, to make people aware of the problem, to introduce policy changes; and from this point of view it has produced good results. This kind of research has sometimes been influenced by the views of institutional funders, (including NGOs) with a mandate to rescue and protect victims, sometimes with a loss of objectivity.

Such 'rough and ready' inquiry was conducted at the beginning of research on human trafficking. It is no longer as relevant as it was initially. The time has come for maturity. Limitations must be acknowledged, new directions taken, new techniques employed, more objectivity injected. In the end, victims and society as a whole will be those that benefit most from a more mature perspective. And this is what matters most.

It is high time for research on trafficking in human beings to grow up. Without, of course, denying that what has been done hitherto was necessary: just as nobody would deny that their infancy or adolescence have been necessary to achieve adulthood.

Notes

1 The ratio between victims who contact the police/judicial authorities or NGOs and those who do not, can be defined using the results of victimisation surveys or with the help of the national experts on trafficking. A starting point for calculating the ratio between the number of victims recorded by this monitoring study on trafficking and the real number of its victims for studies carried out at Transcrime was a victimisation survey conducted on the victims of sexual offences in the UK (Myhill and Hallen 2002). For this type of crime only two in every ten victims contact the authorities. The ratio between the number of victims reported in official statistics and those who go unreported is thus 1/5. Taking account of: (a) the lack of trust in the authorities shown by the victims of trafficking; (b) their illegal status in the destination country and their isolation; (c) their subjugation to the traffickers; (d) the covert nature of the trafficking, it is possible to argue that this ratio is much lower. It seems likely that the ratio between the victims recorded and the real number of victims oscillates between 1/10 and 1/20. This ratio is very similar to what Kelly and Regan (2000) found for the UK.

2 In order to clarify the method, consider the following example in the context of estimating the number of fish in a lake. The process 'consists of two parts: capture and recapture. In the capture part, an initial sample of fish is drawn, their number counted, and each fish marked with a special inkmarker before being released back in the lake. After a sufficient but short period of time, a second sample is independently obtained (the recapture part), and the number of fish with ink-marks and the number without ink-marks are counted and noted. These numbers are then used to estimate the total number of fish in the lake. The argument goes as follows: if the second sample is representative of the fish population in

the lake, the ratio of marked to unmarked fish in that sample should be the same as in the fish population as a whole. From this relationship, the total number of fish in the lake can thus be estimated' (Belser *et al.* 2005: 16). Likewise, ILO has used the mechanism with two samples (two independent lists) of validated reports of forced labour cases in the world press, which were the basis for estimating the number of reported cases and victims between 1995 and 2004 globally.

References

Adepoju, A. (2005) 'Review of Research and Data on Human Trafficking in sub-Saharan Africa', *International Migration*, 43 (1–2): 75–98.

Anderson, B. and Connell Davidson, J.O. (2003) *Is Trafficking in Human Beings Demand Driven? A Multi-Country Pilot Study*. Geneva: International Organization for Migration.

Andrees, B. and Van der Linden, M.N.J. (2005) 'Designing Trafficking Research from a Labour Market Perspective: The ILO Experience', *International Migration*, 43 (1–2): 55–56.

Belser, P., de Cock, M. and Mehran, F. (2005) *ILO Minimum Estimate of Forced Labour in the World*. Geneva: ILO.

Brooks-Gordon, B. (2006) *The Price of Sex: Prostitution, Policy and Society*. Cullompton, Devon: Willan Publishing.

Bruckert, C. and Parent, C. (2002) *Trafficking In Human Beings and Organized Crime: a Literature Review*. Ottawa: Research and Evaluation Branch, Community Contract and Aboriginal Policing Services Directorate, Royal Canadian Mounted Police.

Brunovskis, A. and Tyldum, G. (2004) *Crossing Borders, An Empirical Study of Transnational Prostitution and Trafficking in Human Beings*. Oslo: Fafo Research Institute.

Carchedi, F., Picciolini, A., Mottura, G. and Campani, G. (2000) *I colori della notte. Migrazioni, sfruttamento sessuale, esperienze di intervento sociale [The Colours of the Night. Migrations, Sexual Exploitation and Experiences of Social Intervention]*. Milano: Angeli.

Carling, J. (2006) *Migration, Human Smuggling and Trafficking from Nigeria to Europe*. Geneva: International Organization for Migration.

Derks, A., Henke, R. and Ly, V. (2006) *Review of a Decade of Research on Trafficking in Persons, Cambodia*. San Francisco, Washington DC, Phnom Penh: The Asia Foundation.

Di Nicola, A. (ed.) (2004) *MON-EU-TRAF II. A Study for Monitoring the International Trafficking of Human Beings for the Purpose of Sexual Exploitation in the EU Member States*. Trento: Transcrime.

Di Nicola, A., Orfano, I., Cauduro, A. and Conci, N. (2005) *Study on National Legislations on Prostitution and the Trafficking in Women and Children*. Brussels: European Parliament.

EU Commission (2001) *EU Press Release: EU Urges Higher Priority for Fight against Trafficking in Women and Children*, 7 March. Brussels: EU Commission.

Experts Group on Trafficking in Human Beings (2004) *Report of the Experts Group on Trafficking in Human Beings*. Brussels: European Commission – Directorate-General Justice, Freedom and Security.

Gozdziak, E.M. and Collett, E.A. (2005) 'Research on Human Trafficking in North America: A Review of Literature', *International Migration*, 43 (1–2): 99–128.

Hughes, D.M. (2005) *The Demand for Victims of Sex Trafficking*. Kingston: University of Rhode Island.

Human Rights Watch (2003) *Borderline Slavery: Child Trafficking in Togo*, 15 (8). New York: Human Rights Watch.

Huntington, D. (2002) *Anti-Trafficking Programs in South Asia: Appropriate Activities, Indicators and Evaluation Methodologies. Summary Report of a Technical Consultative Meeting*. New Delhi: Population Council.

ILO (International Labour Organization) (2005) *A Global Alliance against Forced Labour*. Geneva: ILO.

IOM (International Organization for Migration) – Migration Information Programme (MIP) (1996) *Trafficking in Women to Austria for Sexual Exploitation*. Geneva: IOM.

IOM (2000) *Migrant Trafficking and Human Smuggling in Europe: A Review of the Evidence with Case Studies from Hungary, Poland and Ukraine*. Geneva: IOM.

IOM (2001) 'New IOM Figures on Global Scale of Trafficking', *Trafficking in Migrants, Quarterly Bulletin*, No. 23.

IOM (2005) *Data and Research on Human Trafficking: A Global Survey*. Geneva: IOM.

Kelly, L. (2002) 'Journeys of Jeopardy: A Commentary on Current Research on Trafficking of Women and Children for Sexual Exploitation', Paper commissioned by the Research and Publications Division International Organization for Migration for the *EU/IOM Conference on Preventing and Combating Trafficking in Human Beings: A Global Challenge for 21st Century*. Brussels: IOM.

Kelly, L. (2005) '"You Can Find Anything You Want": A Critical Reflection on Research on Trafficking in Persons within and into Europe', *International Migration*, 43 (1–2): 235–65.

Kelly, L. and Regan, L. (2000) *Stopping Traffic: Exploring the Extent of, and Responses to, Trafficking in Women for Sexual Exploitation in the UK*, Police Research Series, Paper 125. London: Home Office.

Laczko, F. and Gramegna M.A. (2003) 'Developing Better Indicators of Human Trafficking', *Brown Journal of World Affairs*, X (1): 179–94.

Lee, J. (2005) 'Human Trafficking in East Asia: Current Trends, Data Collection, and Knowledge Gaps', *International Migration*, 43 (1–2): 165–201.

Myhill, A. and Hallen, J. (2002) *Rape and Sexual Assault of Women: The Extent and Nature of the Problem. Findings from the British Crime Survey.* London: Home Office.

O'Neill, A.R. (2000) *International Trafficking in Women to the United States: A Contemporary Manifestation of Slavery and Organized Crime.* Washington: US Department of State, Center for the Study of Intelligence.

PACO (Programme Against Corruption and Organised Crime in South-eastern Europe) (2002) *Trafficking in Human Beings and Corruption. Report on the Regional Seminar.* Portoroz: Council of Europe.

Piper, N. (2005) 'A Problem by a Different Name? A Review of Research on Trafficking in South-East Asia and Oceania', *International Migration,* 43 (1–2): 203–33.

Regional Working Group on Child Labour in Asia (RWG-CL) (2002) *Handbook for Action-oriented Research on the Worst Forms of Child Labour including Trafficking in Children.* Bangkok: RWG-CL.

Salt, J. (2000) 'Trafficking and Human Smuggling: A European Perspective', *International Migration,* 2000 (1): 32–54.

Savona, E.U., Belli, R., Curtol, F., Decarli, S. and Di Nicola, A. (2003) *Trafficking and Smuggling of Migrants into Italy.* Trento: Transcrime.

Scheper-Hughes, N. (2004) 'Parts Unknown: Undercover Ethnography of the Organs-Trafficking Underworld', *Ethnography,* 5 (1): 29–73.

Shelley, L. (2003) 'Trafficking in Women: The Business Model Approach', *The Brown Journal of World Affairs,* X (1): 119–31.

Transcrime (2002) *MON-EU-TRAF. A Pilot Study on Three European Union Key Immigration Points for Monitoring the Trafficking of Human Beings for the Purpose of Sexual Exploitation across the European Union. Final Report.* Trento: Transcrime.

Tyldum, G. and Brunovskis, A. (2005) 'Describing the Unobserved: Methodological Challenges in Empirical Studies on Human Trafficking', *International Migration,* 43 (1–2): 1–34.

US Department of State (2003) *Trafficking in Persons Report.* Washington DC: US Department of State Publication.

US Department of State (2004) *Trafficking in Persons Report.* Washington DC: US Department of State Publication.

UNHCHR (2002) *Recommended Principles and Guidelines on Human Rights and Human Trafficking.* New York: UNHCHR.

UNICEF (2006) *Evaluation of Anti-trafficking Policies in Romania.* Bucharest: UNICEF.

UNICEF Innocenti Research Centre (2003) *Trafficking in Human Beings, Especially Women and Children, in Africa.* Florence: UNICEF Innocenti Research Centre.

UNICEF, UNOHCHR, OSCE-ODIHR (2002) *Trafficking in Human Beings in Southeastern Europe.* Belgrade: UNICEF.

UN Office on Drugs and Crime (2006) *Trafficking in Persons: Global Patterns.* Vienna: UNODC.

van Dijck, M. (2005) *Trafficking in Human Beings: A Literature Survey*. Tilburg: Tilburg University.

Vandekerckhove, W., Pari, Z., Moens, B., Orfano, I., Hopkins, R., Nijboer, J., Vermeulen, G. and Bontinck, W. (2003) *Research based on Case Studies of Victims of Trafficking in Human Beings in 3 EU Member States i.e. Belgium Italy and The Netherlands*. Ghent: Payoke, On the Road, De Rode Draad.

Zimmerman, C. and Watts, C. (2003) *WHO Ethical and Safety Recommendations for Interviewing Trafficked Women*. Geneva: WHO.

Chapter 4

A conducive context: Trafficking of persons in Central Asia

Liz Kelly

Introduction

At the beginning of the twenty-first century, there is no doubt that migration, especially its illegal/irregular forms of trafficking in persons and smuggling of migrants, has become a major international policy issue. It acts as a lightning rod at national and regional levels, illuminating practices that were previously hidden and taken for granted and, at times, igniting or fanning flames of nationalist exclusionary sentiment. In the case of Central Asia, it is an element of the ongoing processes of state formation and the re-configuration of relationships between the five nations: Kazakhstan, Kyrgyzstan, Tajikistan, Turkmenistan and Uzbekistan. These five Central Asian Republics (CARs) are strategically located between Russia, China, South Asia and the Caucasus. All have had difficult transitions and face uncertain futures following independence in 1991. The conditions which are conducive to trafficking, and exploitation of labour more broadly, are features of contemporary life in the CARs. Large movements of people are taking place against the background of ongoing economic problems of transition, uneven development between the five republics, and limited progress in creating effective and transparent institutional frameworks. Throughout the region the capacity to create enforceable legal norms remains limited, with the restricted reach of the state creating spaces that are filled by corruption and informal markets.

Whilst Central Asia may not be a recognised trafficking 'hot spot' currently, there are huge irregular flows of people within the region and out of it. Intra-regional migratory flows reflect legacies of the Soviet past, seasonal factors and the differential economic performance and prospects across the five republics – with movement of impoverished Tajiks, Kyrgyzs and Uzbeks into wealthier Kazakhstan. Designating risk groups, when high proportions of populations engage in irregular migration in most of the CARs is problematic, since all irregular migrants are vulnerable to trafficking. Previous studies found that most trafficking was for sexual exploitation, but trafficking for labour exploitation is now widespread as well. There are also complex links to drug trafficking, especially in the Ferghana Valley. Some destinations are common across sexual and labour exploitation (United Arab Emirates (UAE), Israel, South Korea), whereas others are primarily for sexual exploitation (Turkey, Greece, Western Europe) or labour exploitation (Kazakhstan, Russia).

This chapter considers the contours and conducive contexts of trafficking in persons in Central Asia, drawing on research undertaken for IOM (International Organisation for Migration) in the region (Kelly 2005), which included two field visits. It highlights the difficulties of drawing clear and consistent boundaries between trafficking, smuggling and irregular migration alongside raising the question of whether the concept of a continuum might more accurately reflect the human rights abuses involved. Finally, it concludes with reflections on the lessons that trafficking in the CARs presents.

Trafficking for sexual exploitation

The impossibility of accurately assessing the scale of trafficking for sexual exploitation has been well documented, leading researchers to turn to a range of indicators from which one can draw educated inferences. These include, for example, detections in country, returns/repatriations of nationals who claim to have been trafficked from other countries and those assisted by support agencies. In the CARs context, data may be extremely elusive, in part because both destination and origin countries seek to minimise or disguise the scale of problems, and because counter-trafficking initiatives are relatively new developments in this region. Nevertheless, there is evidence to suggest that:

- there are increased and organised flows from the CARs into established sex industries where trafficking is known to take place;

- since the impoverished are not in a position to pay for or arrange their own movement out of the region, at the very least most will have been in a situation in which they will be subjected to some form of bonded labour. Where they have been recruited and some form of deception was involved this would fulfil the elements of the UN definition of trafficking.

The increasing numbers on a variety of measures suggest that trafficking for sexual exploitation has increased, and the detection rates in locations such as Israel, Thailand and UAE support this contention. Local experts concurred that there was evidence of increasing internal trafficking and intra-regional flows. One interviewee in Uzbekistan noted that there had been a number of stories pointing to trafficking of men from the northern zones who were probably sexually exploited in Russia and Kazakhstan, but because the issue was 'sensitive' it was minimised – professionals, including law enforcers, took the position that, if men are recruited, they know what they are going to, so if they are then in trouble, it is their own fault.

Recruitment

Patterns of recruitment reflect those documented in existing research, but with a number of regional variations. The much-documented approaches by acquaintances are evident, as is the use of women as recruiters, as the following case example illustrates.

A woman was approached by a female neighbour who was explicit about offering work in prostitution. She moved in with her along with another young woman and was introduced to the female pimp. Both were 15 and in the flat were two other minors aged 15/16. One was sent to UAE, while the others operated as a team in flats around Kyrgyzstan. After a month all were taken by the pimp/trafficker to UAE, each was given €3,000 to make it look as if they were shuttle traders. They worked out of a hotel where each floor was allocated to women of specific ethnic backgrounds. They were told they could pay off their fee in a week and then only had to pay for room and board. But they were charged three times the commercial rate for everything and never managed to save any money. This female trafficker controlled 25–30 girls. The young women estimated they earned €6,000 after paying off debts but they were given

€370 which their trafficker took back when they arrived in Bishkek. All this young woman had to show for this part of her life was a designer handbag (IOM Kyrgyzstan 2000).

In the main, women leave on tourist visas, with the promise of jobs as nannies, domestic workers, positions in the hotel, catering and entertainment sectors. A minority, as in other contexts, know that they will engage in prostitution. The following emerged from interviews and other data as key recruitment contexts:

• travel and employment agencies;
• shuttle traders;
• the 'second wave' (formerly trafficked women);
• adoption from orphanages;
• kidnappings and/or forced marriage, polygamy – primarily with respect to minors.

The limitations on legal migration have created markets for assistance, which have been filled by a variety of unregulated and illegal operators. In each of the CARs there are organised networks of travel, employment and marriage agencies, which play a key role in enabling the 'shuttle trade' – a practice whereby small scale entrepreneurs, most commonly women, travel to neighbouring countries to purchase cheap consumer goods which they resell in local markets. The traders are virtually always operating illegally, since the only way they make a living, let alone a profit, is to evade customs and importation taxes, and most travel on forged or tourist visas. The fact that so few agencies are able to register and operate in a legal and transparent way provides traffickers with reasonable justifications for not having an address, or written material, such as contracts. Also many citizens have no other experience of seeking work. The connections between trafficking and shuttle trading have not been well documented, other than to note the overlap of destinations – China, Greece, South Korea, Turkey, UAE – and that some female traders are also recruiters/pimps/traffickers. It is currently uncertain whether the shuttle trading acts as a front for trafficking or that this illustrates how engagement in illegal trade, where decisions about what to focus on is made in the context of prevailing opportunities. The case example below illustrates how the overlap works.

A 17-year-old from Bishkek with a sick mother and younger brother accepted an offer to work in a new café in Almaty in

2002 where she would earn €130 a month. She and four other young women travelled together where she was left with a market trader. Her trafficker promised to return and explain, but the woman she was left with was a pimp, who removed her documents and controlled her movements and denied contact with parents. She and several other girls were told they had to work through the summer or be sold on to someone else. She could keep half of the money earned but was worked to exhaustion.

The involvement of women as recruiters and pimps deserves more attention. In a context where the price for sexual services has fallen considerably as living standards declined and drugs entered the scene (IRIN 2003), becoming a pimp or recruiter can increase earnings considerably. The so-called 'second wave' refers to women who were trafficked and who have been offered, or perhaps taken, the option of recruitment rather than continued sexual exploitation. According to IOM's Project Office in Tashkent, some stay in UAE to organise at that end, even marrying local police officers, whilst others return to recruit at home.

Another critically important element that demands more detailed attention is the role of diasporas in the organisation of trafficking. One possible explanation of the increased flows from the former Soviet Union to Israel is the émigré Russian community, a minority of whom were and continue to be involved in trafficking. Connections of nationality/ethnicity and family/clan have been key elements in the most enduring and effective organised crime networks throughout the twentieth century and may have a particular salience in the CARs, given the diverse mixtures in the countries.

The realities of sexual exploitation

The reality of trafficking for sexual exploitation in Central Asia shares many of the features we have become all too familiar with at the end of the twentieth century: deceit as to the kind of work that will be undertaken at the destination; deceit as to how much it is possible to earn and remit; and having to pay off a huge debt through working initially for nothing. On arrival, women may be taken to an establishment owned by their traffickers; alternatively the trafficker may sell them to a pimp. The debt owed ranges from €10,000 to €18,000, and the most anyone can earn in a day is €400. If they are working for pimps who charge for accommodation, impose petty fines and even interest on the debt, the chances of earning any money to remit home recedes into the far distance. One estimate (IOM Kyrgyzstan 2000) suggests that each woman in UAE will earn €19–30,000 for their exploiters over three months if they service 15–20 clients a day. A small brothel can, therefore, have a yearly turnover of €1.5 million if they 'work women to death'.

A survey of 100 women in prostitution (IOM Tajikistan 2001) found that only 7 per cent of those who had travelled abroad did so independently, while more than half went as part of a group organised by a trafficker and/or travel agency. A third had been deceived by middlemen and two thirds by employers. Just under two thirds (62 per cent) reported they had been exploited on more than one occasion, half had been subjected to violence, and three quarters had experienced extortion by customs/border guards. One gets some sense of the desperation of these women's lives when you are told that, despite this catalogue of abuses, half intended to try to work aboard again, preferably in UAE. This is undoubtedly a triumph of hope over experience, fuelled here as in other places by the low prices in internal sex markets (it is now about 50 cents on the streets of Tajikistan), alongside the much vaunted – but few in number – examples of women who have managed to lift themselves and their families out of poverty through prostitution. Women choose to believe that 'the next time' it will be different.

Many of the women assisted by IOM in the CARs are older, single mothers, with other family dependents. They dream of finding a way to keep more of the money that is made through their exploitation – a position that makes them vulnerable to re-trafficking. Reducing these risks requires providing livelihood options at home that would enable women to earn enough to support themselves and their families.

Trafficking for labour exploitation

Legacies of the Soviet past (Olcott 2003) and seasonal factors – especially the cotton and tobacco harvests – have played a part in the migration flows in the region. These are increasingly augmented by the differential economic performance and prospects across the five republics. The downturn of the Russian economy in the late 1990s heralded hundreds of thousands of impoverished Tajiks, Kyrgyzs and Uzbeks seeking employment outside their national borders every year. The limited access to transparent and efficient visa and recruitment services means that the majority of these movements are irregular, and a proportion involve trafficking.

One reason why the scale of labour exploitation is greater than that for sexual exploitation is that the majority takes place within the region, and the costs for transport and crossing borders are relatively affordable. Profits to third parties come in part from the much larger flows involved, at the same time the potential to enhance it through trafficking is ever present. Research in Uzbekistan, for example, uncovered stories of guards and police at some borders organising and selling migrants according to their skills and physical condition – such sales are made, whether by traffickers or corrupt officials, either to a 'middleman' or directly to employers, such as farmers.

Movements take place primarily from the poorer republics to the richer Kazakhstan, with migrants seeking to transcend the harsh economic and social situation in their own countries. External flows are primarily to Russia and South Korea, although nationals from the CARs have been found in a wide range of other countries. There can be no doubt that the scale of irregular movement is considerable, and in a context where legal routes are foreclosed, it is unsurprising that so many break laws themselves, and/or seek or accept assistance from third parties. Most of the organisations advertising employment opportunities are not legally recognised, and therefore not subject to any regulation. Such conducive contexts are extremely welcome to smugglers and traffickers, who can profit from the disorganisation and lack of transparency. The sorts of work which irregular and trafficked migrants undertake are similar ranging from harvesting cotton and tobacco to construction work, especially in Russia and factory work in a range of settings. Traffickers and exploiters choose and create locations that allow them to limit the possibility of escape: rural settings miles from the nearest settlements; construction sites surrounded by high walls and with armed guards; relatively isolated factories. 'Accommodation' is always on site, and it is not unknown for clothes and especially shoes to be removed at night.

Patterns of trafficking and exploitation

Thousands of Kyrgyz move each year to undertake plantation work in the Kazakh tobacco harvest (IWPR 2003), a pattern that dates from 1998. Entire families may be involved, since theoretically they can earn five times what is possible to earn at home. Many travel by road and bribe border guards, who they pay €3–6 to leave, but are expected to pay more on their return. Many attempt to make verbal contracts, for example, that they will earn €30 per month, with a third deducted for food and other expenses. It is only at the end of the contract, when the employer withholds payment, alleges poor work or sells individuals on to another farmer that the extent of exploitation becomes clear. Being irregular they have no legal status and therefore no rights if this transpires. The extent to which conditions can be compared to slavery are illustrated by the fact that if people leave or escape they risk being hunted down and beaten. There appear to be tacit agreements between law enforcement and employers about levels of acceptable exploitation, which are undoubtedly stretched through the exchange of money and goods. Undocumented migrant workers are the least protected and undertake the 'dirty, dangerous and difficult' (the 3 D's) work in inhumane conditions.

Labour migration is not confined to men. Fifty Uzbek women were found living and working in an unfinished knitwear factory in Russia (RFE/RL 2003). They had received no wages for six months and their passports had been removed. The local police fined the factory owners and the women. An emerging concern in Uzbekistan and Tajikistan is that fewer and fewer migrants are returning from 'seasonal' migration – there are, for example, reports of villages in the Bukhara area where residents are primarily children and the elderly. It is unclear whether this shift is the outcome of increased trafficking – where limits are placed on movement/return and the exploitation aspect means individuals remain in the destination hoping to earn the money they and their families were relying on. Some interviewees provided examples of male and female migrants who felt they could not return until they had earned enough to change the family circumstances, or repay family and friends who lent money to enable them to migrate in the first place.

An emergent pattern was for individuals or groups to be hired by middlemen, who arrange their transport and border crossing and promise work at the destination. In trafficking cases this individual will 'sell' people directly to farmers and other employers, who recoup the costs through bonded labour. The conditions of work are extreme. In the case of harvesting cotton and tobacco, men and women are expected to work from dawn to dusk in 40 degrees, bringing in the harvest by hand. They live in makeshift huts, and the food they are provided with has been described as 'slops'. Few undocumented workers are registered, meaning that evasion of labour laws is widespread – the hours of work and poor safety standards take a toll on health, as does a high level of accidents. Migrants have minimal access to health care. Those who return home report that what little they have earned was removed by corrupt officials at the borders. One strategy developed to minimise extortion is for groups from the same place to contract for transport to and from the destination.

Conducive contexts

This project made clear that there are social, economic and political contexts that are more or less conducive to trafficking, creating 'fertile fields' for exploitation. Four aspects were especially salient for the CARs.

Impoverishment and lack of sustainable livelihoods

There are a number of specific regional factors which create the fertile fields in which trafficking for sex and labour exploitation takes place in the CARs. The scale of impoverishment, especially since the collapse of the Russian economy in 1997, has created a vast reservoir of people who have no regular source of income or sustainable livelihood. Over half a million Tajiks leave the country to seek seasonal and informal employment opportunities abroad. Whilst most migrants lack the necessary knowledge to make well-informed migration and employment choices, the scale of impoverishment suggests that even if accurate information were to deter some, other slightly more desperate individuals would rapidly take their place. The combination of the sheer scale of numbers, dearth of options and inadequate information, combine to create a large group vulnerable to recruitment and exploitation by traffickers. Only sustainable livelihoods at home will make a difference.

Weak governance/economic infrastructure

The confines of transition in the CARs, with limited transfer of power, imperfect markets and the resurgence of patriarchal and tribal traditions and practices, also contribute to the conducive context. The limited connections between national and local governments and citizens, with officials too often appointed rather than elected, contribute to a polity in which fatalism predominates. People have little sense of being able to effect change and endeavour to manage as best they can within their present reality. A number of key decisions and absences are also part of the complex mosaic. None of the CARs has introduced the kind of labour laws that would comply with ILO (International Labour Organization) treaties and UN policy on migrant labour. Similarly, the legal framework, which provides a foundation for business, and especially small business, remains inadequate. Combined with low wages of public officials this ensures that most of those with oversight functions are disaffected and cynical at best, use their position as an opportunity for income generation at worst.

At the economic level imprudent tax systems rather than generating income for the state, act as a further spur to the informal sector. Small and larger traders alike seek to evade payment of what are widely believed to be unjust impositions. The informal sector, Yoon *et al* (2003) argue, has undergone huge growth because it represents the best, and possibly only, survival strategy in the context of difficult transitions. The continued expansion of informal labour markets/economies in the CARs is also connected to the failure of new financial systems to support and enable small businesses (Kamoza 2005). At the same time, deeply unpopular punitive strategies to prevent/control the shuttle trade were introduced. This resort to authoritarian and bureaucratic methods suggests that many are still working within Soviet style beliefs and practices, rather than developing a more pragmatic and problem-solving approach.

This is just one example of the illegal and irregular status of many workers within their own countries. The risks associated with smuggling and trafficking merely extend their already marginal status:

> [Informal/irregular workers] are not recognised or protected under the legal and regulatory frameworks ... and therefore receive little or no legal or social protection and are unable to enforce contracts or have security of property rights. They are rarely able to organise for effective representation and have little or no voice to make their work recognised and protected. They are excluded from or have limited access to public infrastructure and benefits. They have to rely as best they can on informal, often exploitative institutional arrangements, whether for information, markets, credit, training or social security. (ILO 2002: 3)

Corruption

The theme of corruption is a major feature across the Central Asian societies and is a notable barrier to addressing trafficking. Corruption has its deepest impacts on the poor, since they lack the resources to participate in many aspects of life and takes revenue away from the state that could be invested in public goods, such as education, health and social welfare. The more corruption and the informal sector spread, the more deeply embedded the conditions, which create and support trafficking will become (see, for example, Richards 2004, with respect to labour trafficking).

Whilst we know that corruption plays a major role in trafficking, we need deeper analyses of the precise ways in which it (and the accompanying cronyism and nepotism) works. In Central Asia, even those who act in good faith have to engage in petty corrupt practices to achieve anything. For example, police officers cannot use police cars unless they obtain petrol, and this may require extra payment to be prioritised in queues. So long as daily life is impossible without 'greasing the wheels', and elites are not called to account, campaigns against corruption are doomed to fail, since people will understandably dismiss them as the uninformed ideas of Western 'do-gooders'. One academic, for example, argued that the construction and implementation of aspects of counter-trafficking activities allows the elites to escape sanction, whilst targeting those who have few options.

Illicit trade is both the result and source of corruption, fed by many factors: low/no wages for state officials; lack of training/expertise of state bureaucracies; decades of patronage; lack of confidence in the state; weak state institutions; and semi-autonomous law enforcement. Only a strategy that builds widespread public support, operates in transparent ways and, simultaneously, addresses everyday frustrations and elite profiteering can hope to have any impact. It is to be hoped that implementation of the UN Global Programme on Organised Crime, and the Convention Against Corruption, agreed in Merida in December 2003, will provide demonstration projects that offer concrete steps towards more effective interventions.

Declining status of women

On a range of indicators, including political participation, women's status has declined during the transitions in Central Asia. Concurrently, the conditions of women's lives have worsened, primarily due to the loss of welfare and support systems – including childcare and benefits for single mothers – and the differentially high rates of female unemployment. Overall, women in households that are struggling or deeply impoverished have less time than ever to participate in the associational or civic life that political freedoms have now made possible. Multiple determinants have pushed more and more women into the informal sector, which both the World Bank and USAID believe contributes to a decrease in their status and bargaining power within the household.

The under-employment of women, their expanded responsibilities for dependents and engagement in the informal sector all increase the likelihood that they will encounter traffickers. Several interviewees also noted that the expansion of sex industries in their countries was playing a part. Prostitution in the region increased significantly after the breakup of the Soviet Union, and many argued that the number of women willing to sell sex when they had no other sources of income was higher today than at any time in living memory. Formal gender equality in the public sphere was a significant achievement of socialist countries. That transition has recreated inequality and poverty to an extent not known for much of the twentieth century is a bitter irony (Pierella 2002).

Women have been significant losers across the Commonwealth of Independent States (CIS), including in processes of privatisation and entrepreneurial opportunities. As concerning have been the re-emergence of notions of honour and practices of bride price ('kalym'), polygamy and 'wife stealing'. A number of these may act as veils for trafficking, and, in any event, constitute what a study of Afghanistan (IOM 2003b) refers to as 'trafficking-like practices'. The resurgence of traditional notions of honour has worrying implications for any trafficked woman wishing to reintegrate into her family/community/village. Local practices such as patrilocalism mean that there are no strong links between women and their families of origin following marriage. All of these matters not only contribute to contexts of vulnerability for some women, but also need to inform interventions designed to facilitate reintegration or prevention.

The clear danger here is a return to cultural beliefs and practices, which regard women and girls not as individuals with rights, but rather as the property of their families/male 'protectors'. Such ideas, alongside traditional practices in several of the republics, which encourage the giving of children to older male relatives in times of hardship, form part of the fertile field in which trafficking can thrive. Feminists in Central Asia have also raised concerns about how, in the context of state building, the use of ethno-nationalist discourse often results in women's rights being held hostage to their positioning as guardians of identity and authenticity. Whilst certain Muslim traditions, such as the veil, never took root in the CARs, an ideology of domesticity is emerging, with implicit standards of acceptable femininity that will even further isolate victims of sexual violence/exploitation (Samuiddin and Khanam 2002).

Intersections

The explorations above illustrate that conducive contexts involve intersections of aspects of political economy with layers of inequalities. It is always necessary to examine how male privileges/entitlements operate locally. Whilst many international donors and commentators note the declining status and position of women in the CARs, little priority has been accorded in development and transition programmes to gender equality legislation or implementation mechanisms.

Similarly, ethnicity and nationality are always in play, with ethnic markers and colonial histories used to justify inhuman practices, recreating cultures in which superiority and shame replace notions of rights and duties. Within these structures of meaning, the exploitation of female nationals by those of different origins can become attached to notions of national shame for men. This in turn is used – sometimes in a tacit way – to justify ignore or minimise the extent of trafficking. This was most evident in Tajikistan. Reflecting on trafficking of women in the CARs also requires consideration of the complexity of the ways in which women can be regarded as a commodity. That, in some contexts, they can be legitimately traded/exchanged within the social group, within rules and traditions which older males control, is seldom seen as connected to the commercial trade in women.

These reflections illustrate the necessity of deeper explorations of the many ways in which gender and ethnicity play a part in the complex structuring and diverse consequences of trafficking in persons.

Managing migration

The difficult transitions within the republics, coupled with the impacts of conflict in Tajikistan, are conditions in which the desire to migrate is not only heightened, but may be regarded by some as their only route to betterment. The limited transformations of the states have yet to create open and fair systems capable of managing these processes in an organised way. Continued disorganisation can only serve the interests of corrupt politicians and officials, smugglers and traffickers. Closer scrutiny of trafficking for labour exploitation reveals the need to supplement documentation of routes and flows with the elucidation of the sometimes complex links between origin and destination countries. Legal and illegal migratory flows are often similar, with overlaps of trafficking for sexual exploitation in locations where there are large populations of male migrant workers. Whilst in some instances the connections amount to little more than proximity, in others diasporas and ethnicity are under-explored aspects.

The unplanned and large-scale movements currently taking place across the CARs are potentially destabilising. Within the region tensions are evident in local areas where previous freedom of movement is being controlled through demands for visas even to attend a market that has traditionally served residents on both sides of borders. In the case of the destination countries, a recent report noted anti-migrant sentiment and occasional violence in Russia (IOM 2003a). Increased nationalism and resentments are emerging, but in contexts where labour shortages mean that migrant labour is needed. In the absence of preparation and planning, irregular flows strengthen, thus expanding the opportunities for unscrupulous operators. Traffickers and employers are willing to exploit labour in order to profit from violations of human rights.

Expanding understandings

Whilst on one level the UN protocols have provided us with clear and internationally agreed definitions of trafficking and smuggling, the debates continue as to whether it is possible to draw such boundaries, and the precise meaning of the UN protocol definitions themselves. The UN definition of trafficking makes clear that it requires three elements – recruitment/receipt, movement and exploitation – but this has not resolved the contentious definition issue, especially since the exploitation terms are not clearly defined either here or in other conventions (Anderson and O'Connell Davidson 2003). In addition, serious questions remain to be addressed in research, such as how victims understand and define trafficking, since this affects the extent to which they seek help and, perhaps most importantly, what they say to both police and service providers when asked questions intended to discern if they have been trafficked or 'merely' smuggled. Equally important is how service providers define trafficking and the extent to which narrowed definitions act as a filter into support, especially when resources are scarce (Kelly 2002).

Whilst the protocols make clear and, to an extent, absolute distinctions between smuggling and trafficking, a number of studies (see Kelly 2002) are highlighting that this is difficult to maintain in real world contexts. There are both overlaps and transitions from smuggling to trafficking, with the movement almost always in the direction of increased exploitation. These are most likely where the journey is lengthier and more expensive, since it increases the opportunities for exploitation and the size of debt on arrival. The reliance of many who are smuggled on third parties for employment in the destination country increases the potential layers of control that can be used to create conditions of bondage (Shelley 2002).

There are many cases in the CARs which suggest trafficking is a process that often only becomes clear at the end point. This means that those who are detected at an earlier point, whilst escaping serious exploitation, may also not qualify for designation as a victim of trafficking. Research revealed that many practitioners and policy makers sought to narrow the definition, introducing requirements and elements, which are not part of the protocol; in the process implicit categories of 'deserving' or 'uncontested' victims are created. This process also served to limit the extent of trafficking that was officially recognised. A Ministry of Interior interviewee commented: 'It's hard to prosecute crimes such as trafficking in persons due to lack of clarity and difficulty in determining who is the victim and who is the criminal'.

Focusing on trafficking for labour exploitation extends the question about how the UN Protocol definition is to be interpreted. Should it be a narrow reading, requiring clear markers (such as the presence of force), or a wider one that captures the diversity of situations in which human beings are treated as commodities in conditions similar to slavery? These readings have implications for estimating the scale of trafficking in persons in the region. If the narrow definition is used – requiring forcible recruitment and an unbroken chain of connected individuals in the entire process – there are tens of thousands of cases in the region, with at least four times as many for labour as sexual exploitation. The inclusive definition which views trafficking as a process, where connections need not be direct and personal, but can involve taking advantage of positions of vulnerability will produce hundreds of thousands of cases, possibly even into a million or more, and the proportion of labour exploitation cases increases. Obviously there are a range of intermediate positions where numbers are adjusted according to the exclusions/inclusions within how trafficking is understood and defined.

Either/or or both/and

The data from Central Asia supports extending the continuum concept to encompass the links to and overlaps with irregular migration, clarifying that both sexual and labour exploitation are not confined to trafficking contexts, and that these areas of criminal activity shade into and out of one another on a number of dimensions (IOM 2004; Anderson and O'Connell Davidson 2003). Such a perspective suggests that legal reform and law enforcement responses might be more effective if there was an approach that ensured all the elements of trafficking are dealt with, where appropriate, as specific criminal offences. For example: sale of human beings; removal of legal papers; and withholding of earnings. This would ensure that cases did not have to qualify as trafficking in order for the abuses and human rights violations to be recognised and that there was a synergy between labour law, sexual and physical assault laws and trafficking legislation. Such synergies are likely to facilitate justice since in cases where the evidence may not support a trafficking charge, it might be adequate for other less complex offences (see, for example, Kelly and Regan 2000).

There is also a strong argument for other synergies – such as joining up counter-trafficking work with that of defending the rights of migrant workers. Whilst the UN High Commissioner on Human Rights, Louise Arbour, is surely right to complain that trafficked people should be treated as victims of crime rather than undocumented workers, the UN General Assembly resolutions on migrants seek to assert that they too should be protected from violations of labour law and a range of abuses of human rights such as arbitrary arrest and detention. The question here is not an either/or, but rather a both/and.

Conclusion

There is undoubtedly a serious problem in the region with trafficking in persons, which requires a range of interventions at the national and regional levels. Widespread reforms in the realm of governance are essential in order to address corruption, foster transparency, develop effective regulatory systems and apply political will to legal reform and Plans of Action. In the CARs historical and contemporary factors constitute the ground on which trafficking in persons can emerge and flourish: taken together, they comprise a conducive context.

Understanding and addressing these more structural aspects of the problem must be part of any integrated counter-trafficking initiative. It is not just that there is a trafficking chain linking unscrupulous individuals and networks, but that a set of interconnecting social, political and economic conditions form the fertile fields within which exploitative operators can profit from the misfortunes of others.

Whilst the links between trafficking, cultural traditions and existing inequalities have been mapped out in a number of previous publications (see, for example, IOM 2003b), Central Asia poignantly extends these connections alerting us to the relevance of histories of forced labour/migration and ethnic hierarchies. Perhaps these legacies are part of what enables workers today to be so devalued and abused, creating a context for the apparently unchallenged return of child labour, which may even be facilitated by local politicians. Understanding and analysing trafficking in specific locations requires that we engage with such complex interweaving of the past and present.

Whether individual futures are transformed or not, the scale of migration in Central Asia is transforming social relations. The established gender order is under pressure as many men disappear, or retreat defeated and more and more women have to shoulder the responsibility for family survival. They are not victims in any sense of that word which equates it with passivity, since they are acting and making choices. They are, however, doing so in situations that are not of their own choosing, with limited space for action: this is a far cry from the freedom and autonomy that feminists view as the foundation of gender equality. The republics highlight how wider social forces operating in transition decrease women's worth and standing, which, in turn, makes them vulnerable to trafficking. The devaluing of human beings and human labour has the same consequences with respect to trafficking for labour exploitation. These profound transformations in social relations and ideology form part of the conducive context – or root causes – which must be understood and addressed if trafficking is to be prevented.

The strategic location of the CAR region, internal instabilities and tensions, complex interweaving of legacies of the past and fatalism about the future are not ingredients for strong or stable development. Particularly concerning must be the extent of absolute poverty and the absence of sustainable livelihoods, coupled with declining status of women and emerging ethnic stereotypes and tensions. These are not just fertile fields for trafficking, but also for internal and regional conflict. Central Asia's location between the Middle East, Russia,

China, South and South East Asia makes it attractive to organised crime networks, as does the limited capacity of the states to respond. The risks that this involves extend beyond the peoples of Central Asia, since in the context of globalisation allowing crime groups and cultures of exploitation and slavery to embed has implications that affect us all.

References

Anderson, B. and O'Connell Davidson, J. (2003) *Is trafficking in Human Beings Demand Driven? A Multi-country Pilot Study.* Geneva: IOM.

ILO (International Labour Organization) (2002) *Decent Work and the Informal Economy*, International Labour Conference 2002, 90th Session: Report 6: 3. Geneva: ILO.

IOM (International Organization for Migration) (2000) *Research on Trafficking in Migrants (Kyrgyz Republic, 1999).* Bishkek: IOM.

IOM Tajikistan (2001) *Deceived Migrants from Tajikistan: A Study of Trafficking in Women.* Geneva: IOM.

IOM (2003a) *Labour Migration to Russia and Tolerance Problems*, IOM Open Forum, 6: December, Moscow Migration Research Programme. Vienna: IOM.

IOM (2003b) *Trafficking in Persons: An Analysis of Afghanistan.* Geneva: IOM.

IOM (2004) *Survey of Trafficking in Persons in Central Asia.* Vienna: IOM.

IRIN (Integrated Regional Information Networks) (2003) 'Central Asia: Special Report on Human Trafficking', *IRIN News*, 21 October 2003.

IWPR (Institute for War and Peace Reporting) (2003) 'Kyrgyz "Slaves" on Kazakh Plantations', *IWPR*, 5 August 2003.

Kamoza, T. (2005) 'The Madness of Daring', *New Times*, February 2005.

Kelly, L. (2002) *Journeys of Jeopardy: A Review of Research on Trafficking of Women and Children in Europe.* Geneva: IOM.

Kelly, L. (2005) *Fertile Fields: Trafficking in Persons in Central Asia.* Vienna: IOM.

Kelly, L. and Regan, L. (2000) *Rhetorics and Realities: Sexual Exploitation of Children in Europe.* London: Child and Woman Abuse Studies Unit.

Olcott, M. (2003) 'Ethnic, Regional and Historical Challenges', *Harvard International Review: Central Asia*, 22 (1).

Pierella, P. (2002) *Gender in Transition.* Washington DC: World Bank.

RFE/RL (Radio Free Liberty/Radio Europe) (2003) 'Tajik Slaves discovered in Russian Province, *RFE/RL Newsline*, 3 July 2003.

Richards, K. (2004) 'The Trafficking of Migrant Workers: What are the Links between Labour Trafficking and Corruption', *International Migration*, 42 (5): 147–68.

Samiuddin, A. and Khanam, R. (2002) *Muslim Feminism and Feminist Movement.* Delhi: Global Vision Publishing House.

Shelley, L. (2002) 'The Changing Position of Women: Trafficking, Crime and Corruption', in D. Lane (ed.) *The Legacy of State Socialism and the Future of Transformation*. Maryland: Rowman and Littlefield.

Yoon, Y., Reilly, B., Krstic, G. and Bernabe, S. (2003) 'A Study of Informal Labour Market Activity in the CIS-7', Paper Prepared for the Lucerne Conference of the CIS-7 Initiative, 20–22 January 2003. Washington DC: World Bank.

Chapter 5

Trafficking into and from Eastern Europe[1]

Ewa Morawska

Introduction

> Halyna is 18 years old and she sees no opportunities in her home town of Vinnitsa in Ukraine [...] Sonya, the cousin of a friend from Kiev, tells her about her good time as a waitress in Berlin, and introduces Halyna to some men who are able to arrange documentation and travel. Halyna arrives in Berlin via Poland. As soon as she arrives in Berlin, she is picked up and taken to a flat somewhere in the city, where two Albanian women and one Croatian man are living. The man tells her that her travel debts have to be repaid and he confiscates her documents. After repeated beatings and psychological torture, including threats to her family, she is soon forced to work as a prostitute. (Adapted from Monzini 2005: 1–2)

The enormous expansion of international population flows since the 1980s has been a constitutive component of accelerated globalisation processes connecting different regions of the world through trade and labour exchange, international laws and organisations, and rapidly advancing transportation and communication technologies. These global-scale cross-border population movements represent diverse, often mixed, types, including refugee, labour (low and high skill), educational, and tourist travels, and, of specific interest here, transnational trafficking in people. This latter form of international migration involves first and foremost women, including teenage girls, trafficked for the purposes of sexual exploitation and, on the increase worldwide, children for paedophile pornography. Another, not considered here, category of internationally trafficked persons are (im)migrants transported for cheap (or free) non-sexual labour in thousands of sweatshops servicing the post-industrial capitalist economy mainly in core (highly developed) parts of the world (Zlotnik 2005; International Migration 2003; Chin 1999, 2001; Kyle and Liang 2005; Drew 2002; Freedman 2003; Smith 1997; Kyle and Koslowski 2001).

For the purposes of this discussion, 'human trafficking' is defined as illicit transport of a person or persons across state borders that through deception and/or coercion targets these persons as objects of exploitation for the profit of 'businessmen' who carry out such operations (Laczko *et al.* 2002; see also Bhabha 2005; Monzini 2005; Kyle and Koslowski 2001; Salt 1998; Ruggiero 1997). As such, trafficking in persons violates several human rights of the trafficked: the right to personal autonomy (here, freedom from slavery), the right to enjoy physical and mental health, and the right to work (here, freedom from forced labour), the right to just and favourable remuneration (Fulton 2005; Grant 2005; Salt and Stein 1997; Morrison 1998; Aronowitz 2000).

A new phenomenon?

Defined as above, human trafficking is by no means a new phenomenon, to mention only the prolonged, infamous Atlantic slave trade, and, on its heels and of concern here, the so-called white-slave trafficking in women for sexual exploitation between the Orient and the West and, later on, between South-East Europe and North and South Americas that endured well into the twentieth century (see also Picarelli, Shelley, Lindquist and Piper, Chapters 2, 6 and 7 in this volume). A historian of sexual exploitation of women, Ellen Scully (2001: 74-75), summarised very well the triggering mechanisms of that phenomenon in the regions of origin:

> The new world order [of the turn of the 19th and 20th centuries] beheld rapid and uneven industrialisation, weakening community ties ... These factors collectively abetted a burgeoning traffic in women and children for prostitution, described by contemporaries as the white slave trade. Violence, economic turmoil, and political turbulence pushed local women from Asia and central [and eastern] Europe into brothels as far away as Buenos Aires and Seattle.

A combination of economic and political distress in the sending regions, undiminishing demand for paid sexual services in the rapidly growing urban centres in the West, and greatly improved rail and water transportation in the last decades of the nineteenth century prompted the emergence of the organised transnational trafficking in women. In 1895, the Penitentiary Congress in Paris, followed by a 1899 National Vigilance Association's Conference in London, initiated a campaign for legislation to deal with conditions encouraging prostitution. It led to the first International Agreement for the Suppression of White Trade Traffic (1904; the US signed on in 1908) and, from then on through the inter-war period, repeated international meetings, including gatherings under the umbrella of the League of Nations (equivalent of the contemporary UN), aimed at curbing this criminal activity. These pre-World War II organised efforts to combat human traffic for sexual exploitation, never a priority in national or international politics or public opinion, never really accomplished their objectives (Scully 2001; Monzini 1999; Jaschok and Miers 1994; Barry 1979; Butterwerk 1999).

What makes contemporary human trafficking different from its predecessor is its scale, reach, and organisational sophistication, and the scope of international legal and institutional measures (not very effective, it is true) to curb it and, thus, to restore human rights to the trafficking victims. The incomparably greater numerical scope and more effective organisational infrastructure of present-day transnational human trafficking has to do with the growth of the 'world sex market' (Williams 1999; Monzini 2005), made possible by globalisation of consumer capitalism in which commercial sex plays an important part.

Scale of trafficking

As a number of scholars have pointed out, it has been notoriously difficult to estimate the numbers of internationally trafficked persons (for an up-to-date overview of methodological problems related to research on human trafficking, see International Migration 2005; also Heckmann 2006 and Di Nicola, Chapter 3 in this volume). The existing estimates vary widely from 800,000 to (unlikely) 4 million trafficked persons per year (Kelly 2005: 239; see also Bhabha 2005). The most reliable, and most important in demonstrating the gravity of the problem, has been the evidence, inferred from the 'factual' data on intercepted and assisted victims of trafficking, of the rapid increase of this phenomenon worldwide: the estimated numbers of trafficked persons more than double every 10 years.

Global trafficking in people reflects the general directions of worldwide labour migration, flowing in 'compass' pattern from (semi) peripheral or economically less- and underdeveloped (South-East) to core or more developed (North-West) regions of the world.[2] As in the case of labour migration, the main macro-level 'push' forces that move the trafficking victims to accept offers to travel abroad supposedly to earn better money or a better life through marriage, are the poverty and lack of prospects at home. The macro-level 'pull' forces refer to the aforementioned rapid expansion of global sex market and the facility of international travel.[3] Transnational organisation of trafficking or the push-and-pull mezzo-level mechanism and the operation of micro-level factors that generate and sustain this movement type of international migration will be discussed in the next section.

Reflecting the compass pattern of international trafficking, the primary regions of origin of trafficked persons are Africa, poor countries in South-East Asia and South America with the Caribbean, and East and South-Eastern Europe. The main receiving regions are Western Europe, North America, and Japan. When examined more closely, however, the picture becomes more complex: people are trafficked from the poor-poorest parts of the world to less disadvantaged areas of the same region where they either stay or, more often, move on to more highly developed regions.

Macro-structural push-and-pull forces, numbers and directions of trafficking into and from Eastern Europe

The significance of focusing on Eastern Europe[1] is twofold. First, according to the current estimates of the Council of Europe, it is the source of the majority – nearly three quarters – of women victims of trafficking in western parts of this Continent (www.coe. int/T/E/Com/Files/Themes/Trafficking). Second and related to this, it illustrates very well the links between the rapid expansion of transnational sexual trafficking and the turmoil of economic and political transition in the un(der)developed region of the world that accompanies its incorporation into the global capitalist system.

Mechanisms and directions

The mechanisms and directions of trafficking from and into Eastern Europe generally resemble the worldwide patterns. Although the collapse of the Soviet regime in the region opened the door for the

95

accelerated incorporation of that region into the global system, the long-term processes of capitalist *perestroika* (restructuring) to overhaul and bring up to date unproductive state-socialist economies have not thus far diminished the long-standing gap in economic development between the eastern and western parts of the Continent. Measured by the per capita GNP, the economic performance of East Central Europe in 2000 was only about 40 per cent of that of Western Europe and the US combined (some improvement since 1910 when it was 30 per cent), whereas the ratio of (average) wages between these two parts of the world was 1:4–5 (in 1910 it was about the same). In the eastern- and southernmost corners of East Europe these comparisons are even more dramatic: the East-West per capita GNP ratio in 2000 was 1:15 and that of wages 1:20 to 30 (Morawska 2003; on historical data, see Berend 1996; Chirot 1989; Berend and Ranki 1982).[4] This enduring East-West disequilibrium in economic performance has sustained or, more precisely, revived with the post-1989/90 lifting of international travel restrictions in East and South-East Europe, the early twentieth century geographic pattern of income-seeking migrations from that region. This reflects the worldwide 'compass' or (semi-)periphery-to-core, South-East to North-West population flows, including trafficking of women and children for the purposes of sexual exploitation.

At the same time, the post-Cold War opening of East and South-East Europe to the world and, more precisely, its incorporation into the global capitalist system as its semi- and peripheral parts and the lifting by the region's political authorities of once strict control of international travel, combined with the large stretches of poorly guarded or unprotected borders in eastern- and south-eastern parts of the region, have created an opportunity for the growing movement of population into and through Eastern Europe. These migrants come from even less developed parts of the world such as the impoverished south-east corners of Europe and, further yet, the former Soviet republics in Asia, Afghanistan, and Bangladesh. Besides the earlier noted enduring economic disequilibria among regions in the world capitalist system, two additional factors of a political nature have facilitated the increased population flows, including human trafficking, into and out of Eastern Europe. First, the inclusion in 2004 of ten East Central European nation-States in the European Union (EU) with the accompanying facilitation of international travel, and, second, the still-porous state infrastructure, especially control institutions, and 'gappy' legal systems in the process of *perestroika*, the ongoing political transformation, in many countries in the region.

These combined economic and political factors and the geographic proximity of East (Central) Europe to the core, western parts of the Continent, make this region a perfect hub for international human trafficking (IOM 2005, 2004(a), (b), 2000, 1998, 1995; ILO 2003; Laczko *et al.* 2002; El-Cherkeh *et al.* 2004; Hunzinger and Coffey 2003; Klinczenko 2000; Ivakhniouk and Iontsev 2005). The already-noted enormous expansion of the sex industry in the West fosters the rapidly growing demand for this kind of international 'labour' migrants. Trafficking of East and South-East European women and children for the purposes of sexual exploitation is estimated to constitute a hefty 25 per cent of the worldwide population movement in this category; the proportion of women from other parts of the world trafficked through East and South-East Europe has been slightly lower, around 20 per cent. In actual numbers, following Jonas Widgren's (1994, as cited in IOM 2000: 32) method of estimating the actual number of trafficked persons as 4–6 times larger than the number of apprehensions, and taking the average of 5,000 apprehensions per year, including border and internal seizures, in each of the East (Central and Eastern) and South-East European and bordering Western countries (Germany, Austria, Finland, Italy and – close across the Baltic – Sweden), the volume of human trafficking in and out of that region amounts to 350,000 to 500,000 persons annually.[5]

Trafficking trajectories

Trafficking trajectories in and out of East and South-East Europe reflect the general pattern of world compass migrations and form a complex, criss-crossing map. They have expanded more and more east- and southeastwards over time, with several countries, for instance Poland and Hungary, shifting their status with this expansion from countries of origin, to countries of origin and transit, and countries of transit. After the fall of the Soviet bloc in the early 1990s, the first 'pioneer' wave of commercial sex labourers was trafficked from East Central to Western Europe; the next wave extended to the Balkans, the European post-Soviet Russia and Ukraine; it then stretched further to South-East Europe including Romania, Moldova, Bulgaria, Bosnia and Herzegovina, and Albania, and, next, further yet to former Soviet republics in Asia and beyond.

Today, three major treks can be identified, each with different sub-trajectories. Beginning with longest distance travels, people are trafficked from Central Asia, Afghanistan, and Bangladesh through Russia, Ukraine, Lithuania to Poland, Slovakia, or Hungary, where they either stay or, more often, continue to Germany, Austria, Sweden and further to West European countries. Then, in long-to-middle-distance transfers, the trafficked persons are moved from Russia, Ukraine, and Lithuania in East Eastern Europe and Albania, Moldova, Bulgaria, Romania, Bosnia and Herzegovina in South-East Europe through Slovenia, Poland, Hungary, and the Czech Republic to Western Europe, Israel, the Arab Republics, and further to North America. Finally, diminishing after 2004 but still a distinguishable flow, a middle-to-short distance trajectory involves trafficking women and children from East Central European countries, including Poland, the Czech Republic, Slovakia, and Hungary to Western Europe and, especially, to Germany, Austria, the Netherlands, Belgium, Italy, France, Sweden, and the UK. While East and South-East European trafficked women are estimated, as already noted, to constitute one-fourth of this category of worldwide migration, this proportion varies from trajectory to trajectory: for example, whereas East European women from Russia, Lithuania, and Ukraine represent 70–80 per cent and 30–35 per cent of all trafficked prostitutes in, respectively, Germany and the Netherlands, those from the Balkans, Romania, and Bulgaria predominate (70–80 per cent) or make up a large proportion (45 per cent of all trafficked women) in Austria and Italy.[6]

These diverse streams display basic similarities in the characteristics of the trafficked persons and the mechanisms of their recruitment and cross-border transportation. In the next section I examine these shared characteristics of human trafficking in and out of East Europe in terms of the socio-demographic profile of the trafficked persons, their motivations, ways of recruitment, organisation of transnational transfers, and their situations in destination places. I also note sociologically interesting differences. The focus of the discussion is on the trafficked women (including underage girls), because, as already noted, there is barely any systematic information on trafficked children.

Socio-demographic characteristics of trafficked women, recruitment mechanisms, and the organisation of movement and employment

Women (including underage girls) constitute over 90 per cent of East and South-East European persons trafficked into the western parts of the Continent; the remainder – thus far a terra incognita in terms of sociological research – are young boys trafficked into prostitution. Minors, or 13–17-year-old girls, account for on average 15 to 30 per cent of all trafficked women (but as many as 60–70 per cent are reported in some South-East European countries such as Albania or Moldova). Among the adults, the largest (50–60 per cent) and next largest (20–25 percent) age group are 18–23 and 24–25 years old women respectively, most of them unmarried and without children. The typical gender and age proportions of non-Europeans, mainly Asians, trafficked through Eastern Europe to the West are similar. Most of the adult trafficked women originating from Eastern and South-Eastern Europe have secondary education (partial or completed), and, interestingly, 15 to 20 per cent have some post-secondary schooling; in comparison, women trafficked to and through East Europe from Asia, especially from the regions with strong patriarchal systems where schooling of women is not mandatory, have much lower (if any) levels of education. The majority, more than 70 per cent, of trafficked women originating from East Central and East Eastern Europe come from middle-to-large urban centres; this proportion is considerably lower, 35–40 per cent, among migrants from South-East Europe, and higher – more than 80 per cent – among women trafficked from Asia.[7]

Available case studies that have examined the motivations of young women from Hungary in the early 1990s, and, at the present time, from Romania, Moldova, Bulgaria, and Ukraine who have been recruited for travel to the West, reveal a combination of economic, cultural, and social-psychological 'push' factors. The basic ones are the systematic lower employment rates and lower pay, and, generally more limited opportunities of women to enter, stay, and advance in the region's labour market in comparison to their male counterparts.[8]

The images of affluent and independent women conveyed by globalised (read Westernised) media aggravate East European women's frustration with their low socio-economic position and subordinate gender status at home, while their youth primes them for an adventure and fills their heads with dreams about a fantasy future in the West, be it by earning a lot of money for themselves or finding handsome and rich husbands. Added to this is the realisation by women residents of the (majority) of East and South-East European countries that are not members of the EU with its free cross-border travel that obtaining an entry visa to any of West European countries is quite complicated (if at all possible) and very expensive. In this situation, attractive offers of work abroad made by individuals, agencies, or press advertisements recruiting candidates for westbound travels fall on receptive ears.[9]

Recruitment

Recruitment in East and South-East European countries for trafficking women to the West for the purpose of sexual exploitation takes several forms. One way, estimated to set in motion no less than 30 per cent of young women in the region, is through the initiative of friends or acquaintances of the prospective victim. Halyna, a young Ukrainian, whose story was quoted in the opening extract, was talked into leaving for a supposedly good job as a waitress in Berlin by a friend of her cousin. Vida, from Moldova, was persuaded by a colleague of a friend to go to Poland with promises of certain employment as a maid in Hamburg. Such references increase the trust of the recruited in the sincerity of the invitations and appease their anxiety about potential risks involved, even, as studies demonstrate (Mira Med Institute 1999; Monzini 2005), when they are 'generally aware' of mishaps occurring to their compatriots abroad.

The second, more common form of recruitment, estimated to 'hook' about 60 per cent of prospective travellers, are deceptive offers of assistance in arranging a visa, travel across the border, and a job abroad made by unknown intermediaries/members of transnational trafficking networks who approach the candidates either in their home towns or already en route. A widespread method is thus the so-called 'lover boy' recruitment mode whereby a man (often a foreigner) seduces a girl 'by promising her a marriage or a rosy future' and organises her travel abroad (Monzini 2005: 76). Another popular method is through an elderly woman recruiter, who arouses fewer suspicions than does an unknown male figure. For example, Natasha, a Moscow-based Russian female recruiter, promised underage girls secure and profitable employment in the West and arranged passports for the volunteers by faking their age to avoid the requirement of parental approval (Williams 1999). 'Helpers' to women already en route have also been effective, as in the example of 'Mr. A. standing at the railway station in Prague and waiting for customers. He approaches people in Russian who, in his opinion, might be potential clients for his smuggling services. Judging that they are interested in getting to Germany he offers to organise the transport to the German border and promises they would be met there by his friend to travel further' (Heckmann 2006: 205–6).

Parallel to all the above, recruitment agencies and advertisements in the press offering specific jobs in the West for specific remuneration or marriages to respectable foreigners and (supposedly free) assistance in arranging necessary travel documents, visas, and transportation have mushroomed across East and South-East Europe. Still in the mid-1990s, Hungarian and Polish newspapers regularly published advertisements of job offers in the West for women as babysitters, waitresses, dancers, or bar girls in night clubs, and tempting announcements of West European single well-to-do men seeking to marry nice East European girls who would make good wives and mothers. Ten years later, Albanian, Romanian, Russian, and Ukrainian media largely took over the task. Thus, a typical ad in the Kiev Daily reads: 'Young women needed in Berlin [Helsinki, Vienna, Milan] as maids and babysitters in middle-class homes. Room and board, weekly wage (net) 150–200 Euro, one day off, health insurance provided. Assistance in obtaining travel documents and transportation. Call evenings at …', or 'Nice clean girls, preferably blondes with blue eyes, sought for marriage by good-looking German [Austrian, Italian, Spanish] men'.[10] In the case of Asian women trafficked into and through Eastern Europe, not kin and acquaintance chains or press advertisements, but transnational organised networks tend to be the dominant form of recruitment (Chin 1999; International Migration 2003; Kyle and Liang 2005).

Some commentators on the proliferation of sex trafficking point out the complicity of the victims in carrying out this ugly business: by responding to fake job advertisements and letting themselves be seduced by untrustworthy young men, the women (girls) contribute to their own fate. Indeed, the practices of agents/agencies recruiting for sexual exploitation have been highly professional: offers are presented in a trustworthy fashion, in the media or through the legitimate-looking agencies, with the smallest details of travel arrangements, and employment and income abroad deceptively accurately presented. The victims' inexperience with such employment transactions (there were no official possibilities of income-seeking travels to the West under communism and no independent transnational employment agencies) and their own 'wishful thinking' about their futures, combine to make them susceptible to this kind of deception. The best remedy to such unwarranted, naïve trust among the potential trafficking victims, already put in practice in the growing number of localities in Eastern Europe where human trafficking is widespread, seems mass education – in schools, in the media, in the public places – about the dangers of such credulity and, also, about the ways these recruiters operate.

The scenarios after the women have been lured into travel abroad are similar regardless of their origins and destinations. Like the earlier quoted Ukrainian Halyna, when they arrive at the place of destination or transit, their passports and other personal documents are taken away and they are told they will have to pay back the expenses, between US $700 and $4,000 depending on the distance travelled, incurred in the process of bringing them over. They are put up in a closely surveillanced boarding house or apartment and soon after arrival are forced by physical violence and psychological torment (threats to their families at home) into prostitution. It can take several forms: work in brothels, on the street, in bars or night clubs, at the border serving truck drivers and other interested passers-by, or in pornographic films.

Unless they have the courage or despair enough to escape into the unknown, women thus entrapped find themselves in a helpless situation. They do not have personal documents, and they usually do not speak the language of the host country in which they reside illegally. They do not have any money because whatever they might earn from their forced sexual services is taken away by the traffickers as reimbursement for their 'debts' for the cost of transportation and subsequent expenses of their upkeep. And their movements are tightly controlled by their 'managers' who frequently transfer them from place to place in order to diminish the risk of being caught by the receiver country authorities and losing their 'merchandise'. The physical violence and psychological suffering experienced by young East and South-East European women trafficked into sexual slavery in western parts of the Continent have been noted in all studies of this phenomenon some of which contain sporadic interviews with the victims. They tell harrowing stories of continued abuse ranging from the imposition of excessive working hours, verbal and physical violence, sexual harassment and rape, hunger, isolation, and fear for their own safety and that of their families at home against whom repeated threats are made by the traffickers and their helpers. In addition to this humiliation, they are often used as 'commodities' in the sex trade as the brothel or night club owners often sell them again and again to others when they acquire more attractive (usually meaning younger) victims. The reported prices for East and South-East European women in such transactions range between US $2,500 and $7,000. When they are no longer of use and constitute a burden for their 'employers', they are thrown out to the street.[11]

Organisation and employment

The operation of sex trafficking businesses – from location and recruitment of candidates in their home countries, transportation across borders, to their exploitation in the place of destination – requires an efficient transnational organisation. Most common in trafficking East and South-East European women are professional networks consisting of five to 15 people per international 'circuit': mostly, though not exclusively, men, including the boss in each (origin and destination) country, recruiters and/or managers of special travel agencies in the candidates' countries of origin, assistants responsible for security, transport, contacts (bribery) with the authorities, helpers along transit points during transport from the country of origin to that of destination, and, in the latter, collectors of money, managers and supervisors of trafficked women 'employment' (IOM 2001, 2000; Monzini 2005; Morawska 2003).

Particularly renowned for 'expert' human trafficking into and through the region under consideration and for the management of the victims in Western countries have been Albanian networks, but Poles, Lithuanians, and Ukrainians have also been effective. Thus, since the mid-1990s Albanian trafficking networks have reportedly moved thousands of young women from Uzbekistan, Kazakhstan and Ukraine through Hungary, Slovakia, and the Czech Republic to the Balkans, and further to Italy, France, and the UK where they are known to manage an extensive ring of brothels 'staffed' by these women. A Lithuanian network of four men and one woman has been trafficking underage women from as far as Malaysia into the UK where they have been placed in brothels run by East Asians. Gangs of Poles running job advertisements in Ukraine have been moving women from that country to Yugoslav-ran brothels in Berlin.[12]

Probably the most renowned of all East European traffickers, the Russian network has been the most extensive and best organised. Its close connection to the established Russian mafia global commercial activities including money laundering, extortion, and trafficking of drugs and weapons, makes it more global in scope than other national networks, more efficient and, because of the mafia's well oiled rapport with Russian authorities, less vulnerable to harassment by authorities. Indeed, it has been the Russian sex trafficking networks (besides smaller-scale Chinese chains) that have been responsible for bringing into and through Eastern Europe thousands of women from Asia (Kyle and Koslowski 2001; Williams 1999; Finckenauer 2001; Heckmann 2006; Salt 1998).

Thus far there have been no systematic studies of the return of the East and South-East European trafficked women. What little is known indicates that those who are repatriated or deported encounter serious difficulties: they usually have no passport or other personal documents, they are often harassed by frontier guards, and they are reluctant to return to their home towns because of fear of social ostracism, and because they find it impossible to 'recognise themselves in their previous identity and lifestyle' (Monzini 2005: 134; also Horbunova 1999; IOM 2001, 2004a). The investigation of these returnees' psychological and social re-adaptation to life back in their home countries is certainly awaiting the initiative of human rights specialists, sociologists, and psychotherapists. Not much, either, is known about the apparently growing phenomenon of 're-trafficking', that is, about repeated trading in the same women for sexual exploitation from and through Eastern Europe to the West (but see Erder and Kaska 2003 on this operation in Turkey).

So what has been done to tackle trafficking in women in and from Eastern Europe? In the final section I consider, first, the legal, institutional, and other measures to combat human trafficking using the examples of Romania and Moldova, the two countries in the region under consideration from which high numbers of trafficked originate and transit through. Next, I evaluate the effectiveness of these measures and identify the main reasons why the attempts to curb transnational human trafficking have thus far been unsatisfactory.

Legal and institutional efforts to curb trafficking in women in and from Eastern Europe, and reasons for their (in)effectiveness

Legal proscriptions and organisational bodies as well as non-governmental initiatives created for the purpose of eliminating transnational trafficking in humans at global, (inter)national, and local levels have been growing rapidly since the 1990s when the issue of world-scale white slavery again became a public agenda. All East and South-East European countries, including Romania and Moldova, have accepted and implemented several of these measures and initiatives.

Romania is one of the signatories, to note only the UN resolutions of the last decade[13] of the UN General Assembly's 1997 Resolution on the Elimination of Violence Against Women which specified a number of crime prevention principles in the form of Model

Strategies and Practical Measures to be adopted by member countries. The Romanian government also signed the UN General Assembly Convention Against Transnational Organized Crime and its two protocols: the Protocol to Prevent, Suppress, and Punish Trafficking in Persons, Especially Women and Children, and the Protocol against the Smuggling of Migrants by Land, Air, and Sea. These resolutions, known as the Palermo Protocol, have entered into force in international law in 2003. As a new (October 2006) EU member state, Romania must comply with its *acquis communautaire*, a set of legal provisions and recommendations accepted by member countries, including those concerning human trafficking. They include, to note only recent resolutions, the series of various legal instrument and programmes adopted by the Council of Europe such as STOP I (1996–2000) and II (2001–02), DAPHNE I (2000–03) and II (2004–08), and a framework programme on police and judicial cooperation in criminal matters (AGIS 2004–08). The Romanian government also participates in the 2003 EU Stability Pact for South-East Europe and collaborates with the Organisation for Security and Cooperation in Europe (OSCE), and it adopted the 2005 Council of Europe Convention on Action against Trafficking in Human Beings.

Altogether, since 1999–2000 Romania has subscribed to at least 30 legal initiatives and prevention programmes aimed at combating human trafficking. These directives can be classified into nine types: creation and implementation of legislative frameworks; law enforcement; regional and international cooperation; prevention and raising awareness; assistance to victims of trafficking (legal, material, psychological, reintegration); information campaigns and awareness-raising; training programmes (of judiciary, police, and educators); research and coordination; and networking. The Romanian authorities (Parliament, government and different ministries, Supreme Court) participate in most of these activities in collaboration with governments of countries receiving Romanian human traffic (Italy, France, Israel, The Netherlands, Denmark, the UK), intergovernmental organisations such as the International Organisation for Migration (IOM),[14] International Organisation of Labour (ILO) and the United Nations High Commissioner for Refugees (UNHCR) each of which has a local bureau in Bucharest. Another intergovernmental project whose organisational members (including the Romanian government) participate in several anti-trafficking initiatives in Romania has been the Budapest Group that conceptualises and monitors a harmonised approach to all aspects of trafficking. The Budapest group conducts its activities in collaboration with similar initiatives of the EU and different NGOs (non-governmental organisations), including the International Human Rights Group, La Strada, the Foundation Against Trafficking in Women, ARETUSA, and AntiSlavery International.[15] Local NGOs, including the Romanian Media-for-the Public initiatives, the Red Cross, and the Patriarchy of the Romanian Orthodox Church have also participated in the above-noted anti-trafficking programmes especially in the Assistance to Victims of Trafficking, Information Campaign and Awareness Training, and Research and Assessment initiatives.

About 40 anti-trafficking programmes and organised activities in Moldova make up the same nine types as in Romania, ranging from legislative frameworks and law enforcement, through assistance to victims of trafficking, to prevention and awareness-raising through media and other educational programmes. As in Romania, the Moldovan government adopted the UN Palermo Protocol. Although it is not yet a candidate for EU membership, it participates in the Council of Europe Stability Pact for South and East Europe aimed at monitoring and combating human trafficking, and has a local bureau of the Organisation for Security and Cooperation in Europe. Moldova is also a member of the already mentioned Budapest Group that monitors human trafficking through the region and coordinates the response to it of state-national authorities. The OSCE and other intergovernmental organisations such as IOM, UNICEF, Europol and Interpol collaborate with the Moldovan government to coordinate efforts to combat human trafficking from and into the country, in the enforcement of the existing anti-trafficking laws, and in training for judiciary and police forces.

Several destination-country governments (Russia, Italy, France, Norway, US, Israel, the Arab Republics) through their embassies in Moldova assist local authorities in prevention and awareness-raising programmes, in training of border and urban patrol officers responsible for identifying and detaining the traffickers, and in helping the victims of trafficking. Moldovan and international NGOs join in these efforts: La Strada, the Foundation Against Trafficking in Women, Peace Corps, Human Rights Watch, the Italian Association Papa Giovanni XXIII, the Swedish and Dutch NGOs, and the local church, human rights, and protection-of women organisations.[16]

Effectiveness of initiatives

Considering that, as noted earlier, a similar multitude of legal initiatives and agencies created to combat human trafficking in the region exists in other East and South-East European countries, how can we evaluate the outcomes of their concerted efforts? There is no doubt that during the last decade, bringing the problem of white slavery onto the public agenda of national and intergovernmental legislative and administrative bodies and media in the region has been a significant accomplishment. The very institution and updating of anti-trafficking legislation and cooperative monitoring of its implementation, non-existent in the early 1990s, can be considered a progression towards the elimination of this criminal activity. As the high figures of women still trafficked from and through the region indicate, however, these achievements are far from satisfactory. There has been a constellation of factors, some resulting from the nature of the anti-trafficking efforts, and some related to the mechanisms of trafficking itself, that hinder a more tangible progress in the elimination of white slavery in East and South-East Europe.

First, only a fraction of countries (72 out of 185) many of which are sources of human trafficking through East and South-East Europe have ratified the UN anti-trafficking Conventions, and in those that have, the implementation of these protocols has not been subject to systematic monitoring and verification mechanisms. The relevant EU protocols do not bind non-member countries and their implementation has likewise been far from perfect. In addition and importantly, various governmental and NGOs organisations acting on behalf of the preservation of human rights and, specifically, combating of white slavery, deal with their tasks in different ways, and have different priorities that often conflict with or neutralise each other. Related to the above has been the primary concern of destination governments in punishing the undocumented victims of trafficking rather than eliminating the perpetrators of trafficking crimes. Recently the attention of law enforcing agencies has been gradually shifting to the latter. Of particular relevance here, if properly implemented by all signatory-countries, has been the recent Council of Europe Convention on Action Against Trafficking in Human Beings (May 2005) that contains regulations regarding the protection of victims and specifies the mechanisms to monitor their application (www. wcd.coe.int/ViewDoc/jsp?id=828587).

Second, the globalisation of the sex trade and, especially, its transnationally mobile underground markets ran by traffickers experienced in beating the law makes it difficult for national and even international law-enforcing organs to apprehend them and break their criminal networks. As national and international organisations increase their financial and technological resources and personnel, and update legislative and administrative rules to combat human trafficking, the traffickers respond by shifting their modes of communication and transportation routes and developing better marketing strategies. Widespread corruption in many countries of origin and transit, including East and South-East Europe, further hinders the effective anti-trafficking law enforcement and facilitates the operation of these criminals. Third, there is a lack of sustained cooperation of the potential victims themselves who come from the economically disadvantaged regions and whose own life situations are unsatisfactory, and who are, therefore, particularly prone to manipulation of the trafficking recruiters promising substantial rewards abroad.[17]

And yet, the effectiveness of the anti-trafficking measures will improve over time, I believe, especially as the focus of (inter)governmental agencies and legislative bodies shifts from punishing the victims of trafficking to breaking and eliminating the trafficking networks and the criminals who run them, and as the coordination of actions of the existing anti-trafficking organisations improves and information about the ways these operations work and the risks they carry becomes more widespread. But even the concerted regional and global efforts will not make global human trafficking disappear as long as the mechanisms generating it – economic (core-periphery structural imbalances), political (lack of coordination of law enforcement and corruption of officials), and social (effective transnational criminal networks) – remain in force. It will persist, with the once origin countries becoming transit and then destination countries, like those in East Central Europe, as their economic growth accelerates, and as global sex trade incorporates more and more peripheral parts of the world.

Conclusion

In this overview of contemporary white slavery and, specifically, trafficking in women into and from East and South-East Europe, I have identified the multi-level contributing factors and on-the-ground mechanisms behind this criminal activity. I also examined the multiple global, national, and local agencies working toward prevention of human trafficking in the examples of Romania and Moldova, the two countries from which high numbers of women trafficked to the West originate. Finally, I assessed the effectiveness of these measures and identified a constellation of reasons why they remain unsatisfactory.

Although certain accomplishments towards tackling the problem should be acknowledged, especially in view of how recently such efforts have been instituted, combating human trafficking into and from East and South-East Europe remains a serious challenge and requires the unrelenting attention of law-enforcement agencies and public opinion not only in the region but in the rest of the Continent and in other parts of the world.

Notes

1 This discussion covers East Central (Poland, the Czech Republic, Slovakia, Hungary) and East Eastern (Russia, the Baltics, Ukraine) Europe as well as South-East Europe (former Yugoslavia, Albania, Bulgaria, Romania, Moldova).

2 It should be noted, however, that routes of international trafficking often shift quite significantly in response to changing political and economic conditions.

3 On macro-structural push-and-pull mechanisms of international trafficking, see Kelly 2005; Monzini 2005; Morawska 2003; Williams 1999; see also Sassen 1998 on world-system patterns of labour migrations.

4 It should be noted, however, that there exists considerable differences between countries in the level of economic development within East Central Europe: the 2,000 per capita GNP, for example, in the Czech Republic was 56 per cent and in Poland 47 per cent of the average figure for Western Europe and North America combined. Similar diversity in economic performance exists also in East Eastern and South-Eastern Europe.

5 See Williams 2005; Monzin 2005; Lethi 2003; Laczko et al. 2002; IOM 1998, 2001; El-Cherkeh et al. 2004; Ruyver and Van Impe 2001.

6 See IOM 2000, 2005; ILO 2003; Laczko et al. 2002; El-Cherkeh et al. 2004; Kangaspunta 2003; Ivakhniouk and Iontsev 2005.

7 These estimates are based on the characteristics of trafficked women assisted by aid organisations. Information compiled from Monzini 2005; IOM 2000, 2004(a), (b), 2005; Kelly 2002; OSCE 2002, 2003; El-Cherkeh et al. 2004; Fulton 2005; Kootstra 1999.

8 Over the decade and a half since the collapse of the Soviet bloc, East Central European countries have reached a relatively greater parity in this area than have less economically developed and more patriarchal East Eastern and South-East European countries.

9 See Williams 1999; El-Cherkeh et al. 2004; IOM 2000, 2001, 2005; Shelley 2003; Monzini 2005; Winiecki 2006; Vocks and Nijboer 2000. I have found no comparable information about the motivations of Asian women trafficked into and through Eastern Europe, but I expect they are by and large similar.

10 Morawska's personal archives. See also Monzini 2005; Heckmann 2006; Vandeckerckhove *et al.* 2003; Vocks and Nijboer 2000; Lazaroiu and Alexandru 2003; El-Cherkeh *et al.* 2004; Volks and Nijboer 2000; Ruggiero 1997; Pytlakowski 2006.

11 See IOM 2001, 2004(a), (b); Laczko *et al.* 2002; Monzini 2005; Calandruccio 2005; Morawska 2003; Vocks and Nijboer 2000; Ruyver and Van Impe 2001; El-Cherkeh *et al.* 2004; Salt 1998; Bruinsma and Meershoek 1999; Caldwell *et al.* 1999.

12 From Morawska's ongoing study of the transnational involvement of Polish (im)migrants in Berlin. See also Slany 2005; Cowan 2006; Kelly 2005; IOM 2000.

13 The original Convention for the Suppression of the Traffic in Persons and the Exploitation of the Prostitution of Others passed by the UN General Assembly in 1949 has since been modified by several new resolutions that are continuously revised and updated.

14 Created in 1951 to deal with problems of refugees in Europe, the IOM has since expanded its activities to include, among others, monitoring human trafficking, and initiating and controlling intergovernmental programmes to suppress it through its country-based branches, and annual conferences and publications. Among its latest activities in the region of concern here, in 2004 the IOM Warsaw branch organised an international conference on 'Building Regional Partnerships to Fight Trafficking in Persons in the Context of EU-Enlargement'; it was followed in the next year by a workshop on the same topic in Bucharest, Romania.

15 The most renowned of these, La Strada, was founded in 1995 to prevent trafficking of women in East Central Europe; it has since expanded its activities to include South and Eastern Europe and West European destination countries. The Foundation Against Trafficking in Women, established in 1993, has now 50 member-country organisations. The remaining two NGOs were created in the early 2000s.

16 Information about UN and EU resolutions and programmes adopted by Romania and Moldova compiled from El-Cherkeh *et al.* 2004; Grant 2005; Ollus and Nevala 2001; Fulton 2005; Monzini 2005; wwww.imadr.org/ project; www.osce/org; www.europol.eu/int; www.europa.eu/scadplus/ leg/en/lvb; www.unescobkk.org/culture/trafficking/publication.htm; www.ecre.org/research/smuggle.shtml; www.coe.int/t/e/human_rights/ trafficking; www.org.doc?t=women_trafficking. Information about intergovernmental bodies and international and local NGOs operating in Romania and Moldova from El-Cherkeh *et al.* 2004; Fulton 2005; www.ilo.org; www.unher.ch; www.antislavery.org; www.iom.org; www. hrlawgroup.org/initiatives/trafficking_persons; www.aretusa.net; www. bayswan.org?FoundTraf.html

17 Information on the three obstacles to the effectiveness of anti-trafficking measures compiled from Monzini 2005; OSCE 2001; Heckmann 2006; Salt 1998.

References

Aronowitz, A. (2001) 'Smuggling and Trafficking in Human Beings: The Phenomenon, the Markets that Drive it and the Organisations that Promote it', *European Journal on Criminal Policy and Research*, 9(2): 163–95.

Barry, K. (1979) *Female Sexual Slavery*. London: Coronet Books.

Berend, I. (1996) *Central and Eastern Europe, 1944–1993: Detour from the Periphery to the Periphery*. New York: Columbia University Press.

Berend, I. and Ranki G. (1982) *The European Periphery and Industrialisation, 1780–1914*. New York: Columbia University Press.

Bhabha, J. (2005) 'Trafficking, Smuggling, and Human Rights', *Migration Information Source*, see: http://www.migrationinformation.org/Feature/

Bruisma, G. and Mooershoek G. (1999) 'Organised Crime and Trafficking in Women from Eastern Europe in the Netherlands', in P. Williams (ed.) *Illegal Immigration and Commercial Sex*, pp. 105–18. London: Frank Cass.

Butterwerk, B. (1999) 'Trafficking of Women and Girls for Prostitution: The Case of Central Europe', Paper presented at the International Conference on New Frontiers of Crime: Trafficking in Human Beings and New Forms of Slavery. UNICRI, Verona, 22–23 October 1999.

Calandruccio, G. (2005) 'A Review of Recent Research on Human Trafficking in the Middle East', *International Migration*, 43 (1–2): 267–300.

Caldwell, G. *et al.* (1999) 'Capitalising on Transition Economies: The Role of the Russia Mafia in Trafficking Women for Forced Prostitution', in P. Williams (ed.) *Illegal Immigration and Commercial Sex*, pp. 42–73. London: Frank Cass.

Chin, K.L. (1999) *Smuggled Chinese*. Clandestine Immigration to the United States. Philadelphia: Temple University Press.

Chin, K.L. (2001) 'The Social Organisation of Chinese Human Smuggling', in D. Kyle and R. Koslowski (eds) *Global Human Smuggling*, pp. 216–34. Baltimore: The Johns Hopkins University Press.

Chirot, D. (1989) *The Study of Social Change*. New York: Harcourt Brace.

Cowan, R. (2006) 'Jailing of Lithuanian Sex Trafficker', *International Herald Tribune*, 17 September 2006, p. 10.

Drew, S. (2002) 'Human Trafficking: a Modern Form of Slavery?', *European Human Rights Law Review*, 4: 481–92.

El-Cherkeh, A. *et al.* (2004) *EU-Enlargement, Migration and Trafficking in Women: The Case of South Eastern Europe*. Hamburg: Hamburg Institute of International Economics.

Erder, S. and Kaska, S. (2003) *Irregular Migration and Trafficking in Women: The Case of Turkey*. Geneva: IOM.

Finckenauer, J. (2001) 'Russian Transnational Organised Crime and Human Trafficking', in D. Kyle and R. Kolsowski (eds) *Global Human Smuggling*, pp. 166–86. Baltimore: The Johns Hopkins University Press.

Freedman, J. (2003) 'Selling Sex, Trafficking, Prostitution and Sex Work Amongst Migrant Women in Europe', in J. Freedman (ed.) *Gender and Insecurity: Migrant Women in Europe*, pp. 119–36. Aldershot: Ashgate.

Fulton, A. (2005) *Trafficking in Women from Romania: A Human Rights Analysis*, unpublished MA dissertation, University of Essex.

Grant, S. (2005) 'Migrants' Human Rights: From the Margins to the Mainstream', *Migration Information Source*, see: www.migrationinformation. org/Feature/

Heckmann, F. (2006) 'Illegal Migration: What Can We Know and What Can We Explain?', in M. Bodemann and G. Yurdakul (eds) *Migration, Citizenship, Ethnos*, pp. 197–218. New York: Palgrave Macmillan.

Horbunova, O. (1999) 'Ukrainian Centre for Women's Studies/International Women's Right Centre – La Strada', Paper presented at the NGO meeting Trafficking and the Global Sex Industry. Need for Human Rights Framework, Geneva: Palais de Nations, 21–22 June 1999.

Hunzinger, L. and Coffey P. (2003) *First Annual Report on Victims of Trafficking in South-Eastern Europe*. Vienna: IOM Regional Clearing Point.

Icduygu, A. (2000) 'The Politics of International Migratory Regimes: Transit Migration Flows in Turkey', *International Migration*, September 2000, pp. 357–67.

International Labour Organization (ILO) (2003) *Forced Labour Outcomes of Irregular Migration and Human Trafficking in Europe*. Geneval: ILO.

International Migration (2003) *Special issue on Understanding Migration Between China and Europe*, 41 (3).

International Migration (2005) *Special issue on Human Trafficking: A Global Survey*, 43 (1–2).

IOM (International Organization for Migration) (1995) *Trafficking and Prostitution: The Growing Exploitation of Women from Central and Eastern Europe*. Geneva: IOM.

IOM (1998) *Analysis of Data and Statistical Resources available in EU Member Counties on Trafficking in Humans*. Geneva: IOM.

IOM (2000) *Migrant Trafficking and Human Smuggling in Europe. A Review of the Evidence with Case Studies from Hungary, Poland, and Ukraine*. Vienna: IOM.

IOM (2001) *Victims of Trafficking in the Balkans*. Bucharest: IOM.

IOM (2004a) *Changing Patterns and Trends of Trafficking in Persons, the Balkan Region*. Geneva: IOM Counter-Trafficking Center.

IOM (2004b) 'Assisting Victims of Sexual Trafficking to and from the Russian Federation', report submitted to the Office to Monitor and Combat Trafficking in Persons. Moscow: Year One Final Report.

IOM (2005) *Second Annual Report on Victims of Trafficking*. Geneva: IOM.

Ivakhniouk, I. and Iontsev V. (2005) 'Russia – EU: Interaction Within the Reshaping Migration Space', in K. Slany (ed.) *International Migration. A Multi-dimensional Analysis*, pp. 217–52. Cracow: AGH University of Science and Technology Press.

Jaschok, M. and Miers, S. (eds) (1994) *Women and Chinese Patriarchy: Submission, Servitude, and Escape*. London: Zed Books.

Kangaspunta, K. (2003) 'Mapping the Inhuman Trade: Preliminary Findings on the Database on Trafficking in Human Beings', *Forum on Crime and Society*, 3 (1–2): 81–104.

Kelly, L. (2002) *Journeys to Jeopardy: Review of Research on Trafficking of Women and Children to Europe*, IOM Migration Research Series, 11: 6–13.

Kelly, L. (2005) '"You Can Find Anything You Want": A Critical Reflection on Research on Trafficking in Persons Within and Into Europe', *International Migration*, 43 (1–2): 235–66.

Klinczenko, T. (2000) 'Migrant Trafficking and Human Smuggling in Ukraine', *Migrant Trafficking and Human Smuggling in Europe*. Geneva: IOM.

Kootstra, T. (1999) *La Strada Program: Prevention of Traffic in Women in Central and Eastern Europe*. Utrecht: Dutch Foundation Against Trafficking in Women.

Kyle, D. and R. Koslowski (eds) (2001) *Global Human Smuggling*. Baltimore: The Johns Hopkins University Press.

Kyle, D. and Z. Liang (2005) *Migration Merchants: Organised Migrant Trafficking from China and Ecuador*, unpublished.

Laczko, F. *et al.* (2002) *New Challenges for Migration Policy in Central and Eastern Europe*. The Hague: Asser Press.

Lazaroiu, S. and Alexandru, M. (2003) *Who Is the Next Victim? Vulnerability of Young Rumanian Women to Trafficking in Human Beings*. Bucharest: IOM Mission in Romania.

Lethi, M. (2003) *Trafficking in Women and Children in Europe*, HEUNI Paper No.18. Helsinki: European Institute for Crime Prevention and Control.

Mira Med Institute (1999) *Preliminary Survey Report on Sexual Trafficking from the CIS Countries*, see: www.miramedinstitute.org/trafficking.eng.html

Monzini, P. (2005) *Sex Traffic. Prostitution, Crime and Exploitation*. London: Zed Books.

Morawska, E. (2003) 'Transnational Migration in the Enlarged European Union: A Perspective from East Central Europe', in J. Zielonka (ed.) *Europe Unbound*, pp. 161–90. Oxford: Oxford University Press.

Morrison, J. (1998) *The Cost of Survival. The Trafficking of Refugees to the UK*. London: Refugee Council.

Ollus, N. and Nevala S. (eds) (2001) *Women in the Criminal Justice System: International Examples and National Responses*. Helsinki: European Institute for Crime Prevention and Control.

OSCE (Organization for Security and Cooperation in Europe) (2001) *Trafficking in Human Beings: Implications for the OSCE*. Warsaw: Office for Democratic Institutions and Human Rights.

OSCE (2002) *Country Reports submitted to the Informal Group on Gender Inequality and Anti-Trafficking in Human Beings*. Warsaw: Human Dimension Implementation Meeting, 19–20 September 2002.

OSCE (2003) *First Annual Report on Victims of Trafficking in South Eastern Europe*. Vienna: Task Force on Trafficking in Human Beings, Stability Pact for South Eastern Europe.

Papademetriou, D. (2005) 'The Global Struggle with Illegal Migration: No End in Sight', *Migration Information Source*, see: www.migrationinformation. org/Feature/display.cfm?id=336

Pytlakowski, P. (2006) 'Gangster za Chlebem', *Polityka*, 24 June, pp. 28–30.

Ruggiero, V. (1997) 'Trafficking in Human Beings: Slavery in Contemporary Europe', *International Journal of the Sociology of Law*, 25: 232–44.

Ruyver, B. and Van Impe, K. (2001) 'Trafficking in Women Through Poland: Analysis of the Phenomenon, Causes of Trans-Migration and Proposals to Tackle the Problem', in N. Ollus and S.Nevala (eds) *Women in the Criminal Justice System: International Examples and National Responses*, pp. 182–97. Helsinki: European Institute for Crime Prevention and Control.

Salt, J. (1998) 'Trafficking in Migrant: A Preliminary Literature Review', Paper presented at IOM Workshop in Trafficking, Warsaw, 8–9 June 1998.

Salt, J. and Stein J. (1997) 'Migration as a Business: The Case of Trafficking', *International Migration*, 35: 467–94.

Sassen, S. (1998) *Globalisation and its Discontents*. New York: The New Press.

Scully, E. (2001) 'Pre-Cold War Traffic in Sexual Labour and Its Foes: Some Contemporary Lessons', in D. Kyle and R. Koslowski (eds) *Global Human Smuggling*, pp. 74–106. Baltimore: The Johns Hopkins University Press.

Shelley, L. (2003) 'The Trade in People in and From the Former Soviet Union', *Crime, Law, and Social Change*, 40: 231–49.

Slany, K. (ed.) (2005) *International Migration: A Multidimensional Analysis*. Cracow: AGH University of Science and Technology Press.

Smith, P. (1997) *Human Smuggling: Chinese Migrant Trafficking and the Challenge to America's Immigration Tradition*. Washington, DC: Center for Strategic and International Studies.

Vandeckerckhove, W. *et al.* (2003) 'Research Based on Case Studies of Victims of Trafficking in Human Beings in 3 EU Member States: Belgium, Italy, and the Netherlands', University of Ghent: European Commission.

Vocks, J. and Nijboer J. (2000) 'The Promised Land: A Study of Trafficking in Women from Central and Eastern Europe to the Netherlands', *European Journal on Criminal Policy and Research*, 8: 379–88.

Williams, P. (ed.) (1999) *Illegal Immigration and Commercial Sex: The New Slave Trade*. London: Frank Cass.

Winiecki, J. (2006) 'Rozmnazanie przez Odlaczanie', *Polityka*, 3 June 2006, pp. 54–6.

Zlotnik, H. (2005) 'International Migrant Women in Europe', in K. Slany (ed.) *International Migration. A Multi-dimensional Analysis*, pp. 67–92. Cracow: AGH University of Science and Technology.

Additional resources

European Union Anti-Trafficking Conventions and Protocols, see the
   following websites:
www.coe.int
www.europa.eu.nt
www.ecre.org
www.europol.eu.int/
www.stabilitypact.org/trafficking/
www.europa.edu/pol.rights
www.coe.int/T/E/human_rights/trafficking/

IOM (International Organization for Migration)
Regular reports on human trafficking throughout Europe, see: www.iom.
   int/

NGOs involved in anti-trafficking activities in East and South-East Europe,
   see the following websites:
www.antislavery.org
www.hrlawgroup.org/initiatives/trafficking
www.bayswa.org/FoundTraf.html
www.aretusa.net
www.org.doc?t=women_trafficking

OSCE (Organization for Security and Cooperation in Europe)
Reports on OSCE anti-trafficking activities, see website: www.osce.org/
Legal database: www.legislationonline.org

United Nation Anti-trafficking Conventions and Protocols, see the following
   websites:
www.imadr.org/project/petw
www.unhcr.ch/
www.unescobkk.org/culture/trafficking/htm

Chapter 6

Human trafficking as a form of transnational crime

Louise Shelley

Introduction

Transnational organised crime has been escalating in recent decades as globalisation impacts more regions, resulting in a decline of nation states and border controls. In the 1960s, most of the growth of transnational crime was linked to the growth of the drug trade in such regions as Asia, Latin America, Africa and even Italy, home of the original Mafia. By the late 1990s, the illicit trade in drugs represented an equal share of the legitimate trade in textiles and steel (7.5 per cent of world trade) (UN International Drug Control Programme 1997: 124). Though the drug trade remains the most lucrative aspect of transnational crime, the last few decades have seen an enormous growth in organised human trafficking and smuggling. Many criminals have switched to this area of transnational crime because of the high profits and low risk. Others, not previously involved in transnational crime have entered this trade because of the low initial costs of entry and the large demand for smuggled and trafficked people.

As appalling as human trafficking is, it is a growing transnational phenomenon. International trafficking of women and girls for the sex industry, while not new, has spread to new regions of the world and become a larger part of the illicit global economy. The stunning growth in human smuggling and trafficking occurring in the last 20 years has transpired due to both structural reasons within the international economy, and the increased risk for narcotics traffickers. Moreover, drug traffickers can sell their commodity once, while human traffickers can sell trafficked people repeatedly, thereby deriving extensive profits.

As rational actors, transnational criminals have seen tremendous business opportunities in the human trafficking arena. They are rarely prosecuted because of their ability to neutralise law enforcement through bribes and intimidation. Yet they also thrive in a globalised world because the legal controls are state based, whereas the crime groups are transnational. The criminals' links with the political system exist often not only in their home environment but also in transit and destination countries. Through their flexibility and because of their network structures, they avoid cumbersome legal procedures, which prevent law enforcement from striking effectively at the smuggling networks that cross regions and continents.

Defining the problem

The trafficking problem has existed for decades. As other chapters discuss, the problem of trafficking in women, or the white slave trade, was a concern at the beginning of the twentieth century (see Lee, Morawska, Lindquist and Piper, Chapters 1, 5 and 7 in this volume). International efforts were made then to combat the problem. But in the rest of the twentieth century, the two World Wars followed by the Cold War provided numerous other problems that demanded significant attention. Human trafficking, concentrated primarily in Asia, remained purely a regional concern. With the collapse of the Soviet Union, the problem of trafficking from the former socialist countries emerged on a global scale. Growing international attention was then paid to combating trafficking, including the development of international instruments to combat the phenomenon. The Protocol on human trafficking that was signed in Palermo in 2000 accompanied the United Nations Convention on Transnational Crime. The decision to address human trafficking within the context of transnational crime is highly significant, as it defines the problem not as a small scale one but as a phenomenon tied to international organised crime. Its status as one of the few protocols attached to the Convention recognises the centrality of trafficking to the phenomenon of transnational crime. By defining human trafficking as a crime problem rather than as a migration, human rights or security issue, the international community is recognising that criminal law and law enforcement institutions must play a key role in addressing the problem of transnational human trafficking. Although its causes may be social and economic, the solutions to it lie in the adoption and enforcement of laws.

After years of negotiation among member states, the UN adopted the Protocol to Prevent, Suppress and Punish Trafficking in Persons, Especially Women and Children. This Protocol defines trafficking as:

> The recruitment, transportation, transfer, harbouring or receipt of Persons, by means of threat or use of force or other forms of coercion, of abduction, of fraud, deception, of the abuse of power or of a position of vulnerability or of the giving or receiving of payments or benefits to achieve the consent of a person having control over another person, for the purpose of exploitation. Exploitation shall include, at a minimum, the exploitation of the prostitution of others or other forms of sexual exploitation, forced labour or services, slavery or practices similar to slavery, servitude or the removal of organs. (UN Protocol, Article 3 (*a*))

A different protocol was adopted to address human smuggling. There is some overlap between human smuggling and trafficking but they are really two different phenomena. Many people who engage in human trafficking are small specialised groups who move relatively small number of victims. In some regions of the world, human traffickers are individuals with higher education who have not previously participated in crime. Therefore, their modes of operation differ from the human smugglers who have less education and move large volumes of people.

Dimensions of the problem

Very broad approximations of the size of the trafficking problem by the US government estimate that some 600,000 to 800,000 people were trafficked worldwide according to the United States Trafficking in Persons Report of 2004, of which 80 per cent were women and girls and 70 per cent were trafficked for sexual exploitation (Trafficking in Persons (TIP) Report 2004: 2; for a discussion of such estimates, see Di Nicola, Chapter 3 in this volume). The 2006 Report focuses on the large number internationally engaged in slave or forced labour situations with estimates ranging from 4 to 27 million (TIP Report 2006). These crimes are now globalised. Almost every country in the world is involved in human trafficking either as a source, host or transit country; indeed, some countries function in all three categories simultaneously. In many parts of the world, trafficking occurs within the context of large-scale migration with some of the migrants, especially women and children, winding up as trafficking victims (Human Rights Watch 1995; Singh 2002). This is due in large part to the enormous population migrations into the major cities in Africa, Latin America and Asia. Europe is also facing increasing illegal migration from Africa and Asia, with an estimated 400,000 entering Europe illegally each year (Smucker 2004: 2). The US alone is estimated to have over 10 million illegal migrants (Moreno 2005: A02).

Explaining the growth

The increased speed and ease of communication is an important characteristic of the globalised world. The rise of the internet has had a major impact, as organised crime groups in India and Russia are able to buy and sell women with the ease of a mouse-click. In the countries of the former USSR, hundreds of thousands of websites exist promoting brides and sexual services, and in Europe, websites promote sex tourism, particularly in Latin America and Asia. These activities are facilitated by organised crime groups, which are particularly well-developed in South East Asia, as well as in many other regions such as Latin America (Lintner 2003; International Drug Control Programme 1997: 122–44). In Africa, much smuggling is based out of the Sahara, in particular, Mali (Smucker 2004). The strategic locations both of Turkey and the Balkans have made these countries key routes between Asia and Europe, receiving an increasing number of trafficked individuals. The US–Mexico border remains an important crossing point for traffickers and smugglers moving individuals to the US.

With globalisation, trafficked women and children are often found far from their countries of origin. In many parts of the world, much trafficking occurs within the country or the region; however, women and children increasingly travel long distances to their endpoint. This has been seen particularly in the Asian countries bordering northern India and Thailand (International Organization of Migration 2000: 13; Human Rights Watch 1995). Women from the former Soviet Union are trafficked to Europe, the Middle East, Asia, Latin America and North America (Erokhina 2005; Stoecker 2005). Similarly, women from the Dominican Republic are trafficked to Spain as well as many other European countries (Migration Information Programme 1998: 26–29).

Italy is the primary recipient country of women trafficked from Nigeria, and women from the Balkans wind up in Western Europe (Lindstrom 2004: 45–53). Chinese groups are significantly involved in the sex industry in Thailand and the neighbouring countries (Lintner 2003: 222–23). Thai women are trafficked by Thai and other Asian crime groups to Japan and the US. Japanese organised crime, *yakuza*, are major actors in the Asian sex trade (Kaplan and Dubro 2004), organising sex tourism to Thailand and importing girls from Thailand, the Philippines and Russia to Japan. Not as well known in the international crime literature is Indian organised crime, which is involved in the international trade of girls from Nepal and Bangladesh, to major urban centres, particularly Mumbai (Singh 2002).

The criminal actor

Traffickers are enormously diverse. They range from diplomats and employees of multinational organisations who traffic a young women for domestic labour to the large organisations of Asia which specialise in human smuggling and trafficking. There is every size of organisation in between the family business and the multinational criminal organisation. The high social status of some human traffickers contrasts sharply with that of drug traffickers who originate primarily from poorer families or criminal environments, such as triad (or Chinese organised crime) or mafia families. Women assume a larger role in this form of transnational crime as recruiters, madams and even kingpins of major smuggling operations. This is the only aspect of transnational crime where women assume a leading role.

Human smugglers and traffickers are not always exclusively motivated by profit. Some consciously engage in this activity to fund a terrorist group, a guerrilla movement or an insurgency. A terrorist in prison in Europe ran a prostitution ring of trafficked women from Moldova to fund Hezbollah, a nightclub with trafficked Russian-speaking women in a resort town in Southern Turkey run by Kurdish criminals helps support the PKK, and Marxist guerrillas in Nepal traffic girls to India to fund their cause.[1] Rebel leaders in Africa will traffic the women and children of their defeated enemy just as they sold their captives to slave dealers in earlier centuries.

Smugglers and traffickers are of diverse ethnicities and operate on every continent, often in coordination with each other. The trafficking of Indians to Western Europe requires the cooperation of crime groups across the former Soviet Union, in Turkey and in Western

Europe. Groups that might never cooperate in legitimate businesses work together in trafficking. Illustrative of this is the cooperation of Arabs and Jews in the trafficking of Russian-speaking women from Egypt through the Sinai into Israel.[2]

Groups that have no prior history of involvement in trafficking have moved into this activity because of the significant profits. Illustrative of this is the recent involvement of US motorcycle gangs in the kidnapping of smuggled aliens.[3] Motorcycle gangs have historically engaged in extortion, drug trafficking and many forms of contraband trade but they are also now active in human trafficking. MS-13 gang members have diversified their crime activities to include human smuggling (Abadinsky 2003: 4–18; Swecker 2006).

Women as traffickers

Human trafficking and smuggling are the only areas of transnational crime, where women assume an active and prominent position. The notorious chief of an entire Chinese smuggling organisation, Sister Ping, was recently convicted for alien smuggling, hostage taking, money laundering and conspiracy. Her smuggling operation resulted in 10 deaths, as smuggled aliens unable to swim were forced into freezing waters after the vessel entitled the 'Golden Venture' was detained (Ice News Release 2006). After years of careful investigative work on several continents, it was determined that she ran a multi-national smuggling organisation with tens of millions of dollars in profits. The profits of her business would be acceptable for a mid-size drug trafficker (Bernstein 2006: A1).

Yet this is not the only significant trafficking network run by a women. A major prostitution ring with trafficked women generated $7 million annually in Los Angeles. The ringleader of 'White Lace', Rimma Fetissova, was a Ukrainian women and her chief financial officer was also a woman from the former USSR. This case is illustrative of the role of women in trafficking – as recruiters, entrepreneurs and managers (Los Angeles Police Department Press Release 2002). Many women are also present at the lower levels of trafficking organisations. They can manage the brothels, recruit a few girls for a trafficking network or be bookkeepers of an organisation. Many of these have previously worked as prostitutes, for others it is an opportunity to make more money than is possible through legitimate employment. As one former bookkeeper of a trafficking organisation explained to the author, as an immigrant to the US she was saddled with many unanticipated expenses, including purchase of a car, legal fees to regularise her status and expenses for her daughter. An immigrant in legal limbo with limited English, the offer of employment in a trafficking organisation seemed an ideal opportunity to solve her financial problems. The morality of working for a prostitution organisation did not affect her decision. It was only as she observed the deaths of some prostitutes in other rings and abuses within her own organisation that she began to have reservations (for a discussion of the 'second wave' of trafficked women as recruiters in Central Asia, see Kelly, Chapter 4 in this volume).

Women also rationalise their role in human smuggling. Sister Ping, arrested for her involvement in the ill-fated voyage of the Golden Venture, believed she was providing a public service for the migrants who could not enter the US without her services. Members of the Chinatown community where she resided for many years reinforced this conception as a service provider to the community (Keefe 2006).

Women traffickers are generally not associated with large scale crime groups in Latin America or Western Europe. They differ in this important respect from the groups that specialise in the narcotics trade (Bruinsma and Bernasco 2004: 79–94). Trafficking is a much more important part of the criminal equation of the larger crime groups in Africa, Asia and the former Soviet Union. In Latin America, trafficking is more common among the lesser-known crime groups of the Dominican Republic. Within Europe, Albanian criminals, and smaller crime groups from Russia are key participants. In Asia, however, pre-eminent crime groups, such as the *yakuza* in Japan and the triads of China, often traffic in women. Apart from these major groups, smaller but important crime groups in Pakistan, Nepal, Bangladesh, Sri Lanka and India rely on trafficking to make their profits (Tumbahamphe and Bhattarai 2003). In all regions, the crime groups are able to function effectively because they cultivate close links to law enforcement. In some societies, law enforcement officials are part of the crime groups that traffic the women. In other cases, a significant part of their income is derived through their facilitation of trafficking (Phonpaichit *et al.* 1998).

Criminal groups engaged in trafficking

Many transnational trafficking organisations are large and traverse numerous continents. Yet most prosecuted trafficking cases worldwide consist of only a few individuals, leading to the erroneous perception that the traffickers are only small scale entrepreneurs. As the recent study conducted by the United National Office on Drugs and Crime discovered, there are significant variations in trafficking organisations. Some specialise in human trafficking but more often the groups are multifaceted, engaging simultaneously in smuggling, trafficking and other forms of illicit activity (UN Office on Drugs and Crime (UNODC) 2006: 68).

Many trafficking groups are relatively small scale. But these are often the easiest to catch as they do not have the resources of larger organisations that can pay-off law enforcement in multiple countries. Investigation of a large scale criminal trafficking organisation, such as those which held auctions of Eastern European women at London airports, requires significant financial investment by law enforcement (Bennetto 2006). Extensive resources are devoted to investigations of narcotics trafficking organisations but only limited resources are devoted to the pursuit of human trafficking. More often, these cases become the responsibility of the overburdened and underfinanced vice squad of the local police or become just one more task assigned to an over-burdened smuggling unit of the police.

The resources needed to reach a Sister Ping are significant. Such an investigation requires years of police work, the retention of translators to interview the victims and analyse confiscated records, and the use of sophisticated computer programmes to map the identified networks and their victims. Without this complex analysis, trafficking and smuggling appear as individual and uncoordinated cells that exploit only a limited number of individuals.

Regional differences among traffickers

There is not one model of trafficking. The trade in human beings is not a uniform business and operates very differently in different cultural and political contexts. Human trafficking and smuggling are not unique businesses but share much in common with the trade in legitimate commodities from their region of origin. Traditional patterns of trade and investment shape the trade in human beings as they do the trade in 'other commodities'.

Enormous differences exist in the trade in human beings from post-socialist countries. China, the countries of the former Soviet Union and former Yugoslavia and Albania differ dramatically. China uses trade in people to generate revenue for investment whereas the traffickers from the former USSR sell off human beings as if they were a natural resource like oil or timber with no thought to the future. The Chinese model is based on family ties but Russia, with less historical reliance on the extended family, is more focused on the individual (Shelley 2000). Former Yugoslav groups, influenced by the Civil War and violent conflicts from the Balkans, are the most violent entrepreneurs (Shelley 2004). They, however, operate using traditional clan structures. This suggests that pre-revolutionary traditions of trade, family and historical factors may be more important in determining the business of human trafficking than the common features of the socialist system.

Likewise, human trafficking out of Latin America differs from that emanating from Africa. For example, the volume of women moved for sexual exploitation from Latin America and men for labour exploitation is based on a wholesale market model. The emphasis is on volume of people rather than on the quality of recruits. Profits are made by the sheer numbers that are moved. Consequently, little attention is paid to the survival rates and the conditions on which they are moved. In the case of traffic out of Africa involving multi-faceted crime groups, the contemporary trade in people resembles the historical slave transport. There is serious loss of life and little return of capital to communities of origin (Shelley 2003).

Violations of human rights are greatest in those crime groups where the women are not controlled by the traffickers from recruitment through to their ultimate destination. In trafficking businesses where the women are passed from one set of owners to others repeatedly there is greater abuse. This is the case of trafficked women emanating from the former USSR who are sold off to traffickers from the Balkans, the Middle East or Asia. Violations are more frequent when the recruitment of future victims does not depend on the treatment of previous victims of trafficking. When groups are particularly transnational, they can threaten victims' families, increasing the degree and number of potential victims.

The routes of the traffickers

With globalisation, trafficked people are often found far from their countries of origin. In many parts of the world, much trafficking occurs within the country or the region; however, women and children increasingly travel long distances to their endpoint, as seen in the London airport auctions. Human trafficking victims for labour exploitation often travel equally long or longer routes. Their ultimate destination is a locale with greater need for labour which may be far from their home in Sub-Saharan Africa, Southern China or the mountainous communities of Southern Mexico. Therefore, large numbers of Phillipinos are trafficked to the Middle East as domestic labourers, Fukian Chinese are found by the hundreds of thousands in New York and Paris, and Tajiks and Vietnamese are trafficked labourers in Moscow and Siberia and all of Russia in between (TIP 2005: 40; Plant 2006; Tiuriukanova 2004; UNODC 2003).

Traffickers are the logistics specialists who can move the individuals across vast distances. Often the route is not the most direct because the traffickers knowingly avoid policed roads, border checkpoints and jurisdictions where there is efficient and honest law enforcement. Traffickers require an intelligence capacity to successfully avoid these obstacles to successful transit. Their intelligence may not be as developed as that of large scale narcotics traffickers but it is needed to successfully organise routes and deliver the human product. The end destination for the trafficking victim is often one where there is a diaspora community that can absorb the trafficked people or where there is an allied crime group that can receive and distribute the trafficked labourers.

The following map (see Figure 1) shows the diverse regions of the world that supply trafficked people to the US.

A criss-cross of lines traverses the globe illustrating the truly global dimensions of the trade of the US. But the situation in the US is not unique. The recent UN study on global patterns of organised crime shows that almost all countries are involved in human trafficking as source, transit and destination countries. Some of the most affluent countries are particular destination countries. Trafficking is also highly pronounced in countries with significant domestic organised crime problems, such as Nigeria, the countries of the former USSR and the Balkans (UNODC 2006).

The methods of the traffickers – recruitment, transport and control

Traffickers must recruit their victims, transport them to the locale where they can be exploited, and then maintain control. The variety of recruitment techniques, modes of transport and forms of exploitation are only limited by the imaginations of the traffickers. Their flexibility, opportunism and brutality ensure that they have a constant supply of victims.

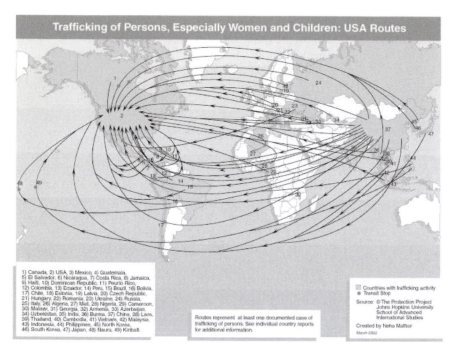

Figure 1 Trafficking of persons, especially women and children: USA routes
Source: The Protection Project John Hopkins University School of Advanced International Studies

Recruitment

Initial victimisation of the trafficked person is usually by a member of his/her own ethnic group. For example, Chinese, Mexican or Russian groups recruit in their own communities. There are many reasons that recruitment occurs within one's own group. Proximity and access are important. But equally important is trust. Trust is important because people often contract with traffickers and smugglers to move them to a particular locale, to pay them a certain amount of money or to keep them in bondage for a particular period. Trust is more easily established with someone from one's ethnic, language or cultural group. The violation of this trust which occurs in every trafficking case may be as devastating to the individual as the physical or psychological abuse applied to the victim.

Recruiters, especially those from Slavic countries, the Indian subcontinent and parts of the Middle East often hand over their victims to other ethnic groups subsequently. Other traffickers such as

Chinese, African and Latin American tend to retain control past the recruitment stage.

Trafficking victims are recruited in a variety of ways (UNODC 2006: 60). Not one source supplies a large number of victims. In this important respect, human trafficking differs from the drug trade. Unlike in the narcotics trade, where tons of raw material are available for shipping in Afghanistan and Colombia, the trafficking business does not rely on quantity. Human smuggling, in contrast to trafficking, may attract hordes of people. The most vivid illustration of this may be the pictures of Africans assembling at the port of ready to border small boats for the perilous journey to the Canary Islands (Bortin 2006: 4). Human trafficking, in contrast to smuggling or the drug trade, has no such ready supply. Significant time and effort must be spent by the traffickers to recruit the individuals they will subsequently exploit.

A wide variety of recruitment techniques are used. The techniques used depend on the levels of education, the expectations of the victims and their families and their financial situation. The widely used techniques in Eastern Europe and the former Soviet Union – advertisements and websites – are absent from the poorer countries of Asia, Africa and Latin America. In much of the world with poorly educated victims, recruitment occurs on a personal basis. All too often, the victim is previously acquainted with his/her trafficker.

Trafficking victims are often recruited by people they know, friends, family, acquaintances and sometimes boyfriends. Some men deliberately befriend vulnerable young women pretending to be their boyfriends and then sell them into prostitution. This was accurately depicted in the Swedish film, 'Lilya Forever'. In India, procurers for brothels look for lost children, befriend them and sell them into prostitution.

In the *Cadenas* case in the southern US, a group of minor girls were entrusted by family members to a known family from their Veracruz community. The parents were assured that the girls would be working with families as domestic helpers, a story that seemed credible to their families as many young Mexican girls travel to the US for employment. The girls only understood that there was something different when they crossed the border and were driven to a store and made to try on sexy lingerie (Florida State University Center for the Advancement of Human Rights 2003).

Such complete deception of the victim is not always the rule. In the *White Lace* case in California, the prostitutes in Los Angeles had previously worked as prostitutes in Lithuania, Russia and Ukraine.

They readily came to the US with the prospect of earning more money. But they were trafficking victims because they had been deceived as to the conditions of their transport to the US and of their employment. They were smuggled into the US after experiencing extreme hardship in Mexico and were forced to work by the head of the ring, even when ill.[4]

Recruiters often inform the adult victims that they have a contract and a debt to the traffickers. But once this debt is paid off, they are free to earn money. In other cases, women are informed that they will work in nightclubs as dancers but are never informed that they are expected to perform sexual services for the customers. The reality always differs from the presentation made to the victim; the extent of deception differs by region and the nature of the traffickers (see for example Morawska, Chapter 5 in this volume).

Women who have been trafficked into prostitution, often return to their home communities with tales of their superior earnings. They talk their friends and acquaintances in to joining them by lying about the conditions of the work and the amount they derive from their employment as prostitutes. These women get bonuses for recruiting or themselves move into the position of brothel keepers enslaving the women they have recently recruited.

Traffickers travel to rural areas of poor countries to recruit victims. This can be as likely in the north of Thailand, the mountainous communities of Nepal or the villages of Central Asia. The traffickers will find the poorest families, those with problems of drug or alcohol abuse or serious medical problems. They will assure the family that they can provide a better future for the child and many offer some nominal payment in return.

In some cases the recruitment is not so benign. Families may also be offered money directly for the child. This method has been used successfully with alcoholics and drug addicts in Russia. But paying parents to sell children also works in other cultural contexts. In a vivid scene captured on film in the Ruchira Gupta film, 'Selling of Innocents', a young Nepalese girl is sold by a father to a trafficker and the child is instructed by the parents to do whatever the trafficker insists. Often these impoverished families, with more children than they can support, face no alternative than reducing the numbers of mouths they have to feed. Selling off their children is not a malicious act but rather is motivated by the possibility of saving their other children through this act.

Some cases of organ trafficking are motivated by the same sense of familial obligation. A trafficker will locate a potential provider of a kidney that will be extracted in an operation outside of the seller's home country. The money derived from the organ sale will be used to support a starving family, to provide medical care for an ill relative or provide investment for the family.

In Eastern Europe and the Soviet successor States, children have been sold out of orphanages for adoption by the administrators. Organised crime groups serve as the intermediaries between the parents and the adoption agency. Notaries are bribed to certify that the parents have surrendered their parental rights. These cases were so frequent in the 1990s that Russia curtailed the number of adoptions of Russian children rather than striking at the crime groups that facilitated these adoptions.

Many ploys are used to recruit victims, including advertisements, and establishment of marriage and employment agencies in the countries of origin. This is particularly the case in Eastern Europe and the former Soviet Union where levels of education are higher and trafficking victims are highly literate. Web and newspaper advertisements for matchmaking services and marriage bureaus may prove to be a cover for a trafficking network. Newspapers carry advertisements for employment abroad as nannies, hotel maids or providers of care for the elderly (Stoecker 2005: 20). As many women from the region manage to obtain such employment, these advertisements carry credibility with many. Furthermore, there is rarely vetting of these advertisements by the newspapers or investigations carried out by local law enforcement.

Traffickers have a ready supply of recruits in conflict zones, war torn regions and after large-scale natural disasters. In the aftermath of the tsunami in 2004, there were reports of trafficking in children and special attention was paid to this by assistance programmes (TIP Report 2005: 17). In the Democratic Republic of the Congo and Rwanda, countries affected by regional conflict, women, men and children have been trafficked as labourers, combatants and sex slaves (TIP Report 2005: 86, 186).

Traffickers face important logistical challenges of moving individuals long distances. These challenges are similar to some faced by narcotics traffickers – they must coordinate transport, evade border and customs controls and ensure entry of the product into the market. But human trafficking poses unique challenges. The human cargo must be fed and housed in transit and delivered in 'serviceable' condition. Small shipments of drugs can readily be moved by couriers; a shipment of human beings cannot be easily disguised.

Traffickers use an enormous variety of techniques to move people and to facilitate their entry into their destination country. Corruption is often an integral part of the transport as border guards, customs officials, consular officers and other diplomatic personnel must be bribed or extorted (Pomfret 2006: 1). Collusive relationships are established with travel agencies or bogus travel agencies to facilitate trafficking.

Investigated trafficking cases reveal every form of known transport from feet to airplanes. Thousands of trafficking victims illegally cross the US–Mexican border in tiny boats, or walk through huge and specially constructed subterranean tunnels. Others cross the border on foot and then walk hundred of miles through the desert. Hundreds die each year of starvation and dehydration having been deceived or abandoned by their traffickers. The victims of the Chinese case mentioned at the start of the chapter had travelled by plane, truck and car to reach their ultimate destination. Others travel by boat, cargo vessels and even small fishing boats as is the case off the coast of West Africa and the Western coast of Turkey. Thousands die trying to enter Western Europe (Aronowitz 2001: 163–94). Individuals travel by uncomfortable bus across large distances.

The challenge of moving significant numbers of individuals is matched only by the need to cross guarded borders. Vast parts of Africa, Latin America, Asia, the former Soviet Union and the Middle East can be traversed with relative ease. Border posts can be crossed with only small payments. Large stretches of border are uncontrolled and can be easily traversed by knowing traffickers and the illicit movement of people can easily be disguised with the licit. The entrance to the Istanbul airport passport control is filled with signs in Russian warning entrants as to the dangers of exploitation by traffickers. But at the same time, young Central Asian women heavily made up and clearly employed as prostitutes have paid the nominal sum for an entrance visa and have passed passport control among the long lines of tourists with facility.

In some cases individuals travel in horrendous conditions – in the holds of cargo vessels, in small boats with no protection from the sun or rain, or in specially constructed and poorly ventilated compartments of trucks. Many become ill but the traffickers, seeking to minimise costs, rarely provide medical care. The conditions of transport recall the abysmal conditions in which slaves were transported in past centuries to the new world (Klein 1978).

Controlling the victim

Victims of trafficking are controlled by acute violence, psychological intimidation, and threats to the families of the victims. Many of the dehumanising practices that were used during the holocaust to produce passive victims are replicated by the traffickers. Trafficking victims are deprived of their identities, moved vast distances away from their families, language and culture in inhumane conditions and are tortured to induce compliance. Individual victims who resist the traffickers are tortured in front of others. Women who continue to resist can be thrown to their deaths from windows of apartment buildings or left to die from the gangrene of the wounds inflicted by the traffickers.[5]

An important difference exists between the facilitators of the holocaust and the traffickers. Many who supervised the execution of the holocaust believed they were serving the state. Their bureaucratic approach to their work led Hannah Arendt to characterise Eichmann on trial as the 'Banality of evil' (Arendt 1977). But there is nothing banal about the heads of trafficking organisations. Wire taps on traffickers and interviews with investigators who have conducted surveillance of traffickers reveal that many are among the most vicious of criminals. They never identify with the suffering of their victims, recalling the brutal guards who loaded the boxcars of humans to deliver to the concentration camps. The discourse of traffickers recalls that of slave traders of previous centuries who referred to their commodities as 'ignorant savages', meriting the brutal treatment they received.

Traffickers routinely confiscate the passports and the documents of the trafficked. Without these documents, the trafficked have no legal status. Loss of identity is key to the dehumanisation of the victim. It also has very practical implication. If trafficking victims escape, they cannot even command the protection of their own country's embassy as they have no proof of their citizenship. Criminal investigators of the recipient countries also cannot investigate.

The central element of trafficking is coercion and deception. Trafficking victims rarely comply immediately with the wishes of their traffickers. Or they subsequently resist. Attempts at escape are brutally punished so that other trafficking victims will not also try. To coerce the victims in these situations, traffickers may retain the services of particularly violent criminals who repeatedly rape and beat the women after they have been brought to their destination. The 'violence specialists' retained by the traffickers are a special subset of the business, comprised often of demobilised soldiers, veterans of civil wars and regional conflicts or the pure thugs of organised crime networks. In some cases their violence towards trafficking victims represents a form of revenge on enemy women. Illustrative of this is the case of Chechens who are used by traffickers to break in Slavic women in western European cities.

The international links of the traffickers allow them to deploy violence at all stages of their network. Their ability to intimidate both the victim and the family at home differentiates contemporary trafficking from the slave trade of earlier centuries. Victim compliance is achieved by threatening family members. The threats against loved ones are not idle but are often carried out, adding veracity to the traffickers' words 'If you do not do what we want, we will hurt your family.'

Prosecuting trafficking

Few traffickers have been prosecuted anywhere in the world. The United States Department of State, through its annual 'Trafficking in Persons' report compiles the cases of trafficking on a national basis. The very limited number of trafficking cases, approximately 5,000 convictions worldwide in 2005, does not reveal the extent of impunity of the traffickers (TIP Report 2006). The UN Research study on trafficking also points to the low levels of prosecution even among such developed countries as the US (UNODC 2006).

The involvement of crime groups in trafficking becomes a rational decision because of their low level of risk. When investigations are mounted and traffickers are prosecuted, the outcomes are negative because many are acquitted. Those who are convicted often receive limited terms of imprisonment, small fines or are sentenced merely to the time they have served during the investigation. This is the only category of serious transnational crime to be treated with such leniency by the courts and criminal investigators. There are several reasons for this leniency. Many law enforcement people perceive trafficking as the age old phenomenon of prostitution and do not see it as a serious problem. In many cases, they believe that the victims willingly participate in this activity and that no crime has been committed. In other cases, massive corruption undermines the capacity of the legal system to combat trafficking because police, border and customs officials have been bought off by the traffickers and smugglers.

Under these conditions, it is certainly clear why human trafficking is growing as a crime of choice. Beccaria, the enlightenment thinker on criminal justice, wrote that the 'certainty of punishment is more important than its severity' (1963, cited in Meehl 1991: 448), but in the case of trafficking there is neither certainty nor severity.

Conclusion

Human trafficking is a large and rapidly growing component of transnational crime. Those who run trafficking networks include both economically motivated criminals and politically motivated transnational crime actors such as terrorists, guerrillas and insurgents. Both categories of traffickers often intersect with the larger world of transnational crime. They obtain false documents for their victims from criminal specialists, hire thugs from outside their network to intimidate the women and trafficked labourers and move their proceeds through established money laundering channels.

The market for trafficked people is growing so rapidly and the business is so globalised that trafficking groups can co-exist rather than kill each other off as occurs regularly in the drug trade. Unfortunately, the violence is directed almost exclusively at the trafficking victims rather than criminal rivals.

Trafficking requires complicity from the legitimate community. Newspapers run advertisements for escort services, apartment owners rent to brothel keepers. Hotels even facilitate trafficking rings by providing women to their customers. Factories contract with human smugglers and traffickers to provide them needed manpower even though these employers know these workers have no work permits. They then proceed to pay them below the minimum wage and ignore labour, health and safety laws.

The problems of complicity from the business community and the prevalence of corrupt and transnational relations between the criminals and governmental figures in different countries combine to make effective anti-trafficking measures difficult to implement. The profits involved and the demand for trafficked people are so significant that awareness campaigns are not enough to prevent the continued growth of trafficking and smuggling.

Human trafficking is a growing and central element of international organised crime. The disparities between the developed and the developing world is a prime driving force for this growth. The tardiness in which the international community has responded to this problem has made many organised criminals switch to this area of criminal activity from other forms of transnational crime. Some crime groups traffic in human beings at the same time that they engage in other criminal activity. Therefore, human beings may move drugs and arms at the same time that they are trafficked.

Crime groups which run integrated business operations and control the trafficked human beings from recruitment through exploitation make enormous profits. The proceeds of this crime feed the political corruption as pay-offs are made to police, border guards and politicians to sustain this activity. Therefore, there is not only significant harm to the individuals who are trafficked but many larger harms to the society. The rise of AIDS, the destruction of families and gross abuses of human rights are additional problems beyond the corruption of the state.

The defences against human trafficking are not presently sufficient in either the law enforcement, the intelligence community, civil society or in foreign assistance programmes. Governance programmes, initiated by foreign aid communities, focus on prevention and education failing to understand that organised crime groups are key actors in human trafficking.

 The fact that many officials and political parties may benefit from the proceeds of trafficking means that there is often little incentive to crack down on the problem. Many seeking to address trafficking ignore the fact that organised crime groups help finance elections. In Thailand, party financing comes, in part, from the profits generated in the sex industry (Phongpaichit et al. 1998). In parts of India, organised crime groups are significant actors in the political process Therefore, there is a need to understand the role that campaign financing provides in the perpetuation of this activity. Just as American policy in Colombia looked at the drug traffickers financing of the presidential political campaign, there is a similar need for this in the trafficking area of organised crime.

Corrupted law enforcement or those who fail to differentiate between trafficking and prostitution means that the legal response is inadequate to the challenge. Much intelligence focuses on understanding drug flows and crime groups but does not provide the same attention to human trafficking. There is a need to increase intelligence gathering on the human trafficking groups to develop an effective law enforcement response in receiving countries which have effective law enforcement.

Unfortunately, the growth of human trafficking and smuggling in the twenty-first century seems inevitable. The consequences of this will be increased human exploitation, a strong social reaction against many illegal migrants in the developed world and a desire to use coercive measures to address the problem. The trade in human beings may be as significant a transnational crime problem in the twenty-first century as drugs became in the last half of the twentieth century.

Notes

1 The Hezbollah information is obtained from an individual who observed this in a Western European prison; the Kurdish information was obtained by the author through observation and interviews; and the Nepal situation is reported in the *Trafficking in Persons* June 2004 report issued by the State Department, p. 216.
2 Interview with Mohamed Mattar, Director of the Protection Project, February 2006.
3 Interview with Lou DiBacco, US Civil Rights Division, Department of Justice, 2004.
4 Interview with the lead investigator, Los Angeles, 2005.
5 Interviews with law enforcement and intelligence sources who have worked on these cases with fatal outcomes.

References

Abadinsky, H. (2003) *Organized Crime*, 7th edition. Belmont, CA: Wadsworth.

Arendt, H. (1977) *Eichmann in Jerusalem: A Report on the Banality of Evil.* Hammondsworth, New York: Penguin.

Aronowitz, A. (2001) 'Smuggling and Trafficking in Human Beings: The Phenomenon, The Markets that Drive It and the Organisations that Promote It', *European Journal on Criminal Policy and Research*, 9 (2): 163–94.

Bennetto, J. (2006) 'New Vice Squad to Tackle Airport Sex-Slave Auctions', *The Independent Online*, 7 June 2006. Accessed 7 June 2006 at: www.news. independent.co.uk/uk/crime/article625093.ece

Bernstein, N. (2006) 'Making it Ashore and Still Chasing the U.S. Dream', *New York Times*, 9 April 2006, p. A1.

Bruinsma, G. and Bernasco, W. (2004) 'Criminal Groups and Transnational Illegal Markets', *Crime, Law and Social Change*, 41: 79–94.

Erokhina, L. (2005) 'Trafficking in Women in the Russian Far East: A Real or Imaginary Phenomenon', in S. Stoecker and L. Shelley (eds) *Human Traffic and Transnational Crime: Russian and American Perspectives*, pp. 79–94. Lanham, MD: Rowman and Littlefield.

Florida State University Center for the Advancement of Human Rights. (2003) 'Florida Responds to Human Trafficking'. Accessed 20 July 2006 at: www.cahr.fsu.edu/H%20-%20Chapter%202.pdf

GTZ (2004) 'Armed Conflict and Trafficking in Women', pp. 13–23. Accessed 15 July 2006 at: http://www2.gtz.de/dokumente/bib/04-5304.pdf

Human Rights Watch/Asia (1995) *Rape for Profit: Trafficking of Nepali Girls and Women to India's Brothels*, 12: 5 (A).

International Organization of Migration (IOM) (2000) *Combating Trafficking in South-East Asia: A Review of Policy and Programme Responses*, p. 50. Geneva: IOM.

Kaplan, D. and Dubro, A. (2003) *Yakuza: Japan's Criminal Underworld*. Berkeley: University of California Press.

Keefe, P.R. (2006) 'The Snakehead', *New Yorker*, pp. 68–85.

Klein, H.S. (1978) *The Middle Passage: Comparative Studies in the Atlantic Slave Trade*. Princeton: Princeton University Press.

Lindstrom, N. (2004) 'Regional Sex Trafficking in the Balkans: Transnational Networks in an Enlarged Europe', *Problems of Post-Communism*, 53 (4).

Lintner, B. (2003) *Blood Brothers: The Criminal Underworld of Asia*. New York: Palgrave MacMillan.

Los Angeles Police Department Press Release (2006) 'Operation White Lace'. Accessed 20 July 2006 at: www.lapdonline.org/press-releases/2002/12/pr02726.htm

Meehl P. (1991) *Selected Philosophical and Methodological Papers*. Minneapolis: University of Minnesota Press.

Migration Information Programme (1998) 'Trafficking in Women from the Dominican Republic for Sexual Exploitation', in *International Organization for Migration*, excerpted in *Trends in Organized Crime*, 3 (4): 26–29.

Moreno, S. (2005) 'Flow of Illegal Immigrants to the United States Unabated', *Washington Post*, 22 March 2005.

Phongpaichit, P., Piriyarangsan, S. and Treerat, N. (1998) *Guns, Girls, Gambling and Ganja: Thailand's Illegal Economy and Foreign Policy*. Chiang Mai: Silkworm Books.

Plant, R. (2006) *Human Trafficking in China: ILO Activities and Lessons for International Policy Coordination*, US Congressional-Executive Commission on China, 6 March 2006.

Pomfret, J. (2006) 'Bribery at Border Worries Officials', *Washington Post*, 15 July 2006, p. 1.

Shelley, L. (2000) 'Post-Communist Transitions and Illegal Movement of Peoples: Chinese Smuggling and Russian Trafficking in Women', *Annals of Scholarship*, 14 (2): 71–84.

Shelley, L. (2003) 'Trafficking in Women: The Business Model Approach,' *Brown Journal of World Affairs*, X (I): 119–31.

Singh, S. P. (2002) 'Transnational Organized Crime: The Indian Perspective', *Annual Report for 2000 and Resource Material Series*, No. 59 (Tokyo: Unafei). Accessed 31 January 2004 at: www.unafei.or.jo/pdf/no59/ch.29/pdf

ICE news release (2006) 'Sister Ping Sentenced to 35 years in Prison for Alien Smuggling, Hostage Taking, Money Laundering and Ransom Proceeds Conspiracy'. Accessed 16 March 2006 at: www.ice.gov/pi/news/newsreleases/articles/060316newyork.htm

Smucker, P. (2004) 'Sahara Town Booms with People Smuggling', *International Herald Tribune*, 25 October 2004, p. 2.

Statement of Chris Swecker (2006) U.S. House of Representatives, Committee on Homeland Security, Subcommittee on Management, Integration and Oversight, 8 March 2006.

Stoecker, S. (2005) 'Human Trafficking: A New Challenge for Russia and the United States', in S. Stoecker and L. Shelley (eds) *Human Traffic and Transnational Crime: Russian and American Perspectives*, pp. 13–28. Lanham, MD: Rowman and Littlefield.

Tiuriukanova, E. (2004) *Prinuditel'nyi trud v sovremennoi Rossii*. Moscow: ILO.

Trafficking in Persons Report 2004 (2004). Washington, DC: Department of State.

Trafficking in Persons Report 2005 (2005). Washington, DC: Department of State.

Trafficking in Persons Report 2006 (2006) Washington, DC: Department of State.

Tumbahamphe, S.M. and Bhattarai, B. (2003) 'Trafficking of Women in South Asia'. Accessed 10 November 2003 at: www.ecouncil.ac.cr/about/contrib/women/youth/english/traffic1.htm

UN International Drug Control Programme (1997) *World Drug Report*, p. 124. Oxford: Oxford University Press.

UN Office on Drugs and Crime (2000) *UN Protocol to Prevent, Suppress and Punish Trafficking in Persons, Especially Women and Children*.

UNODC (2003) *Coalitions against Trafficking in Human Beings in the Philippines*. Vienna: UNODC. Accessed 20 July 2006 at: www.unodc.org/pdf/crime/human_trafficking/coalitions_trafficking.pdf

UNODC (2006) *Trafficking in Person: Global Patterns*. Accessed 27 July 2006 at: www.unodc.org/pdf/traffickinginpersons_report_2006ver2.pdf

Chapter 7

From HIV prevention to counter-trafficking: Discursive shifts and institutional continuities in South-East Asia

Johan Lindquist and Nicola Piper

Introduction

From a global and historical perspective, the discursive construction of human trafficking and its various effects precede that of HIV/AIDS. Whereas the 'white slavery scare' at the turn of the twentieth century was the beginning of the 'international career of the trafficking discourse' (Wong 2005: 76), HIV/AIDS remained unnamed until the mid-1980s, when it quickly gained unprecedented attention as a global problem. Trafficking, in turn, disappeared as a term during World War I only to make a spectacular return on a global scale in the twenty-first century.

Despite the differences between HIV/AIDS and counter-trafficking, the two phenomena are connected in a number of ways as contemporary forms of global problems. In this chapter we are concerned with three types of relationships. First, recent responses to HIV/AIDS and trafficking show a degree of organisational continuity, as international and non-governmental organisations (NGOs) are key actors in both cases. Second, the female prostitute is a critical 'site' of intervention in both HIV prevention and counter-trafficking campaigns. The concern with trafficking has almost exclusively been limited to women and children forced into prostitution (e.g. Wong 2005; Piper 2005), while the focus on female prostitutes in HIV prevention is particularly obvious in developing countries, as demonstrated in our case study from Indonesia. Finally, both phenomena are subject to the control of particular state interests in the absence of political will to implement a rights-centred framework.

In this chapter, these continuities will be highlighted through a case study from the Indonesian island of Batam, which discusses how NGOs that previously worked with HIV prevention have moved at least part of their attention to counter-trafficking. For most NGOs, the shift from HIV/AIDS to trafficking has not, however, led to a radical break in practice, since in both cases the female body, particularly of the prostitute, has been the key site of intervention, in the first case as a vector of disease, in the second as a victim of exploitation.

The intensifying concern among donors, governments, and the mass media with trafficking has been matched by a growing scholarly interest in the topic. Broadly speaking, academic research has tended to take two different starting points: (1) a 'migration' approach, which situates trafficking within the broader phenomenon of irregular migration flows (Skeldon 2000), or (2) a 'sexual violence perspective,' which links trafficking to sexual exploitation, and thus is strictly focused on women and children (Barry 1995; Hughes 2003; Raymond 1998). It is striking, however, that in policy, in the donor infrastructure that has developed around trafficking, and in the media, almost all attention has focused on the sexual violence perspective, and, in particular, the trafficking of women and children into prostitution.

In the mid-1990s Batam, part of the so-called Indonesia-Malaysia-Singapore Growth Triangle, was identified as a high-risk area for the spread of HIV, as the global focus of the pandemic shifted from Africa towards Asia. In Indonesia, large-scale intervention projects were initiated by international institutions such as the World Bank through government agencies and NGOs working on Batam and other parts of Riau Province. The main high-risk groups identified and targeted on Batam were, as in the rest of Indonesia, primarily female prostitutes and transvestites. This should be understood in relation to the government's construction of HIV as a problem associated with marginal groups, which in turn has made the disseminating of information to the 'general public' (*masyarakat umum*) a politically sensitive issue.

Although donor funding for HIV prevention projects has continued to increase in Indonesia, HIV has failed to evolve into a widespread epidemic during the past decade.[1] As a result, HIV has to a certain degree been routinised and fallen out of the media spotlight in Indonesia. This is particularly obvious on Batam and in Riau province where many NGOs that were created and funded through a World Bank project in the late 1990s were closed down when that project ended. This local drop in funding came during a period when a (revived) concern with human trafficking began to generate funding for NGOs in Indonesia and around the world. On Batam, which was identified as a potential hub for trafficking, this led NGOs that had, or continued to work on HIV prevention efforts, to become involved in counter-trafficking campaigns.

In this chapter we take Batam as a case study for considering the institutional and discursive links between HIV/AIDS prevention and counter-trafficking. We are concerned with the power of trafficking discourse and its institutionalisation through international agencies and organisations as well as local NGOs. Rather than taking 'trafficking' for granted as an unproblematic object of discourse and study – that is, as a problem that exists and must be solved – we attempt to position it within a different form of institutional history. Both HIV prevention and counter-trafficking work depend on a common infrastructure of information, funding, and intervention, and, in both cases, female sexuality is of central concern. Highlighting these commonalities allows us to think more critically about trafficking as a topic that must be situated in a social and political context, and to show how particular forms of continuities and concerns shape interventions, thereby excluding more general political concerns about irregular migration from the policy agenda.[2]

The rise and feminisation of irregular migration

The world-wide increase in irregular migration must be linked to the rise of the global service sector, with deteriorating working conditions characterised by high flexibility, low wages, and general insecurity. The intensifying demand for migrant labour has coincided with the closure of legal channels for unskilled migration. In Asia, the number of undocumented migrants is arguably equal if not higher than that of legal labour migrants (Asis 2005).[3]

Labour migration in Asia is arranged in a wide range of scenarios, but generally through the medium of brokers, recruiters, or migrants' own networks, some of which result in abusive or exploitative practices. As Wong (2005) has argued, this requires a model of sociological analysis that accepts that the agency of migrants will vary depending on their position in the migration process, and the different types of licit or illicit brokering they are engaged in before, during, and after arrival. Much of what is classified as 'illegal migration' is directly linked to employment practices upon arrival, as migrants who enter a destination country legally become irregular due to the abusive practices of their employers, such as the withholding of wages and travel documents, or verbal and physical abuse.[4] Throughout Asia, most temporary contract workers are tied to one employer in a specific labour sector and when absconding in search of a better deal, they automatically are treated as illegal by the state.

In this context there is an increasing feminisation of domestic and international migration flows throughout Asia, particularly from Indonesia, Sri Lanka and the Philippines, where women constitute up to 75 per cent of the workers who are deployed legally on an annual basis (Asis 2005). If irregular migrants are factored in, however, the feminisation of migration is even more widespread. Indonesian women are increasingly travelling to Malaysia as irregular migrants, and while Thai women are underrepresented in statistics of legal migration, they predominate among irregular migrants. Thailand has also been the destination for unauthorised migrant women, such as Burmese working as domestic workers and in factories along the Thai-Burmese border.

The demand for domestic workers and so-called 'entertainers' in East and South-East Asia has been a driving force behind the feminisation of migration. While changes are gradually becoming evident not only with regard to the increased volume of female migrants, but also through diversified patterns of migration, including source, destinations, working conditions and skill levels (Yamanaka and Piper 2006), the largest proportion of migrant women continue to work in job categories such as live-in maids, care givers, entertainers, sex workers and in the service sector, more generally (e.g. *Asian and Pacific Migration Journal* 2003).[5]

Migration discourse in its various forms has most generally focused on the dynamics of push-and-pull factors, but more recently the analysis of the exploitation and victimisation of migrants has become increasingly evident. The concern with victimisation has emerged in tandem with the feminisation of migration flows – focusing particularly on the plight of factory workers, domestic servants, and prostitutes. Arguably this has taken its strongest form through contemporary discourses concerning human trafficking and the strict focus on young women and children who are forced into prostitution. Through this concern with exploitation, constraints on women's (and men's) freedom of mobility and choice of employment are typically ignored, and labour rights become irrelevant to the debates.

From HIV to trafficking – the case of the 'Growth Triangle'

Since the early 1990s, Batam has formed part of a cross-border 'Growth Triangle' together with Singapore and the Malaysian province of Johor. In official discourse, this economic zone constitutes an example of a new borderless world in which the nation-state is becoming obsolete. In fact, however, the Growth Triangle depends on a border that facilitates the movement of Singaporeans and Malaysians across national boundaries, while keeping Indonesian labour in place on Batam.

After independence in the mid-1960s, and through the 1970s, Singapore boomed as an export processing zone for the global electronics industry while Batam remained a backwater. With rising wages and costs in the 1980s, however, Singapore was transformed into a financial centre that demanded new off-shore locations for manufacturing. Through this process, Batam has become a site where Singaporean capital has converged with inexpensive Indonesian land and labour, primarily in the industrial estates that cover the island. In less than 40 years, the island has thus been radically transformed and the population has increased from 3,000 to 700,000; most residents are unskilled migrants from across Indonesia, in search of work in the booming economy.[6]

Along with the factories, an economy based on sex and drugs has developed. Singaporean men, many of them part of the working class that is increasingly marginalised in the new economy, take the frequent ferries across the Straits of Malacca and are the main customers in the island's discos, karaoke bars, and brothels. By the late 1990s over one million tourists were entering Batam each year, making it the third tourist destination in Indonesia, after Jakarta and Bali.

On Batam young women are the main source of labour both in the context of factory work and prostitution. The feminisation of labour has thus created an environment in which women's sexuality has become a topic of widespread public interest through newspapers, everyday talk and gossip, and also in various forms of health interventions. On the other side of the border, in Singapore and Malaysia, Indonesian women increasingly work as domestic servants in the homes of the expanding middle class.

It was in this context that Yayasan Mitra Kesehatan dan Kemanusiaan (YMKK), the Health and Humanity Partnership Foundation,[7] was established as a locally-based NGO in the mid-1990s by two female researchers from the Indonesian capital Jakarta. They had identified

Batam as a key area where a variety of health problems would emerge in the context of intensifying migration. By 2006 they had a staff of approximately 15 people. Focusing primarily on women's rights and health issues, YMKK began as an organisation with limited resources, but rapidly became a key actor when Batam was identified as a high risk area for HIV, primarily through the World Bank project in the mid-1990s. Throughout the 1990s, HIV came to dominate YMKK's work as they were approached by a variety of international organisations interested in funding HIV prevention projects. Much of this work concentrated on outreach projects and workshops aimed at female prostitutes and factory workers, both of which were considered to be at high risk for HIV.

In Indonesia's Riau Province, of which Batam is a part, the World Bank project clearly illustrated the emergence of an 'AIDS industry' (Altman 1999), whereby a large number of NGOs were created as funding became available, only to close down as the project ended (Lindquist 2005).[8] In the wake of the World Bank project, and with the temporary demise of funding related to HIV prevention in the late 1990s, YMKK increasingly shifted the focus of their work from HIV to female reproductive health, while continuing to target the same groups, namely prostitutes and factory workers. The bulk of their funding for this project has come from the Ford Foundation in Jakarta, which in recent years has promoted a so-called 'integrated reproductive health approach' that attempts to move beyond a strict focus on reproductive health by including issues such as domestic violence.[9]

With the rise of trafficking as a global problem after 2000, however, YMKK has increasingly been approached by organisations and donors offering funding for workshops dealing with counter-trafficking projects. The focus on trafficking has been heightened by the extensive media coverage of Batam as a supposed hub for human trafficking. One opinion article, for instance, claimed that Batam was not a 'free trafficking zone' (*Batam Pos*, 10 May 2006), while another headline stated in capitalised and bold letters: 'Four Young Women Sold to Singapore' (*Posmetro Batam*, 28 June 2005).

In contrast to the response to HIV in Haiti and Africa during the 1980s, there was already a global infrastructure of knowledge in place when Asia was identified as the new epicenter for the spread of HIV in the 1990s (Pigg 2001: 481). More generally, as in other countries in Asia, HIV has mainly been constituted as something that is expected and emerging, a problem that belongs to the immediate future. Discourses and practices surrounding HIV prevention have thus become increasingly globalised and are framed by international organisations such as UNAIDS and donors such as USAID (United States Agency for International Development) in terms of 'human rights' (Poku 2002).

In Indonesia and Singapore, however, HIV is considered by both governments as a problem of control rather than rights. A 'medical discourse' of HIV/AIDS is prevalent, which primarily is 'concerned with symptoms and depersonalised "seropositives"'; generally sub-divided into various forms of risk groups, for instance, 'prostitutes' or 'homosexuals' (Seidel 1993: 176). As in other parts of the world, this creates tensions between discourses of control and exclusion and discourses of rights and empowerment (Seidel 1993), primarily between local NGOs funded by international donors and the national government. On the level of practice, however, NGOs in Indonesia or Singapore have rarely been in explicit opposition with the government (e.g. Clarke 1998; Tanaka 2002).

There are similar forms of discursive tensions evident with regard to human trafficking, where debates concerning prostitution have been at the centre of attention. While some argue that prostitution should be understood as a form of labour, others view it strictly as a form of exploitation.[10] USAID, for instance, demands that all NGOs that are offered funding sign a contract stating that they oppose prostitution.[11] As in the context of HIV prevention, the exploited female prostitute has become the paradigmatic figure of counter-trafficking campaigns within a discourse of victimisation.

Historicising trafficking

Trafficking was first constituted as a problem during the age of mass migration of Europeans to North America, subsequently undergoing various discursive and focal changes over time (Scully 2001). Initially focusing on young white and primarily western women's deception into prostitution, trafficking discourse later became centred on the movement of Third-World women and children to the Western industrialised world. In the early 1980s, a discourse on behalf of trafficked women began to form, which was rooted in the activism of progressive feminists in the West (Ucarer 1999). This framework situated the sexual exploitation and abuse of women within the larger context of women's socio-economic inequality, and followed from the political campaigning of the international women's movement around the issue of violence against women and the demand that women's rights be considered as human rights. Nevertheless, and as we have already noted, feminists remain divided over the question of identifying prostitution as work or exploitation.

In Asia and South-East Asia, the feminist academic literature has related trafficking historically to the growth of sex tourism in the context of a US military presence and the dramatic expansion of mass tourism after World War II, as well as the more recent phenomenon of 'mail order brides' (Enloe 1989; Hall 1992; Truong 1990; Eviota 1992). In these discussions, researchers have established a link between migration, sex tourism, and particular forms of coercion, as large numbers of migrant women have engaged in prostitution in major tourist sites in search of economic opportunities unavailable in their home communities. Since trafficking has mainly been approached as an issue of sexual exploitation, the concern with the violation of women's rights has tended to be limited to the issue of violence against women. This can for instance be seen in the way in which the the UN Convention on the Elimination of All Forms of Discrimination Against Women (CEDAW) Committee – the Treaty Body monitoring this Convention at the Office of the United Nations High Commissioner for Human Rights – has concerned itself primarily with the sexual exploitation of migrant women.[12]

Trafficking discourse took another turn in the late 1990s when it was integrated into the broader issue of 'illegal' migration by organisations such as the International Organisation for Migration (IOM), a process largely driven by European States' concerns over rising numbers of asylum seekers and subsequent policy changes (Wong 2005: 74). This led to what Wong has called an 'emergent model of the new unholy trinity' that is 'threatening the borders' of the developed world – namely, trafficking, illegal immigration and organised crime – culminating in a 'moralising and criminalising anti-trafficking consensus, of global reach and institutional depth' (ibid: 79). As an effect, there has been a blurring of the distinction between terms such as smuggling and trafficking, and thus, an expansion of the 'problem'.[13] Since IOM adopted a new objective to curtail migrant trafficking, it has become the leading international agency on migration and trafficking (Wong 2005). The ensuing involvement of international donors and UN agencies has resulted in channelling of large amounts of funding for counter-trafficking projects.[14]

Throughout much of Asia, however, trafficking and irregular migration remained non-issues in political terms during the 1990s. It was placed on the agenda of governments starting in 2002 via regional consultative meetings such as the Bali Process initiated by Australia, as well as through donor funding from international agencies and organisations. Although often an internal migration phenomenon, global and state policy responses have mainly focused on trafficking in its international form and, by extension, on the control of the exit and entry of migrants, with the specific aim of preventing irregular migration across borders. This is reflected in the relatively high ratification rate of the 2000 UN Counter-Trafficking Protocol, which supplements the Convention Against Transnational Organized Crime, in contrast to the extremely low ratification rate of instruments addressing the human rights of migrants.[15] This focus on 'criminality' shifts attention away from human rights violations to that of 'illegality' (UNRISD 2005). Furthermore, it obscures the violation of labour rights by leaving employers' illegal and abusive practices outside the frame of discussion. This should be understood in relation to the global policy shift towards 'managing migration' which has resulted in a focus on controlling human mobility rather than expanding rights and protective mechanisms for migrants (Piper 2006).

Implementing counter-trafficking

In Indonesia the insertion of the word *trafficking* into public discourse after 2000 has followed from a process of global institutionalisation, beginning in the 1980s and culminating with the UN Protocol and the United States Trafficking Victims' Protection Act of 2000 (TVPA). Both documents focus primarily on the human trafficking of women and children across borders.[16]

In conjunction with the TVPA, an annual report, the Trafficking in Persons Report (TIP), is published by the US State Department. It ranks countries in three different tiers according to how they are addressing human trafficking. Tier 3 countries are the worst cases of governments who do not fully comply with the minimum standards and who are not making any efforts to do so; Tier 2 is broken down into two categories: Tier 2 (countries whose governments do not fully comply with the minimum standards but are making significant efforts to do so) and Tier 2 Watch List which constitute borderline cases. Those listed in Tier 1 are considered to be fully compliant with the US government's counter-trafficking recommendations. In the 2005 TIP report, both Singapore and Indonesia were listed under Tier 2 (USD 2005: 42).

There are two important points with regard to the effects of the report. First, bottom-tier countries face the threat of losing all non-humanitarian aid from the US government. In the first annual report, Indonesia was placed in the lowest tier (UDS 2002). The immediate response by the Indonesian government was to create a National Trafficking Commission, which raised the country's ranking in the next report to Tier 2 (UDS 2003), a position that it has retained since.

Just across the border from Batam is the city-state Singapore, which was not included in the first two years the TIP report was published. In 2004, however, Singapore was suddenly ranked as a Tier 2 country with a 'significant trafficking problem'. In a four-page rebuttal, the Singaporean Ministry of Home Affairs disputed the ranking and asked the US to disclose – in the name of 'transparency' – the claim that 100 women are trafficked into Singapore each year. Notably, in the 2005 report, Batam was mentioned in the section on Singapore. 'The (Singaporean) government should address child sex tourism by Singaporeans in foreign destinations, and do more to publicise the problem of trafficking for the purpose of commercial sexual exploitations, *particularly Batam, Indonesia*' (emphasis added).

The second effect of the TIP report has been the increasing allocation of funding for counter-trafficking campaigns through international donors, which has created new opportunities for NGOs such as YMKK. In this process, specific provinces and places have been defined as key sites of intervention. Much as it was classified a high-risk area for the spread of HIV in the 1990s, in the 2000s Batam has been identified as both a destination for domestic trafficking and as a hub for international – to Malaysia in particular – trafficking of young women and children into the sex industry (Rosenberg 2003: 178). In both cases the same factors have been highlighted – Batam's geographical location in a border region, the island's large prostitution industry, and the high rates of human mobility in the area.

In Bosnia-Herzegovina, Rosga (2005: 270) has noted that the formation of trafficking as a global problem created a situation in which it made sense both for Bosnia-Herzogovina as a nation and particular individuals and groups to engage in the struggle against trafficking. In places like Batam, which has become identified as a trafficking zone not only for Indonesia, but also Malaysia and Singapore, NGOs such as YMKK become critical points for flows of funding and knowledge.

The continuities of intervention

The continuities between HIV prevention and counter-trafficking campaigns become particularly evident if one focuses on the changing landscape of NGO intervention on Batam. During the last decade there has been a sense of frustration, and occasionally incomprehension, among the staff at YMKK with regard to shifting donor interests. In 2005, when interviewed by Lindquist about YMKK's work on counter-trafficking, one of the staff members asked himself aloud, 'Why is there all this interest in *trafficking*? It is not like it is something new.' In practice, however, counter-trafficking has not led to radically new forms of programmes. For YMKK, which has implemented projects on HIV, reproductive health, and counter-trafficking during the past decade, the key site of intervention has remained the same, namely the female body. This has allowed them to retain a degree of continuity in their work.

In Indonesia USAID and the US State Department, particularly through their partners, the International Catholic Migration Commission (ICMC) and the American Center for International Labor Solidarity (ACILS), but also IOM and the Asia Foundation, are implementing counter-trafficking programmes. Since 2002 YMKK has collaborated with organisations such as ICMC, UNIFEM Singapore, Terres Des Hommes Netherlands (TDH), and the IOM on a number of counter-trafficking campaigns. All of these organisations, except UNIFEM, have their offices in Jakarta. ICMC has primarily funded training workshops, organised several international conferences on Batam dealing with trafficking, as well as published a widely distributed book, *Trafficking of Women and Children in Indonesia* (Rosenberg 2003).

UNIFEM Singapore has offered YMKK funding and organisational support since 2003, which intensified when Singapore was identified as a Tier 2 country in 2004. While initially UNIFEM was concerned with general issues concerning women's empowerment, more recently, increasing attention has been focused on human trafficking, as it has moved to the top of the global policy agenda. Although UNIFEM's concern is with the entire region of South-East Asia, much of their practical work has been focused on YMKK. Furthermore, the collaboration between UNIFEM and YMKK represents a significant shift in the relationship in cross-border development work between Singapore and Batam, which historically has been very limited (cf. Lindquist 2003, Lyons 2005). In contrast, to our knowledge, there is still no substantial cooperation between NGOs on Batam and in Malaysia.

In Indonesia, TDH replaced the Ford Foundation as YMKK's main source of funding in 2006, signalling a move away from 'reproductive health' to 'counter-trafficking' as their key programme. TDH has two types of interconnected programmes in Indonesia. The first is a network programme, Indonesia Acts, supporting 12 NGOs in 9 provinces,[17] which aims to facilitate NGO collaboration around the country. One of the TDH programme officers in Jakarta told Lindquist when interviewed[18] that these types of networks were critical in order to 'destroy trafficking'.[19] The second type of programme aims to fund individual NGOs such as YMKK. According to the programme director, since YMKK earlier had focused on HIV and reproductive health through their work with the Ford Foundation, the World Bank, and other organisations, these became the 'entry points' for engaging with counter-trafficking. The initial focus of YMKK's proposal was on 'capacity building', but according to the TDH programme officer, there were no benefits for the 'target groups'. The proposal was reworked to find this entry point in relation to prostitution, in particular.[20]

It is thus notable that donors such as TDH actively search for continuities between different programmes, in this case 'reproductive health' and 'counter-trafficking'. Beyond these terms, the continuity between the two programmes is based on the fact that the 'risk groups' in both programmes are the same, namely factory workers and prostitutes, in particular, and female migrants, more generally. A critical question, therefore, is what difference there is between the programmes in terms of practice.

YMKK's outreach programme, in which they visit support groups in their place of residence or work, is not only an opportunity for spreading information (*informasi*), but also for collecting data through a standard questionnaire. The results are turned over to data-entry staff at the office in order to create tables for compiling reports that are presented to donors as a basis for evaluating their work. Collecting data is thus a critical part of the work of NGOs such as YMKK.

For YMKK's outreach staff, the shift in focus from HIV prevention and reproductive health to trafficking means adding questions about whether the woman being interviewed during outreach work has been 'trafficked' and if she wants to leave the place she is working, usually a place of prostitution. Finding someone who admits she has been trafficked creates real problems. In the cases where women do want support, the next step has been to contact the police. In 2005, YMKK aided eight women. Five were taken from a so-called *lokalisasi*, a low-charge brothel area, and a sixth was a freelance prostitute who supposedly had been trafficked by her boyfriend. The two other women worked at a karaoke bar in Batam's main town of Nagoya. YMKK reported these cases to the police, who raided the brothel area, imprisoning two pimps in the process.

There are two shelters for victims of trafficking on Batam, both of which accept only women. The first is run by a Catholic organisation, Komisi Migran (The Migrant Commission) where 10 victims have stayed during a two-year period. The second is run by the government organisation, Kantor Pemberdayaan Perempuan (The Office for Women's Empowerment), and was officially opened in 2003 by the Indonesian 'Trafficking Ambassador', actress Dewi Hughes. During the first seven months of 2006, 95 women had been housed there for a maximum of seven days. The shelter can receive at most 10 people at a time. What is of particular interest in both shelters is that domestic servants from Malaysia and Singapore are the dominant cases, while there have been almost no cases of women having worked as prostitutes.

Since 2005, the IOM in Jakarta has been funding the repatriation of trafficking victims through a programme of 'return, recovery, and reintegration'. According to their own figures, between March 2005 and May 2006 the IOM assisted 1,109 Indonesians identified as victims of trafficking, of which almost 20 per cent passed through Batam. Over 95 per cent of these people had been working in Malaysia (75 per cent) and Indonesia (20 per cent) and almost all of them had initially been handled by one of the IOM's over 50 NGO partners. Ninety per cent of the cases were women and over half had worked as domestic servants, while almost 17 per cent were identified as victims of 'forced prostitution'.

When an NGO such as YMKK finds an individual that is identified as a victim they use a standard screening interview form, which is faxed to the IOM. Once accepted by the IOM, the NGO escorts the victim or victims to one of the recovery centres, located in police hospitals in Jakarta, Surabaya, and a more recent one in Makassar. In conjunction with this, there is reintegration funding available for one or two years, with a particular focus on getting children back into school and offering start-up funds for small businesses. On average, there is about 5 million rupiah (about $550 US) per person available for reintegration.

NGOs who report trafficking victims are reimbursed by the IOM once the guidelines have been accepted. In each case it is the head of the counter-trafficking unit at the IOM in Jakarta who makes the final decision.[21] It is therefore not possible to send individuals who have not directly been defined as victims by the IOM. Even though there are limited funds available, the IOM's 'victims of trafficking' project has led to some competition for victims among NGOs on Batam, with NGOs complaining to Lindquist that other NGOs were 'taking' victims in their target areas.

More seriously, however, one effect of earlier raids on brothel areas has been that YMKK's outreach workers have found it difficult to return because they are worried about the reactions from pimps. Clearly short-term and long-term goals are potentially in conflict, as the concern with finding victims stands in opposition to NGOs' aim to gain the trust of women and pimps in the brothel areas. Although the Programme Officer at the Counter-trafficking unit at the IOM clearly stated that they were not supporting 'rescues', it is not clear that their partner NGOs use the same form of reasoning.

According to several NGO workers interviewed by Lindquist on Batam, one effect of counter-trafficking programmes is that pimps are more suspicious. There are also less women in the karaoke bars and brothels. Owners claim that this is because there are less tourists, but some NGO workers suspect that the younger women have been moved to safe-houses because owners are afraid of increasing raids.

More generally, it is clear both from the IOM's own statistics and the reality of the shelters on Batam, that the majority of the trafficking victims identified are female domestic workers from Malaysia, Singapore, and Indonesia. Though there are limited figures available, most reports suggest that the primary abuse suffered at the hands of employers are the withholding of wages rather than sexual abuse.

From sexual exploitation to labour rights

As crossing borders without legal authorisation becomes increasingly difficult, the market for smuggling and trafficking becomes more lucrative. This raises the stakes in this market as the increased costs are passed on to the migrants in the form of higher risks and constraints. As a result, debt bondage has become increasingly widespread, ultimately resulting in the constraint of migrant mobility. The International Labour Organisation's (ILO) framework and definition of trafficking[22] highlights the violation of the fundamental rights and core labour standards relating to forced labour, discrimination and freedom of association, which constitute the antithesis to the ILO's notion of 'decent work'.[23] When trafficking is defined as a form of forced labour, rather then strictly in terms of sexual exploitation, it highlights the abusive practices of debt bondage at various stages in the migration process. Labour performed without contract, no time off, no access to health or social security services, long working hours are all typical in the context of work generally reserved for unskilled migrant workers, not only in commercial sex, but also factories and domestic work.

This broader definition of trafficking opens up the possibility of understanding men as 'victims of trafficking' by including other sectors where forms of debt-bondage labour is widespread, namely agriculture, construction, food processing, and manufacturing. Interviews with South Asian male migrants in Malaysia[24] or Indonesian male migrants deported from Malaysia[25] have shown that their experiences often fits this very definition of trafficking. In this sense, trafficking occurs not only when borders are barriers to labour supplies meeting demands, but when employment itself is illegal or underground, and where work conditions below the legal minimum are tolerated or ignored (ILO 2004). When trafficking is related to more general forms of forced labour, the violations constituting trafficking are endemic in both the documented and undocumented migration processes.

Today, there is in fact increasing recognition that both women and men, boys and girls, may be trafficked not only for sex work but also other forms of exploitative labour. The recent UN World Survey on the role of women in development (2004), for example, notes that trafficking of people refers not only to prostitution, but also forced labour. The UN Special Rapporteur on Violence Against Women also expressed that 'the root causes of migration and trafficking greatly overlap' and it is the lack of rights which is 'the primary causative factor at the root of women's migration and trafficking in women' (UN Economic and Social Council 2000: 19). A complex bundle of rights are thus at stake in the various stages of migration.

In other words, too narrow a definition of trafficking may obscure the different pressures and constraints under which women decide to migrate in search for work in the 'sex and entertainment' industries (UNRISD 2005). What has become clear in existing studies in Asia and elsewhere is that migrant women rarely fit the ideal-type image of the victim of trafficking (Augustin 2005). Many migrants understand prior to migration what their working destination consists of, and even if their choice is constrained by economic and social circumstances, they cannot be understood as innocent victims on a general level. What is needed is a stronger focus on labour rights.

Conclusion

In terms of policy the link between HIV/AIDS and trafficking has been clearly established by the US State Department in its annual Trafficking in Persons report. Apart from being treated as a criminal and human rights issue, trafficking is also seen as having serious public health effects. More specifically, the report states that 'the HIV/AIDS epidemic may be spread by human trafficking' and 'some experts have linked sex trafficking to the spread and mutation of the AIDS virus' (UDS 2005: 49).

Our case study shows, however, that there are other forms of relationships between HIV and trafficking that should be considered on an institutional level. The move of NGO's such as YMKK on Batam from HIV to counter-trafficking projects has been strikingly uncomplicated. Focusing attention on these institutional continuities and the work of various types of organisations on Batam raises questions concerning the effectiveness and the politics surrounding how trafficking becomes defined as a problem on a global scale and how counter-trafficking programmes are being implemented in particular locales. From this perspective, Wong helpfully suggests an alternative history of trafficking. She claims that 'from a poorly funded, NGO women's issue in the early 1980s, "human trafficking" has entered the global agenda of high politics, eliciting in recent years significant legislative and other action from the US Congress, the European Union and the United Nations' (Wong 2005: 69). In other words, it is critical not to take trafficking for granted as a problem that demands an immediate response, but rather to consider why trafficking has been placed on the global agenda, and, more specifically, to pay attention to the actual effects of counter-trafficking programmes.

Notes

1 HIV has reached epidemic among certain populations, IV-drug users and transvestites in Jakarta, and certain areas, most notably Merauke in Irian Jaya (West Papua). In their global report from 2006, UNAIDS estimates that there were 170,000 HIV-positive in Indonesia from a population of over 220 million. (See: www.data.unaids.org/pub/GlobalReport/2006/2006_ GR_ANN1G-L_en.pdf)
2 The empirical data is based on fieldwork conducted by Lindquist on Batam intermittently between 1997 and 2006. Lindquist thanks the Swedish Research Council for funding his research there in 2006.

3 A note on terminology is required here: migrants without documentation or work permits are often referred to as 'illegal' in common parlance which is misleading as it conveys the idea of criminality on the part of the migrant. Many studies have, however, shown that migrants shift between the status of legality and illegality for various reasons, many of which are beyond their control or knowledge. The term 'undocumented' is preferable, but does not cover migrants who enter the destination country legally and only later violate their original entry visa. At the 1999 International Symposium on Migration in Bangkok in 1999, 21 participating countries agreed to use the term 'irregular migrants' which has since then become common practice (UNRISD 2005).

4 See Jones (2000) for the case of Indonesian migrants to Malaysia.

5 A smaller but substantial proportion of women work in the garment sector as well as agricultural and fish farm hands. Women from Bangladesh and Sri Lanka, in particular, have been deployed in Malaysia and the Middle East as garment workers (Dannecker 2005; Dias and Wanasundera 2002).

6 For more background data on Batam, see Lindquist (2002).

7 Previously, Yayasan Mitra Kesehatan (YMK), The Health Partnership Foundation.

8 For an illuminating review of NGOs in the context of these types of processes, see Fischer (1997).

9 Interview with Meiwita Budiharsana, Programme Officer, Ford Foundation Jakarta, 27 July 2005.

10 For an overview of these debates, see Kempadoo (2005).

11 'Organisations advocating prostitution as an employment choice or which advocate or support the legalisation of prostitution are not appropriate partners for USAID anti-trafficking grants or contracts.' (See: www.usaid. org)

12 See *The UN Treaty Monitoring Bodies and Migrant Workers: A Samizdat*, ICMC, 18 December 2004, which can be obtained from: grange@icmc.net and/or: myriam@december18.net.

13 This has led some scholars to refer to trafficking as a 'rumour' (Wong 2005) and 'a problem by a different name' (Piper 2005).

14 In 2001, there were six trafficking projects run by the UN Economic and Social Commission for Asia and the Pacific (UNESCAP), two projects by IPEC-ILO (International Programme on Child Labour by the International Labour Office), eight by the International Organization for Migration (IOM), four by the UN Educational, Scientific and Cultural Organisation (UNESCO), four by the UN High Commissioner for Refugees (UNHCR), 32 by the UN Children's Fund (UNICEF) and two by the UN Development Fund for Women (UNIFEM), all focusing on trafficking of women or children (Piper 2005).

15 See, for instance, the 1990 UN Convention on the Rights of All Migrant Workers and Their Families, and the ILO Conventions 97 and 143.

16 For two different readings of the UN Protocol, see Doezema (2002) and Raymond (2002).

17 This is based on a broader model, International Campaign Acts (ICACTS).

18 Interview with Ruth Eveline, Programme Officer, TDH, Jakarta, 8 August 2006.

19 On the role and force of the 'network' in institutions and the social sciences, see Riles (2000).

20 330 million rupiahs a year for three years covers mainly salary costs and office space for the organisation. The project will be evaluated through bi-annual visits to Batam. TDH funding is only available for NGOs and not the government.

21 Interview with Kristin Dadey, Programme Officer, Counter-trafficking Unit, IOM, Jakarta, 9 August 2006.

22 See Andrees and van der Linden (2005) for a full discussion of the ILO's definition.

23 'Decent work' is defined as productive work under conditions of freedom, equity, security and dignity, in which rights are protected and adequate remuneration and social coverage are provided. See: www.ilo. org/public/english/decent.htm

24 Interviews by Piper in Kuala Lumpur, 2003.

25 Interviews by Lindquist in Tanjung Pinang, 2006.

References

Altman, D. (1998) 'Globalization and the AIDS Industry', *Contemporary Politics*, 4 (3): 233–46

Andrees, B. and van der Linden, M.N.J. (2005) 'Designing Trafficking Research from a Labour Market Perspective: The ILO Experience', *International Migration*, 43 (1–2): 55–78.

Asian and Pacific Migration Journal (2003) 'Gender, Migration Governance in Asia', Special Issue, 12 (1–2) (whole issue).

Asis, M.M.B. (2005) 'Recent Trends in International Migration in Asia and the Pacific', *Asia-Pacific Population Journal*, 20 (3): 15–38.

Augustin, L. (2005) 'Migrants in the Mistress' House: Other Voices in the "Trafficking" Debate', *Social Politics*, 12 (1): 96–117.

Barry, K. (1995) *The Proposition of Sexuality: The Global Exploitation of Women*. London: New York University Press.

Clarke, G. (1998) *The Politics of NGOs in South-East Asia*. London: Routledge.

Dannecker, P. (2005) 'Transnational Migration and the Transformation of Gender Relations: The Case of Bangladeshi Labour Migrants', *Current Sociology*, 53 (4): 655–74.

Dias, M. and Wanasundera, L. (2002) *Sri Lankan Migrant Garment Factory Workers: Mauritius and Sultanate of Oman*, Study Series No. 27. Colombo/ Sri Lanka: Centre for Women's Research (CENWOR).

Doezema, J. (2002) 'Who gets to Choose? Coercion, Consent and the UN Trafficking Protocol', *Gender and Development*, 10 (1): 20–27.

Enloe, C. (1989) *Bananas, Beaches and Bases: Making Feminist Sense of International Politics*. Berkeley: University of California Press.

Eviota, E.U. (1992) *The Political Economy of Gender – Women and the Sexual Division of Labour in the Philippines*. London: Zed Books.

Fisher, W. (1997) 'Doing Good? The Politics and Anti-politics of NGO practices', *Annual Review of Anthropology*, 26: 439–64.

Hall, C.M. (1992) 'Sex Tourism in South-East Asia', in D. Harrison (ed.), *Tourism and the Less Developed Countries*. London: Bellhaven Press.

Hughes, D. (2003) 'The Driving Force of Sex Trafficking', *Vital Speeches of the Day*, 69 (6): 182–84.

Human Rights Watch (2006) 'Maid to Order – Ending Abuses Against Migrant Domestic Workers in Singapore'. New York: HRW.

Human Rights Watch (2004) 'Help Wanted – Abuses against Female Migrant Domestic Workers in Indonesia and Malaysia'. New York: HRW.

ILO (International Labour Organization) (2004) 'Towards a Fair Deal for Migrant Workers in the Global Economy'. Geneva: ILO.

Jones, S. (2000) *Making Money Off Migrants: The Indonesian Exodus to Malaysia*. Hong Kong: Asia 2002 Ltd and Centre for Asia-Pacific Transformation Studies, University of Wollongong.

Lindquist, J. (2002) 'The Anxieties of Mobility: Development, Migration, and Tourism in the Indonesian Borderlands', PhD dissertation, Department of Social Anthropology, Stockholm University.

Lindquist, J. (2003) 'Putting Transnational Activism in its Place: HIV/AIDS in the Indonesia-Malaysia-Singapore Growth Triangle and Beyond,' in A. Uhlin and Nicola Piper (eds) *Transnational Activism, Power, and Democracy: Contextualizing Networks in East and Southeast Asia*. London: Routledge.

Lindquist, J. (2005) 'Organsing AIDS in the Borderless World: A Case Study from the Indonesia-Malaysia-Singapore Growth Triangle', *Asia Pacific Viewpoint*, 46 (1): 49–63.

Lyons, L. (2005) 'Transient Workers Count Too? The Intersection of Citizenship and Gender in Singapore's Civil Society', *Sojourn*, 20 (2): 208–48.

Pigg, S.L. (2001) 'Languages of Sex and AIDS in Nepal: Notes on the Social Production of Commensurability,' *Cultural Anthropology*, 16 (4): 481–541.

Piper, N. (2006) 'The Management of Migration – An Issue of Controlling or Protecting? Normative and Institutional Developments and their Relevance to Asia', ARI Working Paper Series No. 69. Singapore: ARI (www.ari.nus. edu.sg/docs/wps/wps06_069.pdf).

Piper, N. (2005) 'A Problem by a Different Name? A Review of Research on Trafficking in South-East Asia and Oceania', *International Migration*, 43 (1–2): 203–33.

Piper, N. and Ford, M. (2006) 'Migrant NGOs and Labour Unions: A Partnership in Progress?', *Asian and Pacific Migration Journal*, 14 (9).

Piper, N. and Yamanaka, K. (eds) (2003) 'Gender, Migration, and Governance', Special Issue, *Asian and Pacific Migration Journal*, 12 (1–2).

Poku, N.K. (2002) Global Pandemics: HIV/AIDS, in D. Held and A. McGrew (eds), *Governing Globalization: Power, Authority, and Global Governance*. London: Polity Press.

Raymond, J.G. (1998) 'Prostitution as Violence against Women: NGO Stonewalling in Beijing and Elsewhere', *Women's Studies International Forum*, 21 (1): 1–9.

Raymond, J.G. (2002) 'The New UN Trafficking Protocol', *Women's Studies International Forum*, 25 (5): 503–14.

Riles, A. (2000) 'The Network Inside Out', Ann Arbor: University of Michigan Press.

Rosenburg, R. (2003) *Trafficking of Women and Children in Indonesia*. Jakarta: International Catholic Migration Commission and American Center for International Labour Solidarity.

Rosga, A.J. (2005) 'The Traffic in Children: The Funding of Translation and the Translation of Funding', *PoLAR*, 28 (2): 258–81.

Scully, E. (2001) 'Pre-Cold War Traffic in Sexual Labour and Its Foes: Some Centemporary Lessons', in D. Kyle and R. Koslowski (eds), *Global Human Smuggling: Comparative Perspectives*. Baltimore: The Johns Hopkins University Press.

Seidel, G. (1993) 'The Competing Discourses of HIV/AIDS in sub-Saharan Africa: Discourses of Rights and Empowerment vs Discourses of Control and Exclusion', *Social Science & Medicine*, 36 (3): 175–94.

Skeldon, R. (2000) 'Trafficking: A Perspective from Asia', *International Migration*, 38 (3): 7–30.

Tanaka, Y. (2002) 'Singapore: Subtle NGO Control by a Developmentalist Welfare State', in S. Shigetomi (ed.) *The State and NGOs: Perspective from Asia*. Singapore: Institute of Southeast Asian Studies.

Truong, T.D. (1996) 'Gender, International Migration, and Social Reproduction: Implications for Theory, Policy, Research and Networking', *Asian and Pacific Migration Journal*, 5 (1): 27–52.

Ucarer, E.M. (1999) 'Trafficking in Women: Alternative Migration or Modern Slave Trade?', in M. Meyer and E. Pruegl (eds) *Gender Politics in Global Governance*. Boulder, CO: Rowman and Littlefield.

UN Economic and Social Council (2000) *Report of the Special Rapporteur on Violence Against Women, its Causes and Consequences* (Ms. Radhika Coomraraswamy), E/CN.4/2000/48, 29 February 2000. New York: UN.

UNRISD (UN Research Institute for Social Development) (2005) *Gender Equality – Striving for Justice in an Unequal World*. Geneva: UNRISD.

UDS (US Department of State) (2002) *Trafficking in Persons Report*. Washington: UDS.

UDS (2003) *Trafficking in Persons Report*. Washington: UDS.

UDS (2005) *Trafficking in Persons Report*. Washington: UDS.

UN (2004) *World Survey on the Role of Women in Development – Women and International Migration*. New York: UN.

WAO (Women's Aid Organisation) (2003) 'Protection of Foreign Domestic Workers in Malaysia: Laws and Policies, Implication and Intervention', Paper prepared for Programme Consultative Meeting on the Protection of Domestic Workers Against the Threat of Forced Labour and Trafficking, Hong Kong SAR, 10–16 February 2003.

Wong, D. (2005) 'The Rumour of Trafficking: Border Controls, Illegal Immigration and the Sovereignty of the Nation-State', in W. van Schendel and I. Abraham (eds) *Illicit Flows and Criminal Things: States, Border and the Other Side of Globalization*. Bloomington: Indiana University Press.

Yamanaka, K. and Piper, N. (2006) 'Feminised Migration in East and Southeast Asia: Policies, Actions and Empowerment', UNRISD Occasional Paper no. 11. Geneva: UNRISD.

Chapter 8

Immigration detention in Britain

Mary Bosworth

Introduction

> The strength of a liberal democracy is measured not by how it treats the majority but by how it cares for minorities and those at the margins of society. The best tests for humanity and decency are conducted in its dark places: in prisons, psychiatric hospitals, and in institutions for failed asylum-seekers and other migrants. (Shaw 2005: 3)

The number of people confined in Britain under the Immigration Act powers rose by over 20 per cent between 2003 and 2004. Although they amount to a reasonably small number of 1,950 individuals, when compared to the total prison population of 77,029 on 31 July 2005 (National Offender Management Service 2005: 1), their presence poses considerable practical challenges to the daily operations of the Immigration and Nationality Directorate (IND) and the Prison Service who share responsibility for their care. Who must be confined and on what grounds? What should be done with those who are detained? What form should their detention take? Do these people pose a threat? If so, of what nature? If not, why are they held in secure housing? The detention of foreigners, particularly those who have not been convicted by the criminal courts, also poses more conceptual challenges, both to the IND and Prison Service, and to society at large. Whom do we welcome to our shores and whom do we reject? Who belongs and who does not? Who is a victim and who is an offender? What is the relationship between security and citizenship anyway?

Many of the organisational difficulties created by immigration detention arise from the variety of reasons for which people are held as well as the sheer range of establishments in which they may be located. Others relate to the lack of clarity about the size and nature of the population in question (Stewart 2004; Flynn 2005). Of those held exclusively under the powers of the Immigration Act, for example, nearly 80 per cent (1,515) in 2004 were asylum seekers. The rest were made up of non-citizens who had been convicted of criminal offences, and foreigners found in violation of immigration rules (such as, for example, by over-staying their visa or endeavouring to work without one). All of these people may be held in any one of a range of establishments. The majority (85 per cent) are placed in immigration removal centres, most of which have been contracted out to private companies, although some are run by HM Prison Service according to the 2001 Immigration Detention Centre Rules. Of the rest, a small but significant proportion (13 per cent) are confined in prison, usually following their completion of a criminal sentence as they await removal or asylum proceedings. The remaining 2 per cent are placed in short-term holding facilities (Dudley *et al.* 2005: 13).

In addition to these individuals, there is a much larger number of non-citizens serving criminal sentences in the nation's prison system. Foreign nationals constitute around one in five of women in prison, for example, while about 12 per cent of the male population behind bars do not hold British citizenship. Altogether it is estimated that currently there are around 10,200 such individuals in the nation's penal institutions, a figure that has trebled over the past 10 years (Denham 2006: 518; HMIP 2006b). Here again, there is some confusion, since it is not always certain that those behind bars should always be considered criminal. Though the vast majority of foreign women, for example, have been convicted of drug trafficking offences, it is possible that, despite burgeoning attempts that have been enshrined in legislation to protect such individuals, at least some of the foreigners (in both prison or immigration detention) might themselves have been trafficked. Although at present statistics are simply not available on this matter in Britain (Hansard 2003), trafficked women have ended up in prison in other countries like Australia, Japan and the US so we would be naïve to assume it does not happen here (Human Rights Watch 1999).[1]

Statistically, the overlaps and disjunctions among the non-citizen population are awkward. Intellectually, however, they do not pose the same problem. Even though it is important to try to identify the particular and specific treatment of each group, since refugees and asylum seekers will usually have suffered greater hardships than other non-citizens, it is also strategic at times to put them together in order to reflect on broader concepts of inclusion, exclusion and citizenship (Young 1999). Also, if, as Don Flynn (2005: 464) has persuasively argued, the British government is undertaking 'a programme of reform which is aiming at *the comprehensive management of all forms of migration*, whether forced or voluntary', then we may learn more about the goals and justifications of current practice and the role of detention within them by grouping non-citizens together than by considering them separately. This is, after all, what the government itself does (Home Office 1998, 2002, 2005).

Of course, wherever they are housed, all non-citizens should ultimately fall under the care and control of the IND. However, as a number of events in April and May 2006 revealed, the relationship between the prison service and the IND is far from seamless (*The Guardian*, 27 April 2006). Not only were 1,078 foreign nationals released rather than deported when they reached the end of their prison terms, but nearly twenty non-citizens absconded from Ford Open prison over a two-week period in May 2006 apparently in response to the government's plan to enforce removals.[2] Although great effort has since been expended to rationalise and systematise the relationship between the prison service and immigration directorate by reworking prison service orders and by changing the responsibilities of key staff within the IND, the sheer complexity of the population in question and the range of places in which they reside undermines any attempts at totally controlled management. In turn, although immigration detention and indeed, other aspects of the immigration service, increasingly rely upon a criminal justice vocabulary and institutional format, the disorganised nature of much of the daily operations of the IND ensures that, despite itself, the criminalisation of foreigners is, as yet, incomplete.

Such organisational and institutional confusion suggests that it is an apposite moment to ask why states like Britain are opting to detain ever-increasing numbers of foreigners. What, precisely, is the prison or detention centre being employed to do? In order to answer these questions – and thus come to some sense of the broad appeal of immigration detention – this chapter will attempt to unravel the complicated relationship between the Immigration and Nationality Directorate and the Prison Service. Although I shall concentrate on the treatment of refugees and asylum seekers I shall also, at times, consider the larger criminal population of foreign nationals. In my analysis I shall use ideas drawn from a wide, and generally theoretical, body of literature on citizenship and belonging to interpret information drawn from recent government reports, investigations and analyses of immigration detention. In this way, I hope to explore the role played by places of confinement in maintaining practical and symbolic borders of the British nation state.

Immigration detention

The Immigration Act 1971 allowed for the detention of foreigners seeking entry to the UK. Yet, until the 1990s, the authorities used this power only in exceptional circumstances – such as following the disintegration of Yugoslavia and in response to the 1980s mass exodus of Tamils from Sri Lanka (Zetter *et al.* 2003: 86). Starting in 1993, however, the then Conservative government began building new sites to hold foreign nationals and converting older institutions into immigration detention centres. Campsfield House, just outside Oxford, which was previously a male young offender institution and, before that, an army barracks, was the first of these detention centres to be opened at the end of 1993. Rebranded as 'removal centres' by the Labour government in the Nationality, Immigration and Asylum Act 2002, such places have become central to an immigration and asylum policy in which the UK holds the dubious honour of confining proportionally the most asylum seekers for the longest periods of time in all of Europe (Malloch and Stanley 2005; see also Schuster and Solomos 2004; Young 2003).

In addition to tightening its asylum legislation, since 1997 the Labour government has put in place new administrative procedures for dealing with foreigners who are in violation of immigration law, some of which may result in them being detained prior to removal. Thus, people who have committed what are otherwise civil offences regarding their immigration status – by failing to renew their visa ('overstayers'), or by working while in the UK on holiday – may be treated in the same manner (detained), as if they had violated criminal law, by stealing property or committing some kind of violent act. Deportation orders, which prevent the re-entry of such individuals for at least three years, in addition to the more recent administrative removal orders are just part of the arsenal of powers held by Immigration officers (Immigration Act 1971: Part 13, sections 362 and 395F). New criminal laws have also been created to tackle those involved in trafficking non-citizens, many of whom are particularly vulnerable individuals who are brought into Britain by organised groups of smugglers using dangerous, sometimes lethal methods (Lee 2005). Finally, as an adjunct to these laws, legislation is constantly being developed to prevent, regulate and punish acts of terrorism (see, for example, the Terrorism Act 2000 and the Anti-terrorism, Crime and Security Act 2001). In all this legislative reform, confinement has become a vital part of the government's management of non-citizens and, as a result, the criminal justice and immigration systems have become increasingly intertwined. Not only are foreigners held in all parts of the criminal justice system as offenders, and, on occasion (despite international strictures against this practice) while their applications for refugee status are considered, more commonly, they remain in prison after completing their sentence while awaiting deportation. In addition, administratively there are a number of telling overlaps between the two systems as the IND increasingly appears to rely on staff and governance methods drawn from the criminal justice system.

Managing migration: The Immigration and Nationality Directorate

According to its website, the Immigration and Nationality Directorate is responsible for 'securing our borders, preventing abuse of our immigration laws and managing migration to boost the UK' (www.ind.homeoffice.gov.uk/aboutus/). Although it is part of the Home Office, and thus answerable to the Home Secretary, it is run as an independent agency by a Director General who is assisted by a board made up of eight directors who, in turn, oversee a number of employees in specific areas. Recently reorganised and rebranded following the foreign prisoner scandal, the IND lists its five primary operational areas in a so-called 'Organogram' as Borders, Enforcement and Removals, Managed Migration, Asylum and UK visas. The remaining three departments oversee the internal workings of the organisation under the headings of Resource Management, Change and Reform and the Office of the Deputy Director General.

Though individuals under detention and/or removal orders may be dealt with by staff working in more than one of these sub-sections within the IND, for the purpose of this chapter, the twin areas of 'Borders' and 'Enforcement and Removals' are the most relevant since they are the departments most directly concerned with policing, confining and deporting foreigners and in preventing those deemed 'undesirable' or 'undeserving' from entering in the first place. They are also the departments with the closest ties to the criminal justice system. Not only does the section for 'Immigration and Removal' deal with criminal cases, for example, but its director at this time is a former Chief of Police. Likewise, the person presently in charge of 'detention services' is a former prison governor. Similarly, the current director of borders, Mr Brodie Clark, who, until the 2006 scandal about the release of foreign prisoners was director of operations at the IND, was formerly not just a prison governor but Head of Security for the whole of the Prison Service of England and Wales.

It is not only in the high level administration of the IND that this kind of overlap exists between the immigration and criminal justice systems. Staff trainers, from psychologists to security officers are also drawn from the penal estate and police departments, while those investigating disturbances are as well (see, for example, McAllister 2004). Even the two independent watchdogs, who have been some of the most vocal critics of immigration detention are, more usually, charged with investigating prison conditions and prisoner complaints: The Prison Inspectorate and the Prisons and Probation Ombudsman for England and Wales.

Another way in which immigration detention resembles the criminal justice system, and particularly mimics the prison system, is apparent in the involvement of private security companies in the daily operations of immigration facilities. Currently, for instance, there are ten Immigration Service Removal Centres, seven of which have been contracted out to private companies. There are also four Immigration Short-Term Holding Facilities, at least 16 short-term non-residential holding facilities at various ports and airports and an undisclosed number of prisons holding individuals under the Immigration Act across the country (Home Office 2002: 67; S4.74; Heath and Jeffries 2005: 71). Individuals caught trying to enter the UK illegally from France may also be held by the IND in short-term non-residential facilities at Calais Seaport, Coquelle Freight and Coquelles Tourist. At the time of writing, HM Prison Service runs three of the seven Immigration Removal Centres for the IND according to the 2001 Detention Centre Rules in buildings that were either formerly used as prisons or are still in part operating as such. Private companies have responsibility for the remaining seven; Global Solutions Ltd (GSL) (formerly Group 4 Falck/Wackenhut) which operates four, SERCO and its subsidiary Premier Prison Services which run two, and UK Detention Services (UKDS) that manages just one. The short-term and non-residential units are all contracted by the IND to private companies, mostly to GSL.

Of course, private companies have for some time now, been building, running, and servicing penal facilities in the UK and elsewhere. However, the involvement of capital in state punishment remains somewhat contested and is, at least in terms of having overarching responsibility of running the institution, the exception rather than the norm. While companies increasingly provide many of the day-to-day services that inmates used to do themselves – laundry, food preparation, maintenance etc – they are only fully in charge of the day-to-day operations of a handful of UK prisons. In the immigration estate, however, this relationship is reversed. The state runs less than one half of the removal centres, and even those, it seems, will eventually be contracted out to the private sector. Employees of these same companies are also often used to remove individuals from their home if they are living in the community, ferry them from their attempted point of entry to detention, move them between detention centres and to expel the from the country by escorting them to the border.

Managing difference

The Detention Centre Rules, that were thoroughly revised in 2001 and tinkered with again in 2005, are meant to dictate daily practice in whichever institution individuals held under the Immigration Act are placed. Although modelled on the Prison Rules, they are meant to carve out the particular needs, expectations and responsibilities of immigrant detainees. To that end, they should ensure not only that any cultural differences of asylum seekers and other foreigners are respected, protected and understood, but also that individuals detained under the Immigration Act are given as much freedom as possible within a system that attempts to contain their physical movements. 'The purpose of detention centres' according to these rules shall:

> be to provide for the secure but humane accommodation of detained persons in a relaxed regime with as much freedom of movement and association as possible, consistent with maintaining a safe and secure environment, and to encourage and assist detained persons to make the most productive use of their time, whilst respecting in particular their dignity and the right to individual expression. (Detention Centre Rules 2001, para 3(1))

Detainees, in other words, despite being housed in institutions that might have once been penal institutions (or indeed that might still be part of a functioning prison), and despite being guarded by individuals who may have been trained by someone from the prison service, and despite being overseen by administrators who previously worked in the criminal justice system, are not offenders. To use the words of the Chief Inspector of Prisons Anne Owers, 'An Immigration Removal Centre is not a prison. Detainees have not been charged with a criminal offence, nor are they detained through normal judicial processes' (HMIP 2002: 4). Yet, significant evidence, from the prison inspectorate to groups working with refugees, suggests that detainees experience their incarceration as imprisonment.

In the report of an unannounced repeat visit to Yarl's Wood, for example, the Prison Inspectorate included testimony from a number of children who spoke about their experiences at the hands of representatives of the IND and of their detention. One, who described at some length the frightening process of being taken from his home to detention was clearly deeply traumatised by the event:

> When they came to the house like an earthquake the way they knock. I think there were ten of them spread all around our house ... The way they look at you is like you are a criminal; they had big padded jackets and handcuffs, like police stuff. They handcuffed me and my Mum through Terminal 4, through public area and into the van. My two hands were cuffed in front; I was crying in the van, they were removed when we arrived. That is why I just stay in my room – I keep thinking about the handcuffs. (age 13) (HMIP 2006a: 15)

Another, in describing the same kind of experience said he was 'Scared because police broke my door down [and] Upset, [because] I felt like I was in jail' (age 10) (HMIP 2006a: 14). Elsewhere, in a joint research project on women's experiences of immigration detention, Asylum Aid and Bail for Immigration Detainees (BID) depict similar reactions to treatment by the IND. On being taken into custody for example, one woman, said 'I didn't realise it was a detention centre with gates and security officers ... you feel like a criminal ...' (Cutler and Ceneda 2004: Executive Summary: 2).

Such experiences appear again in the 2005 report by Amnesty International *Seeking Asylum is not a Crime*. Taken by police from their homes in the middle of the night, and then handed over to custodial officers with whom they could barely communicate, individuals articulate high levels of fear, anxiety and resentment. As one of them put it, 'I felt like an animal [and I was] Treated like cattle – like a caged animal' (Amnesty International 2005: 15). It is, moreover, not simply aspects of the 'enforcement and removals' process that resemble the actions of the criminal justice system. Rather, the Prison Inspectorate commonly depicts a range of everyday practices drawn from the criminal justice system including the use of the Samaritans 'Listeners' scheme, 'routine handcuffing' and the employment of staff trainers from the penal estate (see, for example, HMIP 2004: 39).

When the population in question is actually held in prison, following the completion of their criminal sentence, the similarities become even more marked. Thus, although the most recent *Foreign Nationals Bulletin* released by the National Offender Monitoring Service (NOMS) urges that 'prisoners who have completed the custodial element of their sentence and are being detained under immigration rules must be treated as unconvicted and receive the privileges that accompany that status', it also makes clear that 'Immigration detainees can continue to be held in an establishment that does not normally hold convicted prisoners' so long as they 'consent to the withdrawal of their unconvicted privileges' (NOMS 2006: 2). In fact, although media attention has focused on the release rather than deportation of foreign prisoners at the end of their sentence, other, more informed groups, including the Prison Inspectorate (HMIP 2006b) and the Home Affairs Committee (Denham 2006) are just as concerned about the (financial implications and legality of the) practice of holding foreigners beyond the end of their sentence while they request permission to remain in the UK or await deportation. Thus, the same *Foreign Nationals Bulletin* sets out new guidelines for Prison Service Order 4630: Immigration and Foreign Nationals in Prison. To prevent non-citizens being held beyond their sentence, it states that prisons must identify all non-citizens and refer them to the IND for consideration of removal at first reception (NOMS 2006: 1). More recently still, in a somewhat different kind of illustration of the interdependence of these two arenas, in autumn 2006 Home Secretary John Reid offered financial incentives to foreign prisoners prepared to return to their country of origin, there to serve out their sentences in order to free up space in the severely overcrowded prison system of England and Wales.

Foreign nationals bring with them a whole host of needs, experiences and expectations, many of which prisons and detention centres are simply not well suited at managing. While the Detention Centre Rules 2001 clearly state that, 'Due recognition' will be given to 'issues of cultural diversity', (S. 3, para. (2)), it is clear from reports issued by the Prison Inspectorate and the Ombudsman that significant practical problems and conceptual difficulties remain. Moreover, matters do not have to escalate into violent or outright racism for problems to ensue, although some evidence exists to suggest a certain institutionalised level of both such problems (Shaw 2004, 2005). Rather, as these reports also frequently enumerate, far more banal problems tend to emerge on a daily basis in the areas of language, food, family contact and education (HMIP 2006b).

In prisons, removal centres and short-term holding facilities, many basic services and information may not be available to detainees due to language barriers. In a 2002 survey of detainees at IRC Lindholme, for example, the Chief Inspector of Prisons found that 'under half (49 per cent) were told why they were being detained in a language they could understand' (HMIP 2002a: 12). Similarly, at Haslar the 'majority of notices in the holding room' were in English only, although the Inspectorate team also commended a 'helpful' 'Welcome to Haslar' leaflet that was available in 18 different languages (HMIP 2005: 15).

Increasingly, in part because of the population growth of foreigners as well as in response to greater attempts at monitoring the impact and experience of racial and cultural difference within institutions, prisons and removal centres are being encouraged to respond creatively to the cultural experiences of their foreign populations. One common strategy, which is used to explain the meals on offer to those who are either illiterate, or unable to read English, is to produce a pictorial menu. At IRC Oakington outside Cambridge, which uses this system, the pictorial menu also differentiates between Halal and non-Halal offerings (HMIP 2020b: 52). Despite such practices, detainees in almost all of the Inspectorate reports, criticise the food. Best practice, instead, appears to be found in the prison service where the Catering Manager of HMP Morton Hall won the 'Public Sector Caterer of the Year Award' due, in part, to his knack for dealing with difference. Presiding over a team of inmate cooks, Saint managed to cater for a population of 53 different nationalities and translate his menu into 11 different languages. Using the expertise of prisoners, he injected some variety into this rather ordinary part of prison life by running themed days around British, Spanish, Caribbean, African and Chinese food.

More generally the Home Office now translates most of their policy material relevant to prisoners and immigration detainees into a number of languages. Thus, even though staff will rarely speak anything other than English, some written information can be delivered in this way. Nonetheless, language barriers remain significant in the day-to-day workings of all institutions holding non-citizens and, in the recent thematic review of foreign prisoners by the Prison Inspectorate, rates very high in their list of concerns (HMIP 2006: 6). Signs, in both prisons and immigration detention centres routinely appear only in English. Legal Aid representatives and visitors who can communicate with all ethnic groups may also be hard to find, as are translators. Under these circumstances, people's individual rights are easily compromised and the flow of information may break down. One initiative currently underway at HMYOI Lancaster strives to address this problem specifically as it pertains to the formal complaints procedure (NOMS 2006: 4). Prisoners at this young offender institution may submit their written complaint in any language. The form is then scanned and emailed to Language Line which will interpret the complaint and inform the prison of the nature of it in English. The English response is then emailed to Language Line which translates this back into the prisoner's mother tongue. This system, which is not mentioned in any of the reports by the Chief Inspector of Prisons, contrasts starkly with more ad hoc systems such as that at Haslar where the institution is forced to rely on detainees to 'interpret for other detainees during sensitive and confidential discussions involving an element of risk assessment' (HMIP 2005: 30).

As Anne Owers observes in her introduction to the Prison Inspectorate thematic report on foreign nationals in prisons, non-citizens 'though a divergent group, have a recognisable cluster of specific needs' in the areas of language, immigration and family contact. 'The three are interlinked' she claims, and when inadequately addressed 'can result in isolation, depression and confusion' (HMIP 2006: 1). Non-citizens, the report suggests, are a particularly vulnerable group and prisons and detention centres struggle to deal with them humanely.

Securing the border

What does it mean that so much evidence suggests that immigration detention centres are being run (and often experienced) 'like prisons'? Of what significance is it that a number of high-level administrators, staff trainers and even those who guard and care for detainees are drawn from the Prison Service? And what can we make of the role played by private companies in the detention of foreigners? Should immigration removal centres and other holding facilities be shaped by assumptions and practices that are drawn from prison management? If not, how else could or should they be run?

To some extent, of course, answers to such questions require some sense of the purpose and form of imprisonment. Why, after all, do we incarcerate anyone and who do we think we should employ to do so? Evidently, there is a well-rehearsed literature on this topic, ranging from philosophical notions of the goals and justifications of punishment to more the limited policy-related aims of the prison service. It is clear that prisons and their employees have always had to juggle and somehow appease vastly conflicting ideas about their purpose. They are, on the one hand, meant to deter, while, at the same time, reform. Above all, these days, they must be seen to punish. To some extent, whatever one's views may be about the absolute legitimacy of imprisonment, prisons can be justified simply as institutions designed to house those found guilty by the courts. To that extent, they serve, at minimum, a role of separating these individuals from other, more law-abiding (or perhaps more fortunate or otherwise canny) folk. In contrast, the justification for immigration removal centres, even on this most basic level, is significantly less clear. Not only do questions remain about the presence of those who have been victimised within the UK as trafficked persons, but questions of culpability and danger of those who fail to meet the legal requirements of refugee status is also highly contested as their desire for greater (economic, educational, safety) opportunities in Britain are often hard to fault.

Administratively too, there are a number of shortcomings which should challenge the legitimacy of imprisoning non-citizens. Though the Labour government is making increasing attempts to use detention as the final stage before deportation, and thus to turn removal centres into short-term holding pens, the Chief Inspector of Prisons and other critics frequently describe cases of people living behind their walls for many months at a time. Similarly, those who are held in prison beyond the completion of their sentence pose particular challenges to ideas of fairness and desert in sentencing. Furthermore, if only because of the range of reasons for which foreign nationals might be held under Immigration Act powers, there can be little consistency in the justification for holding them all.

Most broadly still, many would question the legitimacy or fairness of border control itself. Immigration Detention, for the most part, after all is designed to hold those who have been designated as 'failed' asylum seekers. As many of the other chapters in this collection explain (see Grewcock and Hudson, this volume), few individuals successfully obtain refugee status according to the 1954 UN Convention on the Status of Refugees because the requirements are so narrow. Not only must individuals prove that they would face persecution at home, but if they have passed through any country en route to the UK that is designated by British authorities as 'safe', they will, in all likelihood, be returned there to process their claim. In other words, despite considerable attempts by human rights lawyers and political theorists to argue that it is not and should not be considered illegal to try to improve one's lot in life by seeking refugee status (nor indeed by seeking paid employment in another country), the UK, in common with most other democratic, industrialised, first world countries, insists on treating (and labelling) those who arrive without formal documentation as illegals (Carens 2000; Amnesty International 2005; Benhabib 1999, 2004). It is here, in the very ambiguity of ascertaining people's 'right' to asylum, that immigration detention and the interdependence of the IND and the criminal justice system is both most troubling and most (symbolically and practically) productive. It is here too that we may find part of the explanation for the enthusiasm of capital in the maintenance of such places.

Foreigners, whether asylum seekers, offenders, trafficking victims, or even those who have been legally recognised as students or 'economic' migrants, although very different groups of individuals, are united by their liminal status within British society. Denied the rights and protections accorded by citizenship, and thus, in fact, formally relatively powerless, they are nonetheless continually represented as risky and dangerous. In particular, when labelled as 'bogus' asylum seekers and criminals they are all too easily painted as threats to the economic well-being and safety of the wider British community. Increasingly, and as part of this process, their cultural, linguistic and religious differences are also constructed as threats to the social cohesion of the state as well.

Placing such figures in institutions that look like, feel like and to many intents and purposes are, prisons, merely confirms these fears. Immigration detention, in other words, identifies foreign nationals potentially as always and already criminal. Such is the symbolic power of the prison. Moreover, the state does not have to detain many for this association to be widespread. The immigration estate can remain relatively small (and therefore affordable), while tainting the entire population of non-citizens.

Detention is, as the prison has always been, a sign of the undeserving nature of its inhabitants. It is also, when used as a means of immigration management, a kind of border. As with any border, the ability to cross it rests on citizenship. And it is the very absence of this final element that may partly explain the enthusiasm of the private sector to take responsibility for so many diverse aspects of immigration management and detention. After all, the scale of involvement of private companies in the immigration 'enforcement and removal' sector is notable, particularly given the volume of criticism which has been directed at the same companies when they have ventured into the administration of regular penal institutions. Why then are security firms so keen to take on this endeavour?

To some extent of course, there are quite practical and financial answers to this question. As the number of individuals seeking greater opportunities for themselves and their families as well as relief from tyranny in their home countries continues to increase – and it shows no sign of diminishing – immigration detention is clearly a 'growth market'. And indeed, the management of immigrants has seemingly re-energised the financial power of the security corporations, making them more attractive for investors all over the world (Greene 2002). GSL which was acquired in full in 2004 by two investment banks, Englefield and Electra Partners Europe (since renamed Cognetas), for £202.5 million provides a case in point. Previously owned in the UK by Group 4/Falck, itself a wing of the multi-national company Wackenhut that runs many private prisons throughout the US and Australia, GSL operates most of those facilities which the IND have contracted out to private companies.

Yet, it would be a mistake to imagine that immigration detention is attractive to the corporate world simply because of potential or actual profits. Rather, there are few barriers to the involvement of private industry in this field and, moreover, much desire from the government that such corporations participate. Most obviously and strikingly, unlike private prisons, there are few moral or ethical barriers to the involvement of capital. As criminologists Michael Reisig and Travis Pratt (2000: 211) point out in their discussion of the private prisons in the US, 'at the heart of the private prison management debate is the relationship between the state and its citizens'. Immigration detention centres, in contrast, do not encounter this kind of dilemma, since by definition they are not dealing with citizens of the host country.[3] More profoundly, the absence of this relationship enables such institutions to be more readily viewed as both a kind of service and as a form of risk management, that private companies are particularly well-suited at operating.

While the state is expected to bear responsibility for managing risk, it is no longer required in the UK to bear full risk for all government matters. Instead, as typified by the efflorescence of both Private

Finance Initiatives (PFI) and Public Private Partnerships (PPP) under New Labour, the private sector has increasingly become a legitimate 'partner' in risk management. These schemes, which are not quite the full privatisation of the Thatcher and Regan years, but certainly far from total public control, dilute both the government's financial and its moral responsibilities. This in turn helps to explain why private companies are increasingly being used to manage previously public-funded enterprises like health, welfare and prisons. While the government would claim that such arrangements enhance the efficient use of public funds, and are well-regulated, other advocates point to a blurring of the moral dimension when the healthy 'bottom line' becomes paramount. Thus, it comes as no surprise to learn that Immigration Detention is just one of many strings to GSL's custodial bow, since the company also runs a number of private prisons (in the UK and abroad) as well as secure escort services. Moreover, GSL is not 'just' in the business of custody. It also operates business services and even public services in healthcare, education and local authority.

In this corporate take-over of what might otherwise have been a state matter, certain elements of state responsibility and more complex questions of justice and morality are erased. The particularity of these institutions also disappears as they become just one of a variety of kinds of 'managed care'. In this sleight of hand, the potential (moral) responsibility of the state, to address global matters of inequality, is, once again, neatly avoided.

Conclusion

In recent years, confinement has become central to immigration legislative reform, and thus crucial to the management of a diverse range of non-citizens. Though there are some quite banal explanations for the utility of confinement as a strategy when sorting out individuals who might otherwise seek to evade official scrutiny, the suitability of the prison for its new role does not lie merely in such utilitarian explanations. If the sole concern were to be security, close community monitoring and effective reporting to immigration agents would, after all, be sufficient for the vast majority. And indeed, asylum seekers who are not confined in detention centres are required to report to various agencies including the police, while their cases are under consideration. They are also expected to provide the state with details about their residence and financial situation. Detention is, in other words, merely one of a number of strategies available to the government.

The point is that prisons and detention centres – 'removal centres' or not – are singularly useful in the management of non-citizens because they provide both a physical and a symbolic exclusion zone. The actual and metaphorical similarities between 'removal centres' and gaols mean that those who are confined within them are always already somehow under suspicion. Detention excludes non-citizens from British society while their appeals are processed or while they await removal or deportation. It denies them freedom of access to the community by the bars and fences of their establishments, and prevents them from attaining or appealing to the rights and protections of citizenship. By appealing to criminal justice imagery, detention centres legitimate the construction of new, secure borders within the geographical integrity of the nation state while at the same time contributing to a more generalised fear and suspicion of foreigners that contributes to a more general toughening of the actual borders elsewhere.

Just as they have traditionally been a means of excluding the 'undeserving' poor from the broader society (Garland 1985; Simon 1990), institutions of confinement, whether they are Immigration Removal Centres, regular penal institutions or some other kind of secure Immigration housing, now act as a sorting mechanism for determining the rights and entitlements of foreigners. In this way, not only are they operating as a tool of risk management in concert with Immigration and Asylum legislation, but also as a strategy of social engineering underpinning a particular vision of British national identity.

Notes

1 According to Anti-Slavery International, there are cases of trafficked persons being detained before they have been identified as trafficked in Britain. Furthermore, some trafficked persons are also prosecuted for immigration offences or for use of false passports. The main problem is that these people are often not identified as trafficked at all, or identified only after a long time when someone has gained their trust or eventually listened to their story (personal communication, November 2006).
2 Dealt with swiftly by the Prison Service, who moved 141 other foreign nationals from Ford to closed facilities elsewhere in the country, their escape nonetheless was, somewhat predictably, seized

upon by the media and members of the government as yet further evidence of both the lax treatment of foreigners and the potential risks they pose.

3 In Australia, at any rate, there have been cases not only of citizens being held at length in the nation's immigration detention centres, but even deported to the country of assumed citizenship.

References

Legislation:

Immigration and Nationality Act 1971
Asylum and Immigration Act 1999
Terrorism Act 2000
Anti-terrorism, Crime and Security Act 2001
Detention Centre Rules 2001
Nationality, Immigration and Asylum Act 2002
Asylum and Immigration (Treatment of Claimants, etc) Act 2004

Secondary sources:

Agamben, G. (1998) *Homo Sacer: Sovereignty and Bare Life*. Stanford, CA: Stanford University Press.
Amnesty International (2005) *Seeking Asylum is Not a Crime: Detention of People who Have Sought Asylum*. London: Amnesty International.
Benhabib, S. (1999) 'Citizens, Residents, and Aliens in a Changing World: Political Membership in the Global Era', *Social Research*, 66 (3): 709–44.
Benhabib, S. (2004) *The Rights of Others: Aliens, Residents and Citizens*. Cambridge: Cambridge University Press.
Bosworth, M. (2007) 'Identity, Citizenship and Punishment', in M. Bosworth and J. Flavin (eds) *Regulating Difference: How Race and Gender Shape Punishment in America*. New Brunswick, NJ: Rutgers University Press.
Cutler, S. and Sophia C. (2004) *'They Took Me Away': Women's Experiences of Immigration Detention in the UK*. London: Bail for Immigration Detainees and the Refugee Women's Resource Project at Asylum Aid. Available online at: www.asylumaid.org.uk
Denham, J. (2006) *Immigration Control: Fifth Report of Session 2005–06: Vol. 1 Report, together with formal minutes*, House of Commons papers 775-I 2005–06. London: HMSO. Available online at: www.publications.parliament. uk/pa/cm200506/cmselect/cmhaff/775/77502.htm. Accessed 9 October 2006.
Dudley, J., Roughton, M., Fidler, J. and Wollacott, S. (2005) *Control of Immigration: Statistics UK 2004*. London: Home Office.
Flynn, D. (2005) 'New Borders, New Management: The Dilemmas of Modern Immigration Policies', *Ethnic and Racial Studies*, 28: 463–90.

Garland, D. (2001) *The Culture of Control: Crime and Social Order in Contemporary Society*. Oxford: Clarendon Press.

Greene, J. (2001) 'Bailing out Private Jails', *The American Prospect*, 12: 23–27.

HM Inspectorate of Prisons (2002a) *An Inspection of Oakington Reception Centre*. London: HMIP.

HM Inspectorate of Prisons (2002b) *An Inspection of Lindholme Immigration Removal Centre*. London: HMIP.

HM Inspectorate of Prisons (2005) *Report on an Announced Inspection of Haslar Immigration Removal Centre*. London: HMIP.

HM Inspectorate of Prisons (2006a) *Report on an Unannounced Short Follow-up Inspection of Yarl's Wood Immigration Removal Centre*. London: HMIP.

HM Inspectorate of Prisons (2006b) *Foreign National Prisoners: A Thematic Review*. London: HMIP.

Home Office (1998) *Fairer, Faster and Firmer: A Modern Approach to Immigration and Asylum* (Cm 4018). London: Home Office.

Home Office (2002) *Secure Borders, Safe Haven: Integration with Diversity in Modern Britain* (Cm 5387). London: Home Office.

Home Office (2005a) *Statistics on Race and the Criminal Justice System, 2004. A Home Office Publication Under Section 95 of the Criminal Justice Act 1991*. London: Home Office.

Home Office (2005b) *Controlling Our Borders: Making Migration Work for Britain. Five-year Strategy for Asylum and Immigration* (Cm 6472). London: Home Office.

Home Office (2005c) *Integration Matters: A National Strategy for Refugee Integration*. London: Home Office.

Human Rights Watch (1999) *World Report 1999*. New York: Human Rights Watch.

Human Rights Watch (2003) *World Report 2003*. New York: Human Rights Watch.

Jones, R. (2000) 'Digital Rule: Punishment, Control and Technology', *Punishment and Society*, 2: 5–22.

Lee, M. (2005) 'Human Trade and the Criminalization of Irregular Migration', *International Journal of the Sociology of Law*, 33: 1–15.

Malloch, M.S. and Stanley, E. (2005) 'The Detention of Asylum Seekers in the UK: Representing Risk, Managing the Dangerous', *Punishment and Society*, 7: 53–71.

McAllister, S. (2004) *Report of an Investigation into the Disturbance at Harmondsworth Immigration Removal Centre on 19 & 20 July 2004* (HC 1265). London: HMSO.

National Offender Management Service (2005) *Population in Custody, Monthly Tables July 2005, England and Wales*. London: Home Office.

Reisig, M. and Pratt, T. (2000) 'The Ethics of Correctional Privatization', *The Prison Journal*, 80 (2): 210–22.

Sanchez, L. (2007) 'The Carceral Contract: From Domestic to Global Governance', in M. Bosworth and J. Flavin (eds) *Race, Gender and*

Punishment: From Colonialism to the War on Terror, pp. 167–83. New Brunswick, NJ: Rutgers University Press.

Schuster, L. and Solomos, J. (2004) 'Race, Immigration and Asylum: New Labour's Agenda and its Consequences', *Ethnicities*, 4: 267–300.

Shaw, S. (2004) *Report of the Inquiry into the Disturbance and Fire at Yarl's Wood Removal Centre*. London: Prisons and Probation Ombudsman for England and Wales.

Shaw, S. (2005) *Inquiry into Allegations of Racism and Mistreatment of Detainees at Oakington Immigration Reception Centre and while under Escort*. London: Prisons and Probation Ombudsman for England and Wales.

Simon, J. (1998) 'Refugees in a Carceral Age: The Rebirth of Immigration Prisons in the United States', *Public Culture*, 10 (3): 577–606.

Stewart, E. (2004) 'Deficiencies in UK Asylum Data: Practical and Theoretical Challenges', *Journal of Refugee Studies*, 17 (1): 29–49.

Travis, A. (2006) 'Warning Signs that went Ignored', *The Guardian*, 27 April 2006, see: www.politics.guardian.co.uk/labour/story/0,,1762307,00.html. Accessed 9 October 2006.

Welch, M. and Schuster, L. (2005a) 'Detention of Asylum Seekers in the UK and USA: Deciphering Noisy and Quiet Constructions', *Punishment and Society*, 7: 397–417.

Welch, M. and Schuster, L. (2005b) 'Detention of Asylum Seekers in the US, UK, France, Germany, and Italy: A critical view of the Globalizing Culture of Control', *Criminal Justice*, 5 (4): 331–55.

Young, J. (1999) *The Exclusive Society*. London: Sage.

Young, J. (2003) 'To these Wet and Windy Shores: Recent Immigration Policy in the UK', *Punishment and Society*, 5 (4): 449–62.

Zetter, R., Griffiths, D., Ferretti, S. and Pearl, M. (2003) *An Assessment of the Impact of Asylum Policies in Europe, 1990–2000*. Home Office Research Study, 259. London: Home Office.

Chapter 9

Shooting the passenger: Australia's war on illicit migrants

Michael Grewcock

Introduction

Border policing operates as one of the deeper and murkier undercurrents of Australian politics. In a dismal exercise in realpolitik, the depths were plumbed during the 2001 federal election campaign, when the incumbent Liberal-National Party Coalition used the wretched sight of a few hundred asylum seekers aboard leaking and overloaded fishing boats to persuade a hitherto disenchanted electorate that 'border protection' and a 'war against people smuggling' were necessary pre-requisites for the maintenance of 'Australia's way of life' (Marr and Wilkinson 2003).

However, Prime Minister Howard's declaration during the Coalition's opening campaign rally that 'We will decide who comes to this country and the circumstances under which they come'[1] was more than hyperbolic justification for the full-scale military mobilisation he had ordered along Australia's northern maritime borders; it was confirmation that controlling human movement across Australia's borders is a central focus for national and regional security policy. This is not new in a country with a foreign policy historically based on fears of invasion from more heavily populated Asian states (Burke 2001) and which adhered to a White Australia Policy until 1972 (Jupp 2003). Nevertheless, the emphasis of government policy since 1992, when the federal Labour government formalised the mandatory detention of 'unlawful non-citizens',[2] increasingly has been on restricting the illicit means by which unauthorised migrants, particularly asylum seekers, have sought to enter the country.

Central to this has been the 'war' against 'smugglers' and 'traffickers' – terms used with little precision within Australia's mainstream and largely bi-partisan political discourse but which conjure up images of predatory and dangerous criminal gangs. In order to prosecute this war, there has been a substantial expansion of agencies such as the Australian Federal Police (AFP) into the Asia Pacific region as part of a more generalised war against transnational crime and terrorism. But while those who prosecute this war claim some success – the number of unauthorised arrivals in Australia fell from 4,137 people on 54 boats in 2000–01 to nil in 2004–05 (DIMIA 2005: 29) – the cost of the war on the lives and well-being of the illicit travellers it intercepts, encamps, detains, re-routes, returns and abandons remains high. This raises an important question regarding the wider role of the anti-smuggling and trafficking agenda in reaffirming the legitimacy of the Australian state. Put simply: Is the war on human smuggling and trafficking driven by domestic and geopolitical considerations, rather than any serious commitment to the human rights of asylum seekers and other unauthorised migrants?

In order to address this question, Australia's war against people smuggling and trafficking is critically examined in the context of three related themes: the construction of Western exclusion zones; the 'Pacific Solution'; and the implications of Australia's border policing practices for forced and unauthorised migrants.

The Western exclusion zone and transnational organised crime

In the developed world, state responses to unauthorised migration are neither uniform nor internally consistent. Nevertheless, since the mid 1970s, we have witnessed the emergence of three comparable zones of exclusion – the European Union (EU) ('Fortress Europe'), North America (especially along the US/Mexico border) and the area covered by Australia's 'Pacific Solution' (Green and Grewcock 2002). Each zone has its own local characteristics, but combined they reflect that controlling the physical and legal routes through which forced or unauthorised migrants can acquire some form of legitimacy is a dominant imperative of Western border policy.

Externalisation of border controls

The most fundamental feature of the exclusion zone is the externalisation of border controls through three levels of enforcement. Internally, it rests on measures such as the detention of 'unauthorised non-citizens'. At the border, exclusionary measures range from restrictive visas through to full-scale military mobilisations. Externally, it provides a virtual border – outposts of Western asylum and immigration services (including non-government organisations in their absence) that process visa applications in countries of transit or departure; carrier liability measures that engage organisations like airlines in immigration policing; the maintenance of camps and buffer zones; and multi-agency and multilateral efforts to prevent smuggling and trafficking, through measures such as interdiction and disruption.

In short, externalisation amounts to pre-emptive strikes against the entry of illicit workers into areas where there might be considerable demand for their services or against forced migrants and refugees into areas where they might gain access to the human rights machinery that was developed explicitly to protect them. These strikes have had a significant impact, particularly since the declaration of the war on terror. According to the United Nations High Commissioner for Refugees (UNHCR), asylum applications to the main Western states have dropped 40 per cent since 2001. Between 2003 and 2004, the number of asylum requests made to 50 industrialised countries fell by 22 per cent, from 508,100 to 396,400. In 2004, applications decreased by 19 per cent in the EU, by 26 per cent in North America; and 28 per cent in Australia and New Zealand (UNHCR 2005: 3).

Western governments have interpreted such reductions as a vindication of their efforts to police illegal immigration, but externalisation and the formation of Western exclusion zones reflect a fusion of migration and national security policy that enables state institutions to extend their coercive power and authority beyond their territorial borders, including through military invasions,[3] and to employ enforcement methods that elevate migration control over human rights. This consolidates illicit routes of entry and feeds a cycle of further border policing measures. The extent to which this occurs varies according to immediate political circumstances. However, a constant theme used to legitimise the exclusion zone is the need to declare war against human smuggling and trafficking.

Offensives

This so-called war is one of a number of multi-agency policing offensives conducted by the most powerful states against transnational organised crime. In this context, smuggling/trafficking is threatening by definition – it is illegal, clandestine, well organised, beyond official scrutiny and control. It has a shadowy and dangerous character; the capacity to threaten national security, social integration and racial harmony;[4] and while the moral scruples of human smugglers and traffickers may be questionable, the deviance attributed to their activities as illicit migration agents is made more threatening by an unlikely association between illegal migration and terrorism.

Australia has been at the forefront of the anti-smuggling and trafficking offensive, but the notion of a war against organised crime was first popularised in the US during the period of prohibition in the 1920s. During the 1970s and 1980s, it re-emerged in the form of the 'war against drugs' prosecuted by the US and various European governments (Bewley-Taylor 1999; Green 1998). The invocation of a policing war, along with pseudo military titles, such as Operation Desert Safeguard[5] or Operation Relex,[6] for its conduct, adds a sense of legitimacy to the mobilisation of the state's military forces; the militarisation of policing; the acquisition of exceptional extra-judicial powers; the use of invasive and punitive methods of surveillance and control; and the engagement of a range of agencies (for example, government welfare agencies) with no formal policing role.

The broad symmetry between the responses of the US government to Haitian refugees (Dow 1994; McBride 1999; Taft-Morales 2005); the Australian government against 'boat people' from Asia and the Middle East; and the maritime patrols conducted by various EU states since 2002 (Hayes 2003; Statewatch 2005a) demonstrates that at global level, this war has normalised the militarisation of border policing and the routine exercise of the state's most coercive powers. Coastguard, navy and other military forces now regularly board vessels, sometimes in international waters, with a view to removing them to their state of origin or to a 'safe' third country.

Such policing methods place those seeking entry at considerable personal risk. In October 2001, the Australian Navy towed the dangerously leaking boat at the centre of the 'Children Overboard' controversy[7] away from Australian territorial waters for 22 hours. Almost an hour after it began to sink and barely minutes before it finally went under, the boat's 223 passengers were finally taken on board the Australian Navy vessel (Kevin 2004: 115–24; Marr and Wilkinson 2003: 187–93; Senate Select Committee 2002). By contrast, there are serious concerns that insufficient resources and attention are paid to rescuing those in distress. This is central to the controversy surrounding the sinking of the SIEV X during the course of Australia's Operation Relex in October 2001 (discussed further below) and the drowning of 21 people travelling in boats intercepted by Spanish naval patrols as part of Operation Ulysses in June 2003 (Fekete 2003; Hayes 2003).

This collateral damage is not incidental – the human cost of Western border restrictions, and a tangible measure of state crime,[8] can be inferred from the fatal risks taken by those attempting to enter the West by illicit means. Although there are no absolutely reliable statistics, illicit border crossings are routinely lethal, with indications that record numbers of people are dying attempting to enter North America, the EU and Australia.[9] Some deaths arise from direct confrontations between unauthorised migrants and state authorities.[10] More typically though, border deaths arise from the means of travel adopted to evade border controls, a fact used by disingenuous Western governments to justify their anti-smuggling and trafficking war as an exercise in protecting the safety of illicit migrants.

UN Convention and Protocols

At an international level, this war derives much of its legitimacy from – and helped shape – the 2000 UN Convention Against Transnational Organised Crime and its associated Protocols against human smuggling and trafficking.[11] As a normative exercise, these instruments invest a high level of organised criminality in the smuggler/trafficker by aiming to facilitate transnational enforcement measures through the uniform criminalisation of activities related to organised breaches of border controls. Article 5 of the Convention requires signatory states to criminalise participation in an organised criminal group and invokes wide-ranging state powers designed to target various forms of criminal association and organisation. The targets can be relatively modest, given the very broad definition of an organised criminal group as 'a structured group of three or more persons, existing for a period of time and acting in concert with the aim of committing one or more serious crimes or offences' (Article 2) and the considerable variation in the types of organisation engaged in activities such as human smuggling and trafficking (Schloenhardt 1999).

The Convention's emphasis on group activity is consistent with the enforcement paradigm developed by the dominant states and some non-governmental organisations (NGOs) throughout the 1990s. For example, in 1994, the International Organisation for Migration (IOM) proposed that in order to identify and understand human trafficking, emphasis should be placed 'on the nature of the trafficking organisation per se' (Salt and Hogarth 2000). Similarly, the Budapest Group[12] urged attention to the steps involved in 'breaching the border' and such 'key elements of the smuggling enterprise' as 'recruitment', 'transportation', 'corrupted officials', 'guides', 'support services', 'debt collection' and 'management' (Budapest Group 1999: 33–35). Within such a perspective, organised crime is broken down into individual, constituent, criminal parts, each of which can be the target of a law enforcement process. This highlights the multiplicity of the criminality and helps sustain an acceptance of smugglers and traffickers as a threat; the separation of smuggling and trafficking from its operational context; the primary attribution of blame for illicit migration to the agent; and, in some circumstances, where an emphasis is placed on the ethnicity of organisations such as the Mafia or Chinese Triads, suspicion being cast on whole communities. Fundamentally, such a paradigm denies the complex and shifting motivations of those who organise illicit movement, redefining all their actions as a form of criminality.

This process is refined further by the mechanical distinctions made between smuggling and trafficking.[13] According to the Smuggling Protocol, smuggling of migrants means 'the procurement, in order to obtain, directly or indirectly, a financial or other material benefit, of the illegal entry of a person into a State Party of which the person is not a national or permanent resident' (Article 3(a)). This definition of smuggling assumes the smuggled person exercises a degree of free will and in practice, is applied mainly to refugees and migrant workers. The Trafficking Protocol also covers illicit workers but emphasises the coercive and exploitative nature of the trafficking arrangement (Article 3(a)). This does give overdue acknowledgement to contemporary forms of slavery that many forced migrants must endure (Bales 2004) and the extensive human rights abuses, particularly in relation to women and children, that arise from physical and sexual violence and lack of consent (Bales 2004: 19–20; Seabrook 2001). However, while Western states have been willing to embrace the language of human rights and to some degree rely upon the promotion of the Trafficking Protocol by prominent NGOs,[14] these instruments primarily legitimise more border controls.

This is most apparent with the Trafficking Protocol, which requires signatories to facilitate and accept the return of their trafficked nationals and permanent residents with due regard to their safety (Article 8 (1)); exchange information aimed at identifying perpetrators or victims of trafficking, as well as the methods and means employed by traffickers (Article 10); and strengthen border controls as necessary to prevent and detect trafficking (Article 11 (1)). In contrast to these compulsory measures, the Trafficking Protocol includes some optional measures that have the stated aim of protecting victims of trafficking. However, these do not go beyond 'consideration of adopting legislative or other measures permitting victims of trafficking to remain in their territories temporarily or permanently in appropriate cases with consideration being given to humanitarian and compassionate factors' (Article 7). Unsurprisingly, signatory states have been reluctant to entertain a permanent migration outcome for victims of trafficking. To the extent that temporary or renewable stays become available, they are currently dependent on the migrant co-operating with criminal justice agencies, in circumstances where relatives and close associates may be exposed to reprisals.[15]

Hierarchy of legitimacy and human rights

In this context, the measures to police trafficking allow for a cynical manipulation of human rights rhetoric that does little to break the migrant from the cycle of illegality constructed by border controls and the utilisation of illicit means of entry. And while it is important to understand the multiple dynamics and different forms of forced migration, framing these within the legal distinction between trafficking and smuggling creates a hierarchy of legitimacy, with those migrants who voluntarily engage in arrangements to subvert border controls portrayed as the least deserving and most deviant (Green and Grewcock 2003; Lee 2005). This not only denies the complexity of forced migration, but particularly in the case of asylum seekers, also helps legitimise their detention, expulsion or return.[16] The removal of asylum seekers from the orbit of the trafficking discourse also ignores or denies that refugees can be vulnerable through 'political, economic and social insecurity' (Koser 2001: 67) and that they might seek to enter a country via means that might allow them to maintain themselves – even in very exploitative circumstances – rather than risk detention, removal or attention being drawn to their whereabouts.

Further, conceptualising and constructing traffickers as a predominant source of illegal migration deflects attention from the fundamental role of the state in excluding migrants and forcing them to utilise illicit networks (Kelly 2002; Lee 2005; Marfleet 2006). In a global system where the means of communication and travel are increasingly available but where borders for humans are more formidable than for any other commodity, smugglers and traffickers, regardless of their motives, or involvement in other cross-border criminal activity,[17] increasingly fill a role as migration agents alongside a range of official and semi-official agencies (Koslowski 2001). The migrants they assist may be moving relatively willingly as participants in existing social networks disrupted by border controls or changes to asylum policy, or as 'pioneers' taking part in global forms of movement, opened in part by traffickers. Others may be the victims of deceit and intimidation from the outset, and subject to indefinite bondage and abuse at the point of destination. Whatever the degree of individual consent, the exploitation of the migrant ultimately is contingent upon the migrant's legal status and the availability of a market for the migrant's services, rather than just the motives and behaviour of the agent.

State offensives against illicit agents can also operate as a normalising instrument for Western foreign policy. Thus, pursuant to the US Department of State's 2005 Trafficking in Persons Report (USDS 2005), the US President determined that sanctions should be imposed on Burma, Cambodia, Cuba, the Democratic People's Republic of Korea and Venezuela (USDS 2005a). How little this has to do with protecting the human rights of trafficked persons is reflected by the President's determination on Saudi Arabia:

> The Government of Saudi Arabia does not fully comply with the Act's[18] minimum standards for the elimination of trafficking, and is not making adequate efforts to bring itself into compliance. The President has determined to waive all sanctions ... in the national interest of the US ... Over five billion dollars in foreign military sales to Saudi Arabia would have been restricted by sanctions under the Act. A full waiver has been granted in the national interest of providing these sales in order to advance the goals of the Global War on Terror. (USDS 2005a)

Unchallenged, this elision of the war against transnational crime into the war on terror legitimises and complements developed states making development aid and assistance to source or transit zone states conditional on their compliance with Western border policing priorities (Hayes 2003; Marfleet 2000).[19] This has been a central feature of the processes of enlargement in the EU, where policing trafficking is seen as a measure of state competence and suitability for membership of the Western club (Grewcock 2003; European Commission 2005), and is an important aspect of Australia's relations within the Asia pacific region, with respect to countries like Indonesia and Nauru.[20]

Overall, the trend amongst developed states is to merge anti-trafficking with enforcement focused discourses on security and development. For this dominant paradigm to be challenged, we must recognise the common dynamics in the criminalisation of smugglers and traffickers, rather than focus on legal differences devised to help police different types of illicit migration. This requires an alternative methodology that focuses on the ways in which criminalisation by the state is integral to legitimising criminal activity by the state. The immediate purpose of such a methodology is to delegitimise the artificial construct of war used to justify state-organised abuses of unauthorised migrants. The experience of Australia's 'Pacific Solution' illustrates the consequences of failing to do this.

Declaring 'war' in the Pacific

In late August 2001, the Captain of a Norwegian container vessel, the MV Tampa, answered a mayday call and rescued 433 Australia-bound Afghan asylum seekers aboard the unseaworthy KM Palapa 1. The Howard government ensured this simple act of humanitarianism transformed Australia's relatively dormant federal election contest (Brennan 2003; Marr and Wilkinson 2003), generating a national security panic shortly to be intensified by the events of 11 September.[21] The Tampa events, during which the Norwegian ship was boarded by the Australian SAS and its bewildered passengers removed to Nauru by the Australian Navy, gave rise to the Australian government's 'Pacific Solution', which remains a reference point for government policy towards unauthorised migrants in the Asia-Pacific region.

Leaving aside its manipulative use of the refugee issue for electoral purposes through the manufacture of a Tampa 'crisis',[22] the Australian government's position in 2001 was straightforward: unauthorised boat arrivals, regardless of whether they were asylum seekers with legitimate claims,[23] were to be prevented from entering the country. Those who managed to slip through the net would be detained in remote and inhospitable locations, while those undertaking or planning voyages to the potential haven of a Western state proclaiming adherence to the 1951 UN Convention on Refugees, would find themselves intercepted in international waters; returned to their point of embarkation or re-routed to detention facilities far beyond the jurisdiction of Australian courts; and ordered to join the largely fictitious queue that snakes out of the Government's preference for external processing.

The rationale for this position was that 'Australia's refugee determination procedures were leading to it being targeted by organised people smuggling operations' (Senate Select Committee 2002: xix).[24] Consequently, unauthorised migrants, no matter how vulnerable, found themselves subjected to the full force of the Australian state in order to facilitate a highly co-ordinated government-sponsored war against organised crime, popularised within the escalating parlance of 'border protection' and 'anti-terrorism'.[25] While 2001 represented something of a turning point, the Tampa events occurred at a time when an increasing number of policing measures against illicit migrants and their agents were already being implemented (Crock and Saul 2002; Mares 2001; McMaster 2002). They therefore galvanised, rather than generated, an Australian government response based upon the multi-faceted deviance of unauthorised arrivals. Four key elements of this response are considered here: excision; off-shore processing; greater inter-agency co-operation; and interception.

Excision

Excision of Australia's off-shore territories provided a surreal dimension to a discourse emphasising the primacy of physical borders. Under retrospective legislation,[26] nearly 5,000 islands, including important landfalls such as Christmas Island, Ashmore and Cartier Islands and the Cocos (Keeling) Islands, were simply removed from Australian territory for the purposes of the Migration Act (Coombs, 2005). Any person arriving at these places without a visa thus became an 'unlawful non-person'; unable to make a visa application; subject to mandatory detention; and liable to removal to a declared country such as Papua New Guinea or Nauru. The government argued excision was necessary because people smugglers were targeting islands close to the mainland. Removing Migration Act coverage was justified as a means of reducing incentives for people to make hazardous journeys to Australian territories and of making it harder for people smugglers to escape detection and arrest (Coombs 2005; Senate Legal and Constitutional References Committee 2002: 17–18).

Once migration excision had begun, it was only a matter of time before further excisions were announced, usually in response to further boat arrivals.[27] The arrival of 43 West Papuan refugees on Cape York in January 2006 triggered the inevitable endgame when, as part of its efforts to ease the diplomatic tensions with Indonesia arising from Australia's decision to grant temporary protection visas to 42 of the 43, the Australian government announced in April 2006 that 'all unauthorised boat arrivals will be transferred to offshore centres for assessment of their claims' (Vanstone 2006).[28] While the proposed legislation was ultimately withdrawn, it signalled that the government was willing to remove any avenue for asylum seekers or other unauthorised migrants arriving by boat to access Australia's domestic legal machinery. By focusing on the illicit nature of the travel, rather than the individual circumstances of the migrant, and prioritising its campaign against smuggling and secondary movement, the Australian government effectively declared that forced migrants should be corralled and processed entirely in the developing world. This seriously undermines the spirit of the 1951 UN Refugee Convention by removing any political obligation on Western states to provide an operative system of refugee protection.

Off-shore processing

Off-shore processing is officially justified by Australia's humanitarian entry programme.[29] Under this programme, a quota of 13,000 places is allocated annually,[30] mainly for the permanent re-settlement of refugees identified by the UNHCR or for people considered to be in special humanitarian need. Although this system is constantly upheld by the Australian government as an example of its generosity,[31] it also gives rise to the fictional refugee queue and allows asylum seekers to be kept at arms length by the Australian government, even if legally they are determined to be refugees. In 2001, the shift to off-shore processing was central to portraying boat arrivals as deviant and potentially dangerous. Not only were they represented as breaking the rules, but also as potential terrorist threats (Senate Select Committee 2002: 291–92). This instilled a sense of urgency in the government's bellicose response as it shopped around various Pacific states looking for suitable detention and processing sites (Senate Select Committee 2002: 293–95).

The subsequent agreements with the governments of Nauru and Papua New Guinea to host such sites and the decision of the Australian government to construct a purpose built centre on Christmas Island, off Australia's north-west coast, effectively created across thousands of kilometres of ocean an off-shore gulag, which the Australian government can open, shut or extend as it feels fit, and where the inhabitants are cut-off from independent scrutiny; timely and proper legal advice; the norms of Australia's judicial process; and nearly all meaningful social interaction with the outside world.[32] This aspect of the Pacific Solution has been embraced by other Western states. It parallels the use of Guantanamo Bay for Haitian refugees by the US government (McBride 1999: 4–8) and in 2003 prompted the Blair government to propose the EU establish 'processing centres, on transit routes to Europe' on sites including Albania, Croatia, Iran, Morocco, Romania, Russia, northern Somalia, Turkey and Ukraine (Statewatch 2003).

Major NGOs have responded in contradictory ways to such developments. The IOM, which has no protection mandate and seems indistinguishable from a government agency, managed the Nauru and Manus Island Centres, subcontracting security services to private contractors and working closely with Australian Protective Services[33] and local police. UNHCR, while critical of the government's policy, processed some of the applications on Nauru (Senate Select Committee 2002: 316–19).

Shortly after, as part of its Convention Plus proposals, UNHCR suggested the establishment of an 'EU-based mechanism as a step towards a common asylum system' that would 'target caseloads of asylum seekers that are composed primarily of economic migrants and ... reinforce returns of persons not in need of international protection' (UNHCR 2003). Elements of this mechanism would include: closed reception facilities located close to the external borders of the EU where asylum seekers would be required to reside for the duration of the procedure (not to exceed one month); the immediate transfer to these centres from EU member states of asylum seekers of designated nationality; the rapid determination of asylum claims by a consortium of national asylum officers and second-instance decision makers; the 'fair' distribution of persons found to be in need of international protection to the member states; and the rapid return of persons found not to be in need of international protection (UNHCR 2003 and 2004). Convention Plus was formulated as an attempt to fill protection gaps opened up by the exclusionist policies of various European states and has not been implemented. Despite this, and UNHCR's unwillingness to assist the Australian government with any blanket off-shore processing policy (Fitzpatrick 2006), UNHCR's association with some off-shore processing must still risk adding legitimacy to the push for external containment.

Inter-agency co-operation

Greater inter-agency co-operation was an essential pre-requisite for the conduct of the 'war' against people smugglers. At the height of the Tampa events, the government established a People Smuggling

Taskforce (PST), chaired by a senior public servant from the Department of the Prime Minister and Cabinet. This brought together the Australian Federal Police, the Australian Defence Force, Customs, Coastwatch and a number of other agencies and departments (Senate Select Committee 2002: 7–8). The lack of written records makes the PST's exact role and responsibilities somewhat opaque (Senate Select Committee 2002: 160–73) but it clearly 'provided advice on policy and operational issues' (Senate Select Committee 2002: 161). This centralisation of government decision-making raised important questions of accountability, reflected the rise in the role and influence of unelected ministerial staff and was a central theme in the investigation into the 'Children Overboard' affair (Senate Select Committee 2002: 173–94). Overall, the PST operated as a quasi war cabinet,[34] whose political role was to co-ordinate and centralise an agenda of border protection (terminology used little in public debate until this point) at the highest levels of government. Combating people smuggling was no longer to be left as a series of potentially fragmented administrative or political decisions or ad hoc policing operations – it was to be high profile, core state business without margin for inconsistency or ambiguity.

Interception

Interception provided the foundation for the Pacific Solution. From 3 September 2001, the Australian Defence Force (ADF) played a key role through Operation Relex, which aimed 'to conduct surveillance and response operations in order to deter unauthorised boat arrivals from entering Australian territorial waters' (Senate Select Committee 2002: 14). This involved a substantial deployment of 25 RAN vessels from its major fleet units and led to the interception of twelve 'Suspected Illegal Entry Vessels' (SIEVs). It was backed up by 'an extensive inter-agency intelligence capability' that included the Immigration Department; the Australian Federal Police; the Australian Customs Service and Coastwatch; the Defence Department; the Department of Foreign Affairs and Trade; the Australian Security and Intelligence Organisation (ASIO); the Office of National Assessments; and the Office of Strategic Crime Assessments (Senate Select Committee 2002: 19–30).

At the height of this mobilisation, ASIO and the Defence Signals Directorate illegally intercepted phone calls to and from the Tampa, which also had its satellite phone jammed to prevent the Flying Doctor Service providing medical assistance to the refugees on board. This isolation strategy was reinforced by a public affairs plan that gave the Minister for Defence 'absolute control over the facts which could and could not become public during the Operation' and ensured that 'no imagery that could conceivably garner sympathy' for the refugees could be published (Marr and Wilkinson 2003: 132–36; Senate Select Committee 2002: 24–25). Some of the refugees on board the Tampa later complained that the SAS videoed the filthy conditions that had developed after the SAS seized control of 'welfare' from the crew: 'They were filming us to show we are wild people, we are inhuman, we are not worth accepting into civilised society' (Marr and Wilkinson 2003: 103). Such an environment contributed both to the indefensible and untrue allegations that some of the refugees aboard the SIEV 4 threw their children overboard and the demonisation and criminalisation of those seeking protection from the Australian government. And, while there is evidence to suggest that some senior naval staff were sceptical about the nature of the operation (Marr and Wilkinson 2003: 129–41), the sight of the Australian navy turning round and towing boats away from Australian territorial waters played a substantial part in legitimising military involvement in border control and solidifying proactive, forward deterrence measures.

Operation Relex was the most visible element of the disruption strategy; the activities of the Australian Federal Police (AFP) and their Indonesian counterparts were less visible. Some light was shed on these by the AFP Commissioner, Mick Keelty, in his evidence before the Senate Inquiry (Senate Select Committee 2002: 1923–84). Keelty confirmed that since September 2000, the AFP was under a ministerial direction 'to give special emphasis to countering and otherwise investigat(e) organised people smuggling'. He also claimed that the AFP's efforts were 'successful in bringing people responsible for organised people smuggling before overseas and Australian courts' and that 'since February 2000, the Indonesian authorities ha(d) diverted over 3,000 people suspected of intending to enter Australia illegally into legitimate migration processes under the auspices of the United Nations conventions' (Senate Select Committee 2002: 1922–28).[35]

Keelty's defence of his organisation's work overlooked the fact that many of those diverted have found themselves stranded indefinitely in camps or informal settlements such as those on the Indonesian island of Lombok.[36] It also sidesteps serious allegations, denied by the AFP, regarding some of its disruption activities. These were conducted under the auspices of a protocol agreed between the AFP and the Indonesian National Police (INP) in September 2000 in accordance with a Memorandum of Understanding (MOU) signed in October 1995 to co-operate in the investigation of transnational organised crime. Under the Protocol, the INP established five Special Intelligence Units dedicated to people smuggling operations, with the AFP providing training in investigation and surveillance techniques (Senate Select Committee 2002: 10).

The undercover operations conducted by the AFP and INP included INP operatives, under AFP direction, tracking the on-shore movements of smugglers and attaching tracking devices to their boats before they set out for Australia (Marr and Wilkinson 2003: 41). There are also claims that the police were sabotaging, or encouraging the sabotage of smugglers' boats. While this is denied by the AFP, some of the agents recruited to assist with their operations seemed to have few moral scruples. One, Kevin Ennis, 'was paid "expenses" [by the AFP] to travel around West Timor buying information on passengers which the INP then used to arrest them on minor visa and passport charges' (Marr and Wilkinson 2003: 41–42). He 'also robbed asylum seekers by promoting himself as a people smuggler and taking their money which, according to the police, he then handed to the INP' (Marr and Wilkinson 2003: 42). At one stage, he boasted to Australian journalists 'that he and two confederates "had paid Indonesian locals on four occasions to scuttle people smuggling boats with passengers on them"... and that "he was unrepentant saying the boats were sunk close to land so everyone got off safely"' (Marr and Wilkinson 2003: 42).

The nature of the disruption activities and the secrecy surrounding them is clouded further by the sudden suspension of the Protocol by the Indonesian authorities in September 2001 for reasons that neither the AFP nor the Australian government has been willing or able to disclose (Senate Select Committee 2002: 10–12).[37] What is clear is that the disruption activities, combined with more aggressive policing, increased the risks for asylum seekers. As Marr and Wilkinson (2003: 43) put it:

As it became harder for smugglers to get their boats away, vessels were leaving port more heavily overloaded. As Australia denied family reunion to refugees, the boats began filling with women and children. To avoid being tracked by Australian signals interception, the smugglers were sending their boats to sea without radios. Once Indonesian sailors began risking long jail terms in Australia, the smugglers used more incompetent crews ... And there was also the possibility of sabotage to explain, how the engines of boats such as the Palapa failed far out to sea. (Marr and Wilkinson 2003: 43)

The sinking of the SIEV X,[38] with the loss of 353 lives, should be viewed in this context. The overloaded 19-metre vessel sank inside the Operation Relex patrol zone en route to Christmas Island on 19 October 2001. In the absence of any official rescue effort, a fishing boat picked up 44 survivors the following day. The Australian government claims that at the time nothing was known of the sinking and has never been willing to accept any responsibility for this tragedy. Instead, it has preferred to use it as an example to prospective asylum seekers of the risks associated with using smugglers (Senate Select Committee 2002: 195–290). The government also used the episode to pressure the Indonesian authorities to accept the return of illicit vessels and convene intergovernmental discussions on how best to combat people smuggling in the Asia-Pacific region (Kevin 2004: 3–7).

There are many unanswered questions about the SIEV X, especially regarding its link to the disruption programme (Kevin 2004). The alleged organiser of the smuggling enterprise, Abu Quassey, was not tried in Australia, where his contact with Australian agencies and the possibility that he acted as 'sting' agent[39] could be more easily examined; instead, he was extradited to Egypt where in a closed court he was convicted for homicide through negligence and for aiding illegal immigration.[40] However, most official debate about it remains framed by the war against smuggling and avoids more fundamental questions about the role of Australian government policy.

Overall, the four dimensions of that policy discussed above reflect consistent attempts by the Australian Government to establish the entry of unauthorised arrivals as a major domestic and regional policing issue and to legitimise the concept of forward deterrence. Accordingly, the war against people smuggling has played a central role in the considerable expansion of Australian state agencies into the Asia-Pacific region. Australia now boasts an Ambassador for People Smuggling Issues,[41] while on the basis of combating various aspects of transnational organised crime, the AFP has established posts in most South-East Asian countries; undertaken extended deployments in the Solomons and Papua New Guinea; overseen the establishment of the Indonesian Transnational Crime Coordination Centre; and extended its Law Enforcement Cooperation Programme (AFP 2005: 3–4).

At the diplomatic level, Australia plays a pivotal role in the Bali Process, which grew out of the Ministerial Conference, co-chaired by

Indonesia, in February 2002. Its participants include representatives from virtually all governments in the region as well as the IOM and UNHCR. Its stated purpose is to develop bilateral, regional and multilateral responses that emphasise regional co-operation in the fight against people smuggling, trafficking in persons and related transnational crime.[42] From the Australian governments' perspective the standardisation of legal procedures and enforcement methods to match or comply with those in Australia is clearly the priority, especially in matters such as the return of smuggled persons.

The closer ties between the AFP and its Indonesian counterparts also have wider foreign policy implications. In particular, they have facilitated the rebuilding of links between the Australian and Indonesian governments following the Australian-led intervention in East Timor in 1999. And while the assertion of Australian state authority in the region has not been without its difficulties – witness the successful constitutional challenge to the AFP's PNG mission in 2005 and the diplomatic wrangle between Australia and Indonesia over West Papuan asylum seekers in 2006 (AFP 2005: 60–62; Grattan 2006) – a framework for greater policing co-operation around an agenda that suits the Australian state, is now firmly in place.[43] Preventing illicit migration will remain a central part of this agenda for the foreseeable future, with ongoing repercussions for the human rights of unauthorised migrants.

Victims of the policing war

According to Foreign Minister Downer, the scale of the criminal enterprises responsible for illegal movement into Australia is so large that 'a serious response' is required to prevent smugglers and traffickers 'selling their false hope and abusing human rights'.[44] Such representations of border policing as a humanitarian exercise deny the levels of exclusion inflicted upon the migrant. For those trapped within this contradiction, the personal consequences are severe. In particular, prolonged detention and arbitrary removal operate as two poles of a state response that has little to do with human rights. This has not gone unchallenged – a range of bodies has criticised Australia's policies[45] but as the examples of the detention of children and the trafficking of women for sexual exploitation illustrate, even when the government has implemented changes it claims take human rights concerns further into account, these can be undermined by the expansion of measures to police illicit entry.

Children

In May 2004, the Report of the National Inquiry into Children in Immigration Detention was tabled in Australia's Federal Parliament. Conducted by the Human Rights and Equal Opportunities Commission (HREOC), the Report considered the detention as unauthorised arrivals of 2,184 children in mainland centres[46] during the period 1 July 1999 and 30 June 2003. After finding multiple breaches of the Convention on the Rights of the Child, the Inquiry recommended the release with their parents of all children in immigration detention centres and residential housing projects within four weeks; urgent amendments to Australia's immigration detention laws to ensure compliance with the Convention on the Rights of the Child; the appointment of an independent guardian for unaccompanied children; legislative codification of minimum standards of treatment for children in immigration detention; and a review of the impact on children of the 'Pacific Solution' (HREOC 2004: 2–3).

The Federal government immediately rejected the Inquiry's major findings and recommendations. On the day the Report was published, Immigration Minister Amanda Vanstone told reporters: 'What it says to people smugglers is if you bring children, you'll be able to be out in the community very quickly, and that is a recipe for people smugglers to in fact put more children on these very dangerous boats and try to bring them to Australia. We think that is a mistake and we won't be adopting that policy' (ABC Online 2004).

The Minister's focus on people smuggling was extraordinarily glib given the Report's catalogue of widespread institutionalised child abuse. In particular, the Report emphasised the 'connection between long-term detention and the declining psychological health of certain children' (HREOC 2004: 360). Some children were found to be suffering depression and post-traumatic stress disorder, either caused or aggravated by ongoing detention. Little attempt was made to shield children from acts of violence and self-harm. One child detained at Curtin told the Inquiry:

> My world has become like upside down, because I have never seen things like this, I see people who bury themselves alive one day. I wake up in the morning, I see people have buried themselves, I see people go on the tree and just jump down just like that and I see people who cut themselves, I see officers hit woman and children with batons, or use tear gas. I just, it's too much for me, I don't know why and sometimes I wonder you know, it is very stressful to me. (HREOC 2004: 406)

As well as oral testimony from various professionals and the children themselves, primary records confirmed that as a result of detention, children exhibited a range of problems including 'anxiety, distress, bed-wetting, suicidal ideation and self destructive behaviour including attempted and actual self-harm' (HREOC 2004: 359). One case study details the experience of a seven-year-old boy diagnosed with acute post traumatic stress disorder 'as a result of traumatic experiences … in Woomera and Villawood Detention Centres'. His 'life-threatening symptoms' included 'refusal to eat or drink, as well as becoming withdrawn and mute' (HREOC 2004: 347).[47] Internal documents disclosed the range of methods considered by 11 Afghan unaccompanied children to implement a suicide pact – 'throwing themselves into razor wire; drinking shampoo or other products they could obtain; slicing skin with razor blades; hanging themselves; banging rocks into their skulls' (HREOC 2004: 408). A snapshot of self-harm involving children detained at Woomera in January 2002 revealed seven cases of lip-sewing (two children sewed their lips twice); three cases of body slashing (one 14-year-old boy who sewed his lips twice also slashed 'Freedom' into his forearm); two cases of ingesting shampoo; one attempted hanging; two unspecified acts of self-harm; and 13 threats of self-harm (HREOC 2004: 408–9). A quoted report on Woomera by the South Australian Department of Human Services in August 2002 noted, 'Since January 2002 a total of 50 reports of self-harm have been raised on 22 children, ranging from 7 years to 17 years … 60 per cent of these reports related to children 12 years or less' (HREOC 2004: 410).

While most of the concerns regarding child detainees also apply to adults,[48] the HREOC Report helped ensure that the detention of children remained a focus within Parliament for those campaigning to change or overturn the government's mandatory detention policy. By July 2004, the Minister seemed to be retreating from her initial response when she announced that all but one child 'associated with illegal boat arrivals' had been released from detention (Banham 2004). However, including those still detained on Christmas Island and Nauru, 96 children remained in alternative detention while the legal regime so heavily criticised by HREOC remained entirely intact.[49] Amendments to that regime were eventually made in June 2005 when, in response to pressure from sections of its own back-bench, the government announced changes to the Migration Act[50] designed to ensure that children should only be detained as a measure of last resort and that all families with children in detention would be placed under community detention arrangements (Phillips and Lorimer 2005: 10). However, the amendments still did not create enforceable rights. The new accommodation conditions are entirely at the discretion of the Minister and remain a form of detention.

The government's determination to externalise the processing of asylum seekers now threatens to wind back even these modest changes. As noted above, in April 2006, the government announced its intention to transfer all unauthorised boat arrivals to off-shore detention centres, with a view to settling those who were subsequently determined to be refugees elsewhere. Despite the high likelihood that other governments would refuse to accept refugees who had initially landed in Australia, and the refusal of the PNG government to process West Papuan asylum seekers in PNG territory (Rheeney 2006), the Australian government arranged with the IOM and the government of Nauru to upgrade Nauru's detention facilities. However, a group of government MPs associated with the 2005 changes opposed the legislation and a government-controlled Senate Committee recommended 'the Bill should not proceed' (Senate Legal and Constitutional Legislation Committee 2006: ix). Faced with the prospect of the Senate rejecting the legislation, Prime Minister Howard withdrew it in August 2006 but indicated that further restrictions would be proposed.[51] If carried, the amendments would have reintroduced the detention of children much further away from independent scrutiny and support services than was the case when large numbers were detained in centres like Woomera. In such circumstances, there seems little reason to believe that the very damaging impact of detention on children highlighted by the HREOC Report would not continue, with the added protection for the government that its detainees are outside its jurisdiction.

Alvarez case

Similar issues arise in relation to those believed to have been trafficked into Australia. While their treatment has not featured prominently in Australia's border policing debate,[52] some insight into the Australian state's response was provided by the case of Australian citizen, Vivian Alvarez Solon, who was unlawfully detained under the Migration Act and removed to the Philippines in 2001. Following Vivian Alvarez's unlawful removal, which occurred just weeks before the Tampa events, three senior DIMIA (Department of Immigration and Multicultural Affairs) staff were made aware of what happened but failed to follow it up, with one of the three telling the subsequent Inquiry 'there was a lot worse things going on than this particular case' (Comrie 2005:

81). Vivian Alvarez remained stranded in the Philippines for over four years and was one of over 200 cases investigated in 2005 as a result of errors made by the Immigration Department.[53]

Vivian Alvarez was found seriously injured in a park late on 30 March 2001. Her injuries, combined with a history of mental illness, meant she was not interviewed by immigration officers until 3 May 2001, when she was wrongly assumed to be an 'unauthorised, undocumented arrival who might have been manipulated by certain people for sexual purposes' (Comrie 2005: 13). Vivian Alvarez was interviewed again following her discharge from hospital on 12 July 2001. During the course of the interview, the record of which she was unable to sign, Vivian told the officers she was an Australian citizen and that she wanted to remain in Australia. Although it should have been possible, DIMIA officers could not find a record of her under the name of Vivian Alvarez and failed to properly pursue the information she gave them. She was detained and placed under guard at a motel where she had little privacy and no access to medical facilities, despite one of the guards logging her condition as 'basically immobile/she requires assistance for walking, dressing and all basic hygiene needs' (Comrie 2005: 15).

On 16 July 2001, on the basis of no obvious evidence other than her presumed nationality, an undated, unauthorised note was placed on her file: 'Smuggled into Australia as a sex slave. Wants to return to the Philippines. Has been physically abused' (Comrie 2005: 15). On 19 July 2001, a locum doctor, with no access to her medical records, declared Vivian fit to travel. She was removed from the country the following day accompanied by a Queensland Police officer. Despite concerns raised earlier by the Philippines Consulate General in Brisbane, no arrangements were made for Vivian's care on arrival in Manilla and she was simply left at the airport. By chance, she was supported by a charity that cared for her until she was 'discovered' by Australian officials on 12 May 2005.

For the purposes of this discussion, the most significant feature of the Alvarez case was the minimal impact of the Criminal Code Amendment (Slavery and Sexual Servitude) Act 1999, which codified the offences of slavery and sexual servitude, but did not include a specific offence of people trafficking or any meaningful protection for potential witnesses. In practice, this meant that the Immigration Department routinely removed people found working illegally in the sex industry, regardless of whether those people were consenting to their working arrangements and notwithstanding any formal commitments the government had to protect further violations of the victims' human rights (Carrington and Hearn 2003: 6–10).[54] Clearly, the merest hint that Vivian Alvarez might have been trafficked was enough to have her immediately removed in the most negligent manner without any consideration of the impact this might have on her.

Legislative developments

Subsequent legislative and policy developments have neither removed the possibility of such a 'mistake' occurring again nor dissociated the victims of trafficking from the exclusionary realm of policing. Australia signed the UN Trafficking Protocol in December 2002 and ratified it in September 2005. In October 2003, the government announced a $20 million anti-trafficking package (Phillips 2004) that it consolidated in June 2004 in an Action Plan to Eradicate Trafficking in Persons targeting 'the four key areas of prevention, detection and investigation, criminal prosecution and victim support' (Commonwealth Attorney-General's Department 2004). While some attention to victim support suggests a shift in emphasis, and the Immigration Department now has a new protocol for the referral of potential trafficking victims to the police,[55] an indication of the Plan's focus is provided in the Criminal Code Amendment (Trafficking in Persons Offences) Act 2005. Under this legislation, the Attorney-General may issue a 30-day bridging visa to a suspected trafficking victim pending an initial investigation. A victim willing to assist the police might then be granted a Criminal Justice Stay Visa that includes the right to work for the duration of the criminal justice process. When that visa expires, a Witness Protection (Trafficking) Visa may be issued, allowing for temporary or permanent residence.

There are limited statistics[56] with which to measure the utility of these visas, but the insistence that they only be issued on the basis of compliance with the criminal investigation overlooks the consequences such co-operation might have for the victims or their close personal networks. In this regard, the support measures for victims are very much an optional extra, reflecting that conceptually, references to rights protection camouflage a more exclusionary impulse.[57] The changes at a domestic level also beg the question: What happens to those who are intercepted on their way to Australia? Presumably, they are turned around or detained en route outside Australia's jurisdiction. Given that a substantial portion of the AFP's resources in this area are devoted to regional policing measures and the Australian government is involved at a number of levels in trying to establish mechanisms for the prevention of illicit travel into Australia's contracting migration zone, it is difficult to see how Australia's policing of trafficked migrants is fundamentally different to its response to other types of unauthorised entry.

Conclusion

The emphasis on border or migration policy ebbs and flows within mainstream politics but has been a constant theme in the post-Cold War era. This period, during which the dominant Western states have declared wars on various transnational criminal threats, is characterised by an expanding and complex law and order discourse in which new and evolving forms of policing are promoted as necessary for the maintenance of domestic and international order. In an era of rendition and the indefinite incarceration of 'unlawful combatants', the predilection of states like Australia to maintain an externalised policing and detention infrastructure reflects not only their geopolitical influence but a capacity to remove their 'unwanted' from the minimal protections of international and domestic law.

Against this background, the main focus of this chapter has been the exclusionary impact of the 'war' against human smuggling and trafficking on those seeking illicit entry into Australia and how this experience highlights a fundamental disjuncture between border policing and human rights at a global level. This disjuncture arises from a number of sources, not the least of which is the limited nature of many human rights instruments relating to unauthorised migrants, but principally it is a product of the primacy of border controls and the associated policing apparatus.

For those concerned with defending or promoting the rights of unauthorised migrants, especially NGOs directly engaged with proactive Western states, the main conceptual challenge rests in a rejection of the enforcement priorities of the dominant national and international policy makers and the construction of an alternate paradigm that, for example, seeks to develop a more broadly formulated rights-based framework for all forced migrants. Criminologists can play an important part in this process by critically analysing the role played by border controls in the criminalisation of unauthorised migrants and their agents, and challenging the wider security rationales employed by countries like Australia. Failure to do this will result in the perpetuation of a policing war that continues to produce illicit migrants, while systematically abusing their rights to free movement and protection.

Notes

1 The full text of Howard's speech appears at: www.australianpolitics.com/news/2001/01-10-28.shtml
2 See Migration Amendment Act 1992 and Migration Reform Act 1992.
3 For example, the Clinton administration used 'the threat of a mass exodus of refugees' as a principal justification for its military intervention in Haiti in 1994. See Newland (1995).
4 For an elaboration of this argument in relation to national identity within the EU, see Grewcock (2003).
5 Commenced in 2003 to police sections of the US/Mexico border.
6 Commenced in 2001 to police Australia's northern maritime border.
7 The controversy arises from the fact the government falsely accused some of the asylum seekers of throwing their children into the water in order to force the Navy to rescue them in Australian territorial waters.
8 I use the term state crime in the criminological sense of state-organised deviance involving the violation of human rights (Green and Ward 2004: 1–10). See also Green and Grewcock (2002); and Pickering (2005).
9 It is difficult to collate precise figures, partly because they are not published in any systematic or centralised form, but hundreds of people are known to die each year. The US Bureau of Customs has confirmed a record 464 immigrants died attempting to cross the US/Mexico border during the 2004–05 fiscal year (Reuters 2005). The figures for Europe are higher and more fragmented. The campaign group UNITED has documented over 6,300 deaths attributable to 'border militarisation, asylum laws, detention policies, deportations and carrier sanctions', including 3,358 drownings, between 1993 and 2004 (UNITED 2004 and 2005). On 19 October 2001, 353 people aboard the 'SIEV X' drowned in the Indian Ocean en route to Christmas Island in Australian territorial waters. See below.
10 On 29 September 2005, Moroccan police, effectively operating as an advance guard for the EU, shot dead 5 people and wounded approximately 50 more attempting to enter the Spanish enclave of Ceuta on the Moroccan coast. A further 135 were wounded on 3 October 2005 in a similar incident in the enclave of Melilla. In both cases, the Moroccan Police were working alongside the Spanish Guardia Civil and operating under a EU-funded programme to enforce border controls in the region (ECRE 2005; PICUM 2005; Statewatch 2005b).
11 Protocol Against the Smuggling of Migrants by Land, Sea and Air (the UN Smuggling Protocol); and the Protocol to Prevent, Suppress and Punish Trafficking in Persons, Especially Women and Children (the UN Trafficking Protocol).

12 For details of the 'Budapest Process', see: www.icmpd.org

13 For a history of how the distinction developed, see Salt and Hogarth (2000).

14 For example, UNICEF and Anti-Slavery International.

15 One important qualification to this argument is that Article 14(1) of the Council of Europe Convention on Action against Trafficking in Human Beings 2005 requires states to issue renewable residence permits to victims of trafficking if: (a) 'the competent authority considers that their stay is necessary owing to their personal situation'; and/or (b) 'the competent authority considers that their stay is necessary for the purpose of their co-operation with the competent authorities in investigation of criminal proceedings'. The European Commission proposed in September 2005 that all EU states ratify the Convention and its Protocols. For a summary of the European legislation, see Europol (2005). For a summary of the US legislation, see USDS (2005). For a discussion of the Australian legislation, see below.

16 This is despite Article 5 of the Smuggling Protocol prohibiting criminal prosecutions of migrants merely for the act of being smuggled.

17 The extent of the engagement with 'organised crime' varies considerably (Aronowitz 2003: 91), while the image of the ruthless trafficker does not stand up to scrutiny in all cases (Kleemans 2003: 102–04).

18 Trafficking Victims Protection Act (2000).

19 In somewhat opaque language, the European Commission has told EU institutions and member states they 'should intensify efforts to address the issue of human trafficking within the EU and in relations with third countries, for example, by building on efforts to support anti-trafficking initiatives through development co-operation' (European Commission 2005: 4).

20 Nauru received $26.5 million (Aus) aid money for 'hosting' an immigration detention centre in 2001 (Senate Select Committee 2002: xliii).

21 After September 11, the link between terrorism and refugees was made more explicit. On 13 September 2001, the Solicitor General told the Federal Court: 'Today, invasions don't have to be military ... They can be of diseases or unwanted migrants'... [the government must have power to protect Australia from the sort of people] ... 'who did what happened in New York yesterday' (quoted, Marr and Wilkinson, 2003: 145).

22 There is no logical reason why these events had to be seen as a crisis, but it is a measure of the government's success and of the narrow confines of mainstream political debate in Australia that the phrase 'Tampa crisis' has passed into everyday political lexicon. For example, it is routinely used throughout the 2002 Senate Select Committee Report.

23 In its public pronouncements, the government engaged in a sustained campaign to undermine the legitimacy of the refugees' claims through the routine use of terms such as 'queue-jumpers', 'illegals' and 'forum shoppers'.

24 A clear example of government attempts to shape perceptions of unauthorised migrants within the paradigm of organised crime came from Immigration Minister, Philip Ruddock: '... some argue that Australia's recent actions are an unfortunate precedent that dilutes the spirit and intent of the Refugees Convention. The question can be asked another way: did the founders of the Convention envisage that it would become the enabling tool of organised crime' (Ruddock 2001).

25 Negative and racist media representations of asylum seekers, particularly Muslims, during this period are discussed in Lygo (2004); Pickering (2005); and Poynting et al (2004).

26 The excision legislation formed part of a bundle of bills passed on 26 September 2001: Migration Amendment (Excision from Migration Zone) Act 2001; Migration Amendment (Excision from Migration Zone) (Consequential Provisions) Act 2001; Migration Legislation Amendment (Judicial Review) Act 2001; Migration Legislation Amendment Act (No.1) 2001; Migration Legislation Amendment Act (No.6) 2001; and Border Protection (Validation and Enforcement Powers) Act 2001. See also Marr and Wilkinson (2003: 151–57).

27 Under the 2001 legislation, this could be done by regulation. For a chronology of the changes from 2001 to 2005, see Coombs (2005).

28 See Migration Amendment (Designated Unauthorised Arrivals) Bill 2006.

29 A basic outline of the programme can be found in DIMIA Fact Sheets 60 and 65, via the Department's website: www.immi.gov.au/refugee/index. htm

30 The quota was 12,000 in 2001.

31 See, for example, the website of Immigration Minister Amanda Vanstone at: www.minister.immi.gov.au/humanitarian/index.htm

32 For example, in order to gain access to detainees on Nauru, applications must be made to the government of Nauru, which has routinely refused such visa applications.

33 The APS, which is now an operating division of the Australian Federal Police, provides security for property and persons on behalf of the Federal government.

34 Between 27 August and 9 November 2001, the Committee met at least 53 times, sometimes two or three times in a single day (Senate Select Committee 2002: 7).

35 There is a substantial disparity between the often highly publicised allegations of people smuggling and actual prosecutions. Out of approximately 1,000 allegations, there were 19 prosecutions and 17 convictions between June 2000 and June 2005 (DIMIA 2005: 95).

36 As of September 2005, 92 asylum seekers remained stranded on Lombok. Most had been towed back to Indonesia from Australia's Ashmore Reef in 2001 (A Just Australia Newsletter September 2005).

37 It was formally re-adopted with the renewal of the MOU in June 2002.

38 Suspected Illegal Entry Vessel (SIEV) X is the name given to this un-named vessel by Tony Kevin, a former Australian diplomat, who has campaigned for a full judicial inquiry into the incident. See Kevin (2004) and www.sievx.com/

39 This is the proposition argued forcefully in Kevin (2004).

40 For the curious tale of how Quassey ended up in Egypt, see Kevin (2004: 201–13). In December 2003, Quassey was sentenced to five years' imprisonment for homicide and two years for aiding. The latter sentence was later reduced on appeal to three months. See: www.sievx.com/chronology/

41 See: www.dfat.gov.au/illegal_immigration/ambassador_role.html

42 See also the Bali process website: http://www.baliprocess.net/

43 At the enforcement level, co-operation has now extended to Australia renewing training and operational ties with Kopassus, the Indonesian Army Special Forces Unit, widely believed to have been responsible for orchestrating militia attacks in East Timor around the 1999 elections.

44 Alexander Downer, MP, Speech to the Bali Process Senior Officials' Meeting, 8 June 2004, at: www.foreignminister.gov.au/speeches/2004/040608_bali_process.html, accessed 29 March 2006.

45 See, for example, Amnesty International (2005); HREOC (1998) and (2004); United Nations High Commissioner for Human Rights (2002).

46 HREOC was denied access to children detained on Nauru and Manus Island as part of the Pacific Solution on the basis that it did not have 'extra-territorial' jurisdiction (HREOC 2004: 37).

47 The child, Shayan Badraie, was eventually awarded $400,000 in damages by the New South Wales Supreme Court.

48 As I write, allegations are surfacing of widespread sexual abuse in the Villawood and Baxter detention centres. See also Grewcock (2005).

49 Figures provided by the campaign group Chilout, based on information provided by the Minister for Immigration, the Federal Senate and Nauruwire. Using the same sources, Chilout estimated that on 29 September 2004, 87 children remained in immigration detention, 76 of whom were in locked facilities with guards. See: www.chilout.org

50 See Migration Amendment (Detention Arrangements) Act 2005.

51 On the day the legislation was withdrawn, the government indicated its intentions by announcing that eight people detained the previous day after being 'dumped by people smugglers' on Ashmore Reef would be the first people in four years transferred to Nauru.

52 For overviews of the literature, see Carrington and Hearn (2003) and Fergus (2005).

53 The trigger for this investigation was the detention of a mentally ill woman, Cornelia Rau, an Australian resident wrongly determined by DIMIA to be an unlawful non-citizen. The Rau Inquiry, chaired by former Australian Federal Police Commissioner, Mick Palmer, was established on 9 February 2005. On 2 May 2005, the Palmer Inquiry was

also asked to examine the circumstances surrounding the removal of Vivian Alvarez. Some provisional findings regarding Vivian Alvarez were incorporated into the Palmer Report, which was published in July 2005. Responsibility for completing the Alvarez investigation was then passed to the Commonwealth Ombudsman, who was investigating 201 cases of detainees later found to be lawful. In June 2006, it was announced that a further 26 Australian citizens had been illegally detained. See also Grewcock (2005).

54 A further example of this is the case of Puongtong Simaplee, who died from heroin withdrawal at Villawood Detention Centre on 26 September 2001. A Thai national, she had been picked up in a raid on a brothel and was detained pending imminent removal. She received little medical treatment in Villawood and weighed only 38 kilograms when she died. Her inquest was told she had been trafficked from Thailand into prostitution in Malaysia when she was 12, and later into Australia (Fergus 2005: 32).

55 See Migration Series Instruction (MSI) 391: 'People Trafficking'. My thanks to Jennifer Burn of the University of Technology, Sydney, for providing me with this.

56 See, for example, DIMIA (2005: 94).

57 For further discussion of the new visa system, see Burn *et al* (2006).

References

ABC Online (2004) 'Vanstone Critical of Human Rights Commission Report', 13 May 2004, see: www.abc.net.au/pm/content/2004/s1107800.htm, accessed 14 May 2004.

Amnesty International (2005) *The Impact of Indefinite Detention: The Case to Change Australia's Mandatory Detention Regime*, AI Index: ASA 12/001/2005.

Aronowitz, A. (2003) 'Trafficking in Human Beings: An International Perspective', in D. Siegel, H. van de Bunt and D. Zaitch (eds) *Global Organized Crime: Trends and Developments*. Dordrecht: Kluwer Academic Publishers.

Australian Federal Police (AFP) (2005) *2004–2005 Annual Report*. Canberra: AFP.

Bales, K. (2004) *Disposable People: New Slavery in the Global Economy*, revised edition. Berkeley: University of California Press.

Banham, C. (2004) 'Detained Children Freed in Policy Flip', *Sydney Morning Herald*, 6 July 2004.

Bewley-Taylor, D. (1999) *The United States and International Drug Control, 1909–1997*. London: Pinter.

Brennan, F. (2003) *Tampering with Asylum*. St Lucia: University of Queensland Press.

Budapest Group (1999) *The Relationship Between Organised Crime and Trafficking in Aliens.* Vienna: International Centre for Migration Policy Development.

Burke, A. (2001) *In Fear of Security: Australia's Invasion Anxiety.* Sydney: Pluto Press Australia.

Burn, J., Simmons, F. and Costello, G. (2006) *Australian NGO Shadow Report on Trafficked Women in Australia.* New York: UNANIMA International.

Carrington, K. and Hearn, J. (2003) 'Trafficking and the Sex Industry: From Impunity to Protection', *Current Issues Brief*, No. 28, 2002–2003. Canberra: Department of the Parliamentary Library.

Commonwealth Attorney-General's Department (2004) *Australian Government's Action Plan to Eradicate Trafficking in Persons.* Canberra: Commonwealth Attorney-General's Department.

Comrie, N. (2005) *Inquiry into the Circumstances of the Vivian Alvarez Matter*, Report No. 3/2005. Canberra: Commonwealth Ombudsman.

Coombs, M. (2005) 'Excising Australia: Are we really shrinking?', *Parliamentary Library Research Note*, No. 5, 31 August 2005. Canberra: Department of Parliamentary Services.

Crock, M. and Saul, B. (2002) *Future Seekers: Refugees and the Law in Australia.* Sydney: The Federation Press.

Department of Immigration, Multiculturalism and Indigenous Affairs (DIMIA) (2005) *Annual Report 2004–2005.* Canberra: DIMIA.

Dow, M. (1994) 'A Refugee Policy to Support Haiti's Killers', *New Politics*, 5: 1 (new series).

European Commission (2005) 'Fighting Trafficking in Human Beings – An Integrated Approach and Proposals for an Action Plan', *Communication from the Commission to the European Parliament and the Council*, COM (2005), 18 October 2005, 514 final. Brussels: European Commission.

European Council on Refugees and Exiles (ECRE) (2005) 'Melilla Tragedy Underlines Need for Respect for Fundamental Rights within Comprehensive Approach to Asylum System', *Statement to Justice and Home Affairs Council*, 12–13 October 2005, see: www.ecre.org/positions/Melilla.pdf, accessed 1 March 2006.

Europol (2005) *Legislation on Trafficking in Human Beings and Illegal Immigrant Smuggling.* The Hague: Europol.

Fekete, L. (2003) *Canary Islands Tragedy: Did the RAF put Border Security before Human Safety?* London: Institute of Race Relations.

Fergus, L. (2005) 'Trafficking in Women for Sexual Exploitation' *Briefing*, No. 5. Melbourne: Australian Centre for the Study of Sexual Assault.

Fitzpatrick, S. (2006) 'UN "Concerns" over Asylum Policy', *The Australian*, 19 April 2006.

Grattan, M. (2006) 'Can Howard find Refuge?' *The Age*, 14 May 2006.

Green, P. (1998) *Drugs, Trafficking and Criminal Policy: The Scapegoat Strategy.* Winchester: Waterside Press.

Green, P. and Grewcock, M. (2002) 'The War Against Illegal Immigration', *Current Issues in Criminal Justice*, 14 (1): 87–101.

Green, P. and Ward, T. (2004) *State Crime: Governments, Violence and Corruption*. London: Pluto Press.

Grewcock, M. (2003) 'Irregular Migration, Identity and the State – the Challenge for Criminology', *Current Issues in Criminal Justice*, 15 (2): 114–35.

Grewcock, M. (2005) 'Slipping Through the Net? Some Thoughts on the Cornelia Rau and Vivian Alvarez Inquiry', *Current Issues in Criminal Justice*, 17 (2): 284–90.

Hayes, B. (2003) *Cover Up! Proposed Regulation on European Border Guard Hides Unaccountable, Operational Bodies*. London: Statewatch.

Human Rights and Equal Opportunities Commission (HREOC) (1998) *Those Who've Come Across the Seas: Detention of Unauthorised Arrival*. Sydney: HREOC.

HREOC (2004) *A Last Resort? National Inquiry into Children in Immigration Detention*. Sydney: HREOC.

Jupp, J. (2003) *From White Australia to Woomera: The Story of Australian Immigration*. Cambridge: Cambridge University Press.

Kelly, L. (2002) *Journeys of Jeopardy: A Review of Research on Trafficking in Women and Children in Europe*, IOM Migration Research Series, No. 11. Geneva: IOM.

Kevin, T. (2004) *A Certain Maritime Incident: The Sinking of the SIEV X*. Melbourne: Scribe Publications.

Kleemans, E. (2003) 'The Social Organisation of Human Trafficking', in D. Siegel, H. van de Bunt and D. Zaitch (eds) *Global Organized Crime: Trends and Developments*. Dordrecht: Kluwer Academic Publishers.

Koser, K. (2001) 'The Smuggling of Asylum Seekers into Western Europe: Contradictions, Conundrums and Dilemmas', in D. Kyle and R. Koslowski (eds) *Global Human Smuggling: Comparative Perspectives*. London: The Johns Hopkins University Press.

Koslowski, R. (2001) 'Economic Globalization, Human Smuggling and Global Governance', in D. Kyle and R. Koslowski (eds) *Global Human Smuggling: Comparative Perspectives*. London: The Johns Hopkins University Press.

Lee, M. (2005) 'Human Trade and the Criminalization of Irregular migration', *International Journal of the Sociology of Law*, 33: 1–15.

Lygo, I. (2004) *News Overboard: The Tabloid Media, Race Politics and Islam*. Geelong: Southerly Change Media.

Mares, P. (2001) *Borderline: Australia's Treatment of Refugees and Asylum Seekers*. Sydney: UNSW Press.

Marfleet, P. (2000) 'A New Orientalism: Europe Confronts the Middle East', in T. Ismael (ed.) *The International Relations of the Middle East in the 21st Century*. Aldershot: Ashgate Publishers.

Marfleet, P. (2006) *Refugees in a Global Era*. Basingstoke: Palgrave Macmillan.

Marr, D. and Wilkinson, M. (2003) *Dark Victory*. Sydney: Allen and Unwin.

McBride, M. (1999) 'The Evolution of US Immigration and Refugee Policy: Public Opinion, Domestic Politics and UNHCR', *New Issues in Refugee Research*, Working Paper, No. 3. Geneva: UNHCR.

McMaster, D. (2002) *Asylum Seekers: Australia's Response to Refugees*. Melbourne: Melbourne University Press.

Newland, K. (1995) 'Impact of U.S. Refugee Policies on U.S. Foreign Policy: A Case of the Tail Wagging the Dog?', in M. Teitelbaum and M. Weiner (eds) *Threatened Peoples, Threatened Borders: World Migration and US Policy*. New York: The American Assembly.

Phillips, J. (2004) 'People Trafficking: Australia's Response', *Research Note*, No. 20, 2004–2005. Canberra: Department of Parliamentary Services.

Phillips, J. and Lorimer, C. (2005) 'Children in Detention', *Parliamentary Library E-Brief*, 13 October 2005; updated 23 November 2005, see: www. aph.gov.au/library/intguide/SP/Childrendetention.htm, accessed 13 June 2006.

Pickering, S. (2005) *Refugees and State Crime*. Sydney: The Federation Press.

Platform for International Cooperation on Undocumented Migrants (PICUM) (2005) 'Death at the Border', *PICUM Newsletter*, October 2005, see: www. picum.org/, accessed 2 November 2005.

Poynting, S., Noble, G., Tabar, P. and Collins, J. (2004) *Bin Laden in the Suburbs: Criminalising the Arab Other*. Sydney: Institute of Criminology and Federation Press.

Reuters (2005) 'US says Migrant Deaths at Record on Mexico border', *Reuters AlertNet*, 3 October 2005, see: www.alertnet.org/thenews/newsdesk/ N03594921.htm, accessed 4 October 2005.

Rheeney, A. (2006) 'PNG: Somare Says No to Australia Over Asylum Seekers', *Pacific Magazine*, 19 June 2006.

Ruddock, P. (2001) 'Australian Government Position on the MV Tampa refugees', *On Line Opinion*, 15 October 2001, see: www.onlineopinion.com. au, accessed 12 April 2006.

Salt, J. and Hogarth, J. (2000) Migrant Trafficking and Human Smuggling in Europe: A Review of Evidence. Geneva: IOM/UN.

Schloenhardt, A. (1999) 'Organised Crime and the Business of Migrant Trafficking: an Economic Analysis', *AIC Occasional Seminar*. Canberra: Australian Institute of Criminology.

Seabrook, J. (2001) *Children of Other Worlds: Exploitation in the Global Market*. London: Pluto Press.

Senate Legal and Constitutional Legislation Committee (2006) *Provisions of the Migration Amendment (Designated Unauthorised Arrivals) Bill 2006*. Canberra: The Senate.

Senate Legal and Constitutional References Committee (2002) *Migration Zone Excision: An examination of the Migration Legislation Amendment (Further Border Protection Measures) Bill 2002*. Canberra: The Senate.

Senate Select Committee (2002) *Report of the Senate Select Committee on a Certain Maritime Incident*. Canberra: The Senate.

Statewatch (2003) 'UK Asylum Plan for "Safe Havens": full text of proposal and reactions', *Statewatch News Online*, April 2003, see: www.statewatch. org/news/2003/apr/10safe.htm, accessed 14 June 2006.

Statewatch (2005a) 'G5 Meeting in Evian, 4–5 July, Operational Conclusions', *Statewatch News Online*, July 2005, see: www.statewatch.org/news/2005/jul/03eu-g5-meeting.htm, accessed 14 June 2006.

Statewatch (2005b) 'Spain/Morocco: Migrants Shot Dead at Border Fence, Spain Deploys Army', *Statewatch News Online*, October 2005, see: www.statewatch.org/news/2005/oct/01spain-morocco.htm., accessed 2 November 2005.

Taft-Morales, S. (2005) 'Haiti: Developments and US Policy Since 1991 and Current Congressional Concerns', *Report for Congress, Congressional Research Service*. Washington DC: The Library of Congress.

UNITED (2004) *List of 5017 Documented Refugee Deaths through Fortress Europe*, 16 June 2004. Amsterdam: UNITED.

UNITED (2005) 'The Deadly Consequences of Fortress Europe', *Information Leaflet*, No. 24. Amsterdam: UNITED.

United Nations High Commissioner for Human Rights (2002) *Human Rights and Immigration Detention in Australia*, Report of Justice, P.N. Bhagwati, Regional Advisor for Asia and the Pacific of the United Nations High Commissioner for Human Rights. Geneva: UNHCHR.

United Nations High Commissioner for Refugees (UNHCR) (2003) *Summary of UNHCR Proposals to Complement National Asylum Systems through new Multilateral Approaches*. Geneva: UNHCR.

UNHCR (2004) 'Europe's Next Challenge', *Refugees*, 2 (135): 4–13.

UNHCR (2005) *Asylum Levels and Trends in Industrialized Countries, 2004*. Geneva: UNHCR.

United States Department of State (USDS) (2005a) *Trafficking in Persons Report 2005*. Washington DC: USDS.

USDS (2005b) 'Presidential Determination with Respect to Foreign Governments' Efforts Regarding Trafficking in Persons', *Presidential Determination No. 2005–37*. Washington DC: USDS.

Vanstone, A. (2006) 'Strengthened Border Control Measures for Unauthorised Boat Arrivals', *Media Release*, 13 April 2006. Canberra: DIMA.

Chapter 10

The rights of strangers: Policies, theories, philosophies

Barbara Hudson

Introduction: The regulation of migration

The stranger enters our territory, claims our attention, disturbs our sense of the world and of ourselves; he is

> ... making me into the object of action of which he is the subject: all this, as we remember, is a notorious mark of the *enemy*. Yet unlike other, 'straightforward' enemies, he is not kept at a secure distance, nor on the other side of the battleline. Worse still, he claims a right to be an object of *responsibility* – the well-known attribute of the *friend*. If we press on him the friend/enemy opposition he would ... [give no answer] He is a constant threat to the world's order. (Bauman 1991: 59)

This chapter is concerned with the rights of 'strangers' in our midst; that is, the rights of non-citizens. It addresses questions of what are their rights as defined by various laws and policies; what dilemmas are raised by the allocation of rights to non-citizens as well as to citizens, and also raises questions of what ideas are being put forward by political and legal theorists, and what, if any, philosophical grounds these ideas draw upon.

Laws and policies

In discussing laws and policies, the focus will be on the various categories of *irregular immigrants* created by the classification systems in current use. When we turn to arguments, theories and philosophies for the extension of rights among non-citizens, however, the distinctions between, for example, refugees and economic migrants, illegal and legal immigrants, potential citizens and temporary migrant workers, tend to disappear. It is for this reason that I prefer to use the word *strangers* in my title, as this is a word that does not depend on these (often unsustainable empirically as well as vanishing in the literature) differentiating terms. 'Stranger' denotes a person who arrives unasked and who awaits classification; the stranger is the outsider, the non-member, and classification – does she need help, does she deserve help, does she pose a danger to the community, would she be a worthy member of the community – in our present societies is prior to the allocation of rights. Most governments want to know what sort of person they are dealing with before deciding on the extent to which the rights of citizenship can be extended, or whether only those rights which are due to all humans should be respected, or whether even these rights can/should be denied.

Discussion of law and policy will concentrate primarily on the UK and the European Union (EU). The focus will be on themes and trends rather than giving details of all relevant legislation and case law. Such detailed description would be beyond the scope of one chapter, and in any case legislation and policy innovation in this field is so fast-moving that it would almost certainly be out of date by the time the book appears in print. EU legislation and policy is underpinned by the Amsterdam Treaty of 1997, the main purpose of which was to amend the framework of the EU in order to strengthen institutions and to enable enlargement of the union. In the UK, 1997 saw the implementation of the 1996 Asylum and Immigration Act, and there has been a further Nationality, Immigration and Asylum Act in 2002; an Asylum and Immigration (Treatment of Claimants etc) Act 2004, and a further Immigration, Asylum and Nationality Act in 2006.

UK and EU legislation and policy are centred on giving effect to classifications of wanted and unwanted migrants. The categories constructed through attempts to manage migration in the interests of nation-states are the basis of inclusions and exclusions from national and EU territories, and are treated as though they are reflections of real differences in the motivations and circumstances of migrants. Empirically, however, the distinctions are much harder to maintain. The distinction between those fleeing wars or persecution and 'economic migrants' is less clear than legislation and policy suggest: most people move for a mix of reasons, and economic privation itself is often the result of bad governance, or of discrimination against particular ethnic or religious groups. Another distinction, that between trafficked and smuggled persons, is also less clear in empirical reality than in law and policy. The distinction is presumed to be that trafficked persons are coerced into travelling, but many smuggled persons find themselves in bonded labour situations when they arrive at their destination, having to endure dreadful work conditions and slave-like wages in order to repay the costs of their travel; trafficked persons may have travelled voluntarily, thinking they are coming to a desirable and legal job but then finding themselves as coerced sex-workers (Obotaka 2005).

In law and politics, these categories are used as though the distinctions they make are clear-cut, but this is empirically far from the case. It would be hard, for example, retrospectively to classify the 'founding fathers' of the USA. They were seeking to establish a democratic republic, they were seeking to follow their own religion, and they were also seeking to achieve prosperity in a new land. Yet contemporary governments attempt to impose classifications on the 'boat people' of today as though there were no difficulty in distinguishing economic migrants from refugees, coerced from voluntary migration.

The objective of classification, legislation and policy is to regulate immigration, to manage it so that the advantages of immigration can be gained for receiving countries and the perceived pressures (economic, social and political) of influxes of unpopular kinds of migrants can be avoided. This is made clear in the UK by the introduction to the 2006 Immigration, Asylum and Nationality Act which says that the legislation builds on two published policy documents which set out five-year strategies for the management of asylum and immigration: 'Controlling our Borders: Making Migration Work for Britain', published in February 2005, and 'Confident Communities in a Secure Britain', published in July 2004. Making migration work means attracting economically useful migrants: the UK list of desired immigrants includes doctors and dentists, people with capital to start businesses, and other 'highly skilled individuals'. This is summarised in a further Home Office publication in summer 2006, which promises a 'crackdown on illegal immigrants', whilst 'boosting Britain's economy by bringing the right skills here from around the world' (Statewatch 2006).

In the EU, there has been a 'race to the bottom', as the toughest policy has been generalised through the member states rather than the more generous. The Amsterdam Treaty is concerned to reconcile the fight against terrorism, drug trafficking and illegal immigration with the free movement of capital globally and the free movement of citizens of member states within the EU. Its objective is to create an area for 'freedom, security and justice', through co-operation on visas, asylum, immigration, and related matters. Co-operation has been mainly 'negative integration' of processes, for example that asylum applications cannot be heard in more than one country, rather than 'positive integration', such as policies for improving access to benefits and assistance, enhancing rights of appeal, and encouraging better relationships with receiving communities (Peers 2000). As Peers argues, the legal integration that has been implemented not only fails to prevent a race to the bottom, but encourages or compels member states to engage in this race.

External dimension

Not only have the nation-states of Europe engaged in this race to the bottom in their dealings with migrants, they have exported this to other countries through the 'external dimenson' of EU asylum and immigration policies. The Hague Programme 'Strengthening Freedom, Security and Justice in the European Union', adopted in November 2004, re-affirms that while all member states must guarantee protection in accordance with the Geneva Convention on Refugees and other international human rights treaties and conventions, economic migration remains the competence of member states, and does not go further than repeating calls for co-operation in sharing information and in enforcement processes. What is new, however, is the importance given to persuading third countries to take responsibility for managing migration flows.

Recent developments in the 'external dimension' amount, it could be argued, to 'externalisation' of the management of migration (Rodier 2006). EU officials are working in ports and airports in third countries, processing asylum and immigration applications; joint sea patrols between EU countries and Libya attempt to prevent arrivals of migrants from the southern shores of the Mediterranean into the prosperous north; in Morocco, joint Spanish-Moroccan patrols attempt to stem migration through the Spanish coastline. The Spanish enclaves of Ceuta and Melilla in northern Morocco are surrounded by six-metre walls, and this increased protection and surveillance has considerably reduced the numbers of migrants, mostly from sub-Saharan Africa, entering Spain. The Seville European Council in 2002 called for the inclusion of a clause providing for co-operation in combating illegal immigration and for compulsory re-admission of illegal immigrants to be included in any future agreements, association or aid between third countries and the EU.

The EU, like other states of the prosperous north (a concept used in post-colonial literature which includes developed countries such as Australia, in the southern hemisphere (Hudson 2006)), has interpreted 'freedom, security and justice', as meaning the strengthening of external borders against those who would enter from the undeveloped, impoverished 'south'. Freedom, security and justice obtain only within the privileged north; in its dealings with the south, the north is concerned only with its own security and economic advantage. This is shown clearly by the EU external dimension (and similar policies of the USA in its dealings with migrants from central and south America, and of Australia in its dealing with migrants from Indonesia and the Philippines; see Grewcock, Chapter 9 in this volume). The regulation of migration, then, reflects the desire to reap the benefits of an inflow of skilled, young workers into the ageing populations of Western nations, but at the same time reflects the desire to keep out the 'human waste' created in all processes of modernisation, intensified and made more 'turbulent' in the present phase of globalisation (Bauman 2004; Castles and Miller 1993; Papastergiadis 2000).

According to the G8 Ministers of Justice and Interior, illegal migration is 'a source of hiring mercenaries, extremists, a channel for selling weapons, drugs and human trafficking' (Statewatch 2006). Migration has become criminalised in itself through these developments in categorisation and in legislation and policy; migrants are criminalised and demonised further through their depiction as drug dealers and worse (Melossi 2003; Young 2003). In 2006 Britain, it is believed that a large proportion of drug importation is carried out by Pakistanis, that the trade in smuggling of women for prostitution is dominated by East Europeans. In central Europe much crime is blamed on migrants from the former USSR and on Roma migrants; in Greece most crime is blamed on Albanians and Bulgarians; in Spain and Italy, North Africans are 'the usual suspects'. And of course the terrible events in New York, Madrid and London have demonised all non-white Muslims as terrorists, potential terrorists or promoters and supporters of terrorism.

Political-legal theory

Much of political-legal theory in regard to the rights of non-citizens focuses on the tension between the rights of individuals to protection and assistance, and the rights of nation-states to set their own conditions for entry. The discourses of universal human rights and self-determination for peoples and their communities are invoked on the two sides of the argument. A resolution that receives support from many authors is that citizenship should be based on residence rather than nationality. Other, more philosophically derived arguments and theories say that even an easing of citizenship access would not extend the protection of rights of those who do not wish to or who still could not become citizens, temporary migrant workers being a prominent example of this category. Going beyond this limitation towards affording rights to all categories of 'strangers' entails uncoupling the idea of rights from the idea of citizenship, and arguments for this uncoupling are examined. Such uncoupling – either completely or to an extent – is proposed by the emerging theory of *cosmopolitan justice* (Benhabib 2004; Moellendorf 2002).

The rights of irregular migrants

Almost every nation-state differentiates between citizens, residents and aliens in its allocation of rights. Citizens have rights to all the benefits of membership in the state: rights to residence, rights to welfare and income benefits, rights to health care and to education, as well as rights to democratic participation. Persons given the status of legal residents may be granted some or all of these rights, although there are usually some rights that are not afforded to residents who are not citizens (state pension rights, for example). Where there has been a widening or sharing of citizenship, as within the EU, citizens of other member states may enjoy most or all of the rights of citizens of the countries in which they reside, including the right to vote, but residents who are citizens of countries outside the EU will not enjoy these rights. Irregular or undocumented migrants enjoy none of the rights that states grant to their own citizens and legal residents. Irregular migrants enjoy only those rights which are recognised as fundamental and universal rights, applicable to all humans regardless of status. Even these rights, however, have to be interpreted, and the emphasis on security and exclusion in legislation and policy means that these rights are liable to be interpreted as narrowly as possible.

Human rights

The two fundamental and universal human rights are the right to life, and the right to protection from torture and from inhuman or degrading treatment. These fundamental human rights are contained in the UN Declaration of Rights, and are Articles 2 and 3 of the European Convention on Human Rights (ECHR). As first drafted, Article 2 in the ECHR said that: 'Everyone's life shall be protected by law. No one shall be deprived of his life intentionally save in the execution of a sentence of a court following his conviction for a crime for which this penalty is provided by law'. This does not go far in protecting failed asylum seekers or irregular immigrants from being returned to countries where they may be condemned to death. The Article is modified, however, by the Sixth Protocol of the ECHR which provides that 'No one shall be condemned to such penalty or executed'. This Protocol was incorporated into the Human Rights Act 1998 in the UK, and clearly provides much stronger protection.

These two Articles have no exceptions: they are applicable to failed asylum seekers, illegal immigrants, suspected terrorists and persons convicted of serious crimes. There are, however, some difficult issues of interpretation. In relation to Article 3, questions arise as to whether 'degrading and inhuman treatment' means only persecution, or only arises in the context of punishment, or whether withholding or unavailability of welfare or health provisions could amount to degrading or inhuman treatment (Blake and Husain 2003). Clearly if such circumstances were admitted as Article 3 issues, the consequences for immigration would be enormous since many if not most of today's migrants from disadvantaged countries could claim severe health and welfare deprivations.

Where removal of an irregular immigrant would expose her to substantial risk of persecution, it would seem that Article 3 would prevent such removal. As well as the range of 'degrading and inhuman treatment', however, another issue of interpretation is the source of the persecution or treatment. The Article has generally been taken to intend state persecution, torture or degrading punishment, but where cases involve persecution by non-state actors, arguments of applicability of the Article arise. In a series of judgments, a concept of 'sufficiency of protection' has emerged, which means that states have an obligation to intervene to protect their citizens against ill-treatment by non-state actors, and EU countries seeking to remove an irregular migrant have to investigate the effective protection likely to be afforded. Cases have considered the risk of ill-treatment to Roma asylum seekers, and other groups of migrants.[1]

This concept of sufficiency of protection was articulated in a 2001 case concerning whether a permit over-stayer and drug offender should not be deported because she faced a real risk of violence from her former partner. The issue was whether new legislation in her country of origin – Jamaica – provided an effective level of deterrence to make the likelihood of violence unrealistic.[2] Lord Justice Arden concluded that '... to be effective, measures for the purpose of Article 3 must be those which attain an adequate degree of efficiency in practice as well as exist in theory'.

Returning people to countries where they might be tortured is prohibited by Article 3 with no exceptions, but some countries (including the UK) try to satisfy the requirements by reaching agreements with states suspected of using torture. Lord Hoffman in 2001 ruled that whether a sufficient risk, such as to demand non-removal, exists is a question of evaluation and prediction based on evidence, and that the executive enjoys 'no constitutional prerogative' in assessing this.[3] This would seem to rule that it is unlawful for the executive to announce that an agreement has been reached and therefore the individual can be considered safe from torture: evidence of the use of torture is still relevant.

A very different approach to this question has been taken by the Canadian Supreme Court in the case of *Suresh*.[4] Suresh, a Sri Lankan, arrived in Canada and was recognised as a (Geneva) Convention Refugee in 1991. Convention Refugee status gives a series of rights, including the right of 'non-refoulement', non-return to a country where the person's life, physical integrity or freedom might be threatened. Suresh was subsequently judged to have obtained Convention status by 'wilful misrepresentation of the facts' and the Solicitor General and Minister for Immigration and Citizenship commenced deportation proceedings. In overturning the decision to deport, the Supreme Court confirmed that the protection against being returned to a country where there was a real risk of torture applied to everyone regardless of status, and expressed scepticism about the effectiveness of assurances and agreements, regarding them as impossible to monitor, and open to forms of evasion such as contracting out the torture to non-state actors, or claiming to be unable to control the behaviour of all state officials.

Article 13 of the ECHR requires that there must be effective remedies available to prevent expulsions in violation of Article 3. This would seem to prohibit arbitrary time limits and to demand review procedures (Blake and Husain 2003: 96). Much of recent UK immigration and asylum legislation has, however, been in the direction of trying to speed removals, and to reduce opportunities for appeal, both for failed asylum seekers and so-called illegal immigrants.

Detention and removal

Procedures for detention and removal of migrants are politically contentious, and as well as raising issues in relation to Article 13, they also are questionable under Article 5, which provides for the right to liberty and security of the person. Cases concerning the detention of persons at airports and police stations have raised questions of whether the nature of the venues and the availability of facilities for sanitation, food, childcare and so forth amount to inhuman and degrading treatment, and have also raised Article 5 concerns about how prolonged detention can be without amounting to deprivation of liberty. It has been held that detention at airports is permissible as long as the detention is not so prolonged or the conditions so severe as to be disproportionate to the purpose of the interrogation, but that under certain circumstances the detention may amount to deprivation rather than legitimate restriction of liberty.[5]

Other rights

Other rights supposedly available to migrants whether they are citizens or not are the Article 8 right to respect for private and family life, and the Article 12 right to marry and form a family. The right to marry is subject only to the requirements that the individuals concerned are of marriageable age and that they comply with the marriage laws of the state in which they are seeking to marry. Immigration decisions should take into account whether there is a family or private life actually being enjoyed, and whether interference is according to law, whether it is necessary and in pursuit of a legitimate aim, for example preventing crime or terrorism. EU judges have themselves criticised European case law on Article 8 as arbitrary and incoherent (Blake and Husain 2003).

Due process rights are fundamental for the rule of law, and Article 6 provides for fair trials. EU case law has decided, however, that this applies only to criminal trials, and not to immigration tribunals. Appeals, interpretation of rights, interrogation processes and decision-making in relation to migration are therefore comparatively lawless, and it is relatively easy for governments and supra-national institutions to introduce more restrictive regulations and procedures. Anti-terrorism legislation, anti-trafficking policies and the demonisation and criminalisation of migration have meant that there is much public support for exclusions, removals, and suspension of rights, and almost no public demand for enlargement of the rights of migrants, whether legal or illegal.

Human Rights Act

The populist demand for tighter immigration controls should be counteracted by a developing culture of rights in the UK following the introduction of the 1998 Human Rights Act (HRA). Although the HRA may not appear to have much to say about irregular immigrants, it should provide a context for appreciating what fairness in procedures entails, in precluding expulsions to unsafe countries, and in establishing respect for rights as a central concern in all decision-making, counter-balancing utilitarian calculations of economic cost and security. The EU Charter of Rights gives more precise interpretations of the fundamental rights that are due to citizens and migrants than has previously been available. Although it is non-binding, it should provide a context for interpretation of rights within the member states, and it should lead to a coherent expression of European values which could reverse the 'race to the bottom' in immigration policies.

The right to migrate?

The key distinction in the allocation of rights is that between citizen and non-citizen. Apart from fundamental human rights which are supposedly available to all regardless of citizenship status (although, as discussed, these rights are subject to interpretation by states), other rights are privileges of citizenship, and their enjoyment entails either full citizenship, or granting of a status – Convention refugee, citizenship of a member state of an alliance such as the EU, temporary protection, or approved immigrant – which carries some of the rights and privileges of citizenship. Apart from the Geneva Convention, there have been few international conventions giving rights to migrants per se. The UN has introduced an International Convention on the Protection of the Rights of All Migrant Workers and Members of Their Families, which entered into force on 1 July 2003, but by the summer of 2006 this was not signed by a single industrial country (Rodier 2006).

But is there a right to migrate? According to Rodier's report on the external dimension of EU immigration and asylum policy, developments such as the passing of responsibilities to Morocco and Libya to control movement from these states to Spanish enclaves and across the Mediterranean are creating a category of illegal emigration, as well as illegal immigration. She quotes a press release from the

Conference of the Interior Ministers of the Western Mediterranean in May 2006, which welcomes 'the efforts of the countries of the southern Mediterranean to contain illegal emigration to Europe' (Rodier 2006: 20). Rodier also notes that Senegalese authorities announced that they had captured 1,500 'potential emigrants who were preparing to travel by boat to the Canary islands'. She comments that by describing emigrants as criminals, the concept confirms the idea that it would be normal to put a large percentage of the African population under house arrest as the widespread requirement for Africans to have a visa to enter developed countries would prohibit any 'legal prospect of travelling outside their own country' (*ibid*: 20).

As Rodier notes, this concept of illegal emigration is entirely contrary to the Universal Declaration of Human Rights which in Article 13(2) states that 'Everyone has a right to leave any country, including his own …'. The right to emigrate has certainly long been acknowledged in the West. Countries like the USSR and East Germany, for example, which restricted emigration, were strenuously disapproved of. There was widespread rejoicing when the Berlin Wall came down and other Eastern European states opened their borders to allow their own people to go. Apart from demonstrations of approval, however, the main response to states opening their borders and allowing people to leave, has been the Western European states closing their borders and making it difficult for people to enter. Around the globe, it seems as though now that the source states are no longer managing migration by keeping people in, the Western states have taken over the task. In regions like north Africa, and the Indian sub-continent, western nations are trying to persuade the states seen as the source of 'human waste' to manage migration by keeping people in, creating for the first time a 'double wall' of barriers to emigration and to immigration.

The right to leave does not amount to a right to free movement between countries because there is no corresponding right to immigrate. It has been argued, however, that freedom of movement is a fundamental freedom because it recognises 'the ageless quest of individuals for a better life' (Nafziger 1983: 846). While the right of states to control immigration has not been seriously challenged in international law, several theorists are arguing that the current restrictions on migration should be seen as an historical irregularity, and that international laws should be reformed to allow greater freedom of migration (Juss 2004).

Dummett and Nicol (1990) argued that while restriction of movement was by no means unknown in earlier periods, it has never been so systematic or so widespread. They say that restriction of movement is the modernist form of feudalism:

> Instead of being 'chained to the soil' of a feudal landlord, the twentieth century poor gradually became chained to the territory of their countries of origin because other countries' rules forbade them to enter. If they moved abroad to work clandestinely, or under restrictions applied to foreigners, they became a new class of half-free people: lower paid than others, often forced to live apart from spouses, tied to a particular job, or fearing capture or deportation. (Dummett and Nicol 1990: 13)

Sovereignty of nations vs individual human rights

The issue of a right to immigration is usually posed as a clash between states' rights to self-determination, and individual human rights. A state cannot be said to be sovereign and self-determining if it cannot set its own rules for immigration; on the other hand, if looked at from the perspective of individuals, a right to leave cannot realistically be exercised without a freedom to enter somewhere else. The classic articulation of the case against open borders – complete freedom of immigration as well as emigration – is taken to be that by Michael Walzer in *Spheres of Justice* (1983). The book discusses principles for a just distribution of social goods, and he includes membership as one of the goods to be distributed. Walzer argues that the idea of membership entails a distinction between members and non-members, so that there must be some rules of membership and some criteria for distinguishing between those entitled to membership and those not entitled. He says that completely open borders would lead either to the erection of barriers to entry by non-state groups (such as requirements for membership in many gated communities or even new towns in the USA), or to persons having no social identity or cohesion. While he condemns controls on emigration, he says that community and culture depend on closure and control of membership. Walzer offers an analogy between communities and clubs: a club can bar admission to applicants for membership, but cannot bar withdrawal from it.

Access to citizenship

An opposite view is taken by Joseph Carens, who argues that citizenship in a modern state is not a matter of culture and shared values, but a matter of inheritance, and as such is the modern equivalent of feudal privilege (Carens 1987). Carens argues that the only restrictions on immigration should be that persons obey the laws and constraints that citizens of the country have to abide by. Carens, and also Roberto Unger, find the strongest arguments for open borders in gross inequalities in the global distribution of life chances. Unger argues that there are economic and social reasons for freedom of movement, saying that nothing would have a greater impact on world poverty than expansion of the right to migrate (Unger 2006). Not only would a right to immigrate be the most powerful incentive for the rich nations to make meaningful contributions to the economic and social development of undeveloped nations, but it would have a social and moral impact in that humans would be free to move to societies in which they would be able to flourish socially and culturally as well as to prosper economically.

Carens's reasoning in favour of open borders is reminiscent of Rawls 'difference principle', the second of his principles of justice in his celebrated book *A Theory of Justice* (Rawls 1971). Rawls argues that people are born into a more or less advantaged position in life, and they have done nothing to deserve this accident of birth. Any advantages gained from their inherited circumstances are therefore not gained on merit, and so need justification if they are to be maintained. Rawls concludes that inequalities are only permissible to the extent that they are of benefit to the least well off. Rawls's theory demanded that people making decisions about social institutions should do so from behind an imagined 'veil of ignorance', such that they would not know where in the social strata they actually stood. This, he argued, was the only way to prevent the elite – who usually are the decision makers in actual societies – introducing laws and policies which favour the rich. If there were a possibility that they might actually be in the worst-off position, he suggests, people would favour rules of distribution which protect the worst off, while allowing some inequalities so that they would not necessarily forego all advantage if it turned out that they were in a better-off actual position.

Unger and Carens concede that open borders are not likely to be acceptable to nation-states in the near future. In more recent work, Carens has concentrated on making citizenship more easily available to migrants (Carens 2000). He argues that citizenship should be based less on inherited nationality than on residence, and that the longer a person resides within a country – whatever their status at entry – the stronger their claims to the rights of citizenship become. Baubock (1994) argues that after a certain period citizenship should become an entitlement, reducing states' discretionary powers to grant or withhold citizenship. Benhabib also argues that after long-term residence, citizenship should be a legal right, and in *The Rights of Others*, proposes that citizenship should not be based on ascribed characteristics such as nationality, but on residence and work status alone (Benhabib 2004, 2005).

Looking at the UK, Kostakopoulou (2006) criticises the Nationality, Immigration and Asylum Act 2002 for placing too much emphasis on social cohesion. This, she argues, means that applicants for citizenship have to prove their adherence to UK cultural values in advance of enjoying their benefits. She contends that a sense of belonging to a community develops with inclusion in a society and its politics, rather than being something that can exist and be tested at the outset.

The approach in this body of work, advocating the liberalisation of requirements for citizenship, and moving to a residence and registration model in place of the old nationality model has two major deficiencies. First, it assumes that migrants want to become citizens of the country they enter, and has little to offer to the migrant workers who see their residence as temporary and who want to retain citizenship of their countries of origin. Second, it retains the approach to human rights that sees them not as moral universals, but as rights of membership.

Benhabib (2002) takes the debate between a human right to migrate and the states' rights to regulate membership forward by arguing, against Walzer, that rights to exit and entry are not, as he contends, 'morally asymmetric', but must both be recognised if humans' rights to live the life which promotes their own version of the good (culturally as well as economically) are to be realised. On the other hand, she concedes that rights to entry and to association do not amount to full membership rights. She suggests that membership rights can be graded according to categories of temporary residence, permanent residence, civic incorporation, and full political membership, with corresponding gradations in the allocation of rights.

The Law of Peoples

When he extends his principles of justice from the domestic to the global sphere, Rawls does not incorporate his difference principle (Rawls 2001).[6] He argues that what he calls 'well-ordered societies' (that is societies which respect the human rights of all individual and group members, and which have procedures for consultation with their populations in decision-making, even if these procedures do not amount to liberal democracy) have a duty of assistance to 'burdened societies' (societies which do not have the cultural, political or economic resources to become well-ordered societies) to the extent that the latter are able to enter the Society of well-ordered Peoples (*sic*). The duty of assistance does not extend to unrestricted immigration. He states that people have a responsibility to take care of their territory and the size of the population, and that the people as politically organised (that is, the government) must maintain the territory as an asset of the people, and ensure its capacity to support them *in perpetuity* (emphasis in the original). People, he argues, 'must recognise that they cannot make up for failing to regulate their numbers or to care for their land, by conquest in war, or by migrating into another people's territory without their consent' (Rawls 2001: 8).

He discusses the main causes of migration, including the persecution of religious or ethnic minorities; the denial of human rights; political oppression; starvation, and pressure of numbers. Starvation, he contends, is largely a matter of the absence of decent government, whereas population pressure is eased by the granting of equal rights and assured education to women. Assistance to burdened states, and intervention in outlaw states, to promote decent government and human rights would, according to Rawls, resolve the problem of migration. In what he calls a 'realistic utopia' of the coming into being of a global Society of well-ordered Peoples, the question of immigration is not left aside, he claims, but is eliminated as a serious problem. Rawls is making much the same argument as Unger that development of democracy and prosperity in presently underprivileged states would reduce migration, but whereas Unger calls for open borders and claims that one of the benefits would be such development, Rawls calls for development of democracy and prosperity, with one of the benefits being reduction of demand for immigration.

Cosmopolitan justice

Rawls contrasts his views and concerns with the 'cosmopolitan view' of justice. Cosmopolitans, he argues, would support something analogous to his 'difference' principle, whereas he supports the protection of basic human rights, but little by way of global redistribution of resources. He explains that:

The cosmopolitan view ... is concerned with the well-being of individuals, and hence whether the well-being of the globally worst-off person can be improved. What is important to the Law of Peoples is the justice and stability for the right reasons of liberal and decent societies, living as members of a Society of well-ordered Peoples. (Rawls, 2001: 120)

Brock (2005) defines cosmopolitan justice as the belief that institutions and principles of justice should reflect the equal worth of all human beings, regardless of their group membership. It is this starting with individuals rather than states which is the difference between cosmopolitans and other theorists, including Rawls, who consider the requirements of global justice. Rawls's analysis is in terms of *peoples* rather than *persons*; 'peoples' he defines as collectivities (states, nations, people sharing a territory and a culture) rather than individuals. It is only by taking individuals as the unit of analysis and as the bearers of rights that it is possible to divorce the idea of possession of rights from the status of citizenship. In relation to migration, satisfying the needs of all humans to food, shelter, freedom of thought and religion, and to a life of dignity and self-determination would demand a much greater freedom of migration than (merely) ensuring protection from a 'well-grounded fear of prosecution'. It would mean that migration would be recognised as a right of individuals, rather than something to be managed in the interest of nation-states.

Moellendorf explains that international law has two different tendencies, *statism* and *cosmopolitanism*. Statism conceives the basis of international law as the principle of self-determination and respect for the sovereign equality of all states. This principle is recognised in paragraphs 2(4) and 2(7) of the UN Charter which recognise territorial integrity and political independence as the two main interests of states and which shield matters 'essentially within the domestic jurisdiction' against collective UN interference. For cosmopolitanism, the claims of individual persons constitute the basis of international legal obligations. The Preamble, with its statement of the equal worth of all humans, and Article 55 which calls for the promotion of respect for, and observance of, human rights and fundamental freedoms for all, express the cosmopolitan impulse. Moellendorf seeks to defend and extend the cosmopolitan conception of justice (Moellendorf 2002).

He applies Rawls's difference principle to the global sphere, but for Moellendorf the original position requires that behind the veil of ignorance when deriving international principles of justice, decisionmakers represent persons rather than peoples, and that they do not know which state they were members of. He argues that in this situation, deciders would be primarily interested in the freedom and ability of individuals to pursue their own conception of the good life within a fair system of global co-operation. Moellendorf contends that the moral equality of persons requires commitment to a fair equality of opportunity as one of the principles of justice. The present global distribution of resources massively impedes equality of opportunity. Moellendorf gives the example of global equality of opportunity by saying that if it were realized 'a child growing up in Mozambique would be statistically as likely as the child of a senior executive in a Swiss bank to reach the position of the latter's parent' (Moellendorf 2002: 49). Although the example has been criticised as too culturally specific, the point is well made that in any system of global fairness, desirable national, cultural and global positions and statuses should be open to all (Brock 2005: 347).

Limitations on immigration in a globally unequal world, Moellendorf argues, impose barriers to the pursuit of goals because of where they are born on some but not others, and are therefore incompatible with the principle of equality of opportunity. He finds that this principle invalidates the argument that immigration reduces the position of home workers, saying that even if this were true, if a market system of employment is acceptable between compatriots, cosmopolitan justice requires it to be acceptable between compatriots and non-compatriots. He similarly finds that the argument for cultural survival gives little support for widespread restrictions on immigration, since the circumstances in which cultural *survival* (emphasis in the original) of some group is threatened by immigration would be very rare.

The only situation in which immigration might justifiably be limited, for Moellendorf, is where all states had institutions to distribute the entitlements of citizenship and residence fairly, and where global institutions exist to distribute non-state entitlements (human rights, environmental protection). But, as he says, many states violate protection of entitlements, and global institutions of distributive justice scarcely exist. Moellendorf sees no justification for restrictions on movement where these would be accompanied by restrictions on equality of opportunity.

Moellendorf and Rawls both advocate something like the 'peaceful federation' of states suggested by Kant in his essay *Perpetual Peace* (Kant 1970). A global federation of nations with some supranational organisations is seen as the organisational structure needed to spread democratic egalitarian governments and institutions within states, and to regulate relationships between them as well as to ensure that states respect the human rights of all persons. Benhabib also endorses this idea of 'cosmopolitan federalism', which she develops further in *The Rights of Others* (Benhabib 2004). In this book, as well as advocating cosmopolitan federalism in principle, she also proposes processes of 'democratic iterations', discursive procedures whereby the idea of federation and of the principles of human rights and democratic participation would be entrenched and extended.

Duty of hospitality

In both *The Claims of Culture* and *The Rights of Others*, Benhabib supports the idea of a *duty of hospitality*, which means that strangers must be received without violence. This idea is derived from another proposition in Kant's essay *Perpetual Peace*, a proposition drawn upon more by social and moral philosophers than by political/legal theorists. Kant says that humans share a common possession of the earth, and this communal possession means that 'all men are entitled to present themselves in the society of others' (Kant 1970: 106). Because the earth is a sphere rather than a flat space, persons cannot avoid being brought into contact with each other. We behave as though the earth is not only flat, but infinite, so that we can pretend to be able to spread out indefinitely so as to be able to avoid unsought-for contact with others, but this illusion cannot be sustained. If contact is unavoidable, then toleration of the stranger becomes an existential necessity, and we must work out principles for responding to the presence of strangers. A right and corresponding duty of hospitality is the principle Kant advocates: 'Hospitality means the right of a stranger not to be treated with hostility when he arrives on someone else's territory' (*ibid*: 105).

While Benhabib develops her version of an ethics of hospitality mainly through her commitment to discourse ethics which allows for the participation of all, including the marginalised and non-members in decision-making, an ethics of hospitality is most fully developed by Derrida. In works published in the five years before his death, Derrida brings together Kant's idea of a duty of hospitality with Levinas's philosophy of responsibility to the 'other' being prior to the establishment of any relationship or reciprocal obligations, or even of relationships of comprehension and understanding (Derrida 1999, 2000, 2001).

The stranger to whom the duty of hospitality is owned is not a guest; as Simmel pointed out in his famous essay 'The Stranger' which is drawn upon by Bauman in his work on ethics for a postmodern world, the stranger is uninvited (Bauman 1991: 59). Derrida calls this an ethics not of *invitation* but of *visitation*. He sees that this sort of hospitality is risky, but nonetheless entailed by both Kant's and Levinas's ideas:

> Pure and unconditional hospitality, hospitality *itself*, opens or is in advance open to someone who is neither expected nor invited, to whomever arrives as an absolutely foreign *visitor*, as a new arrival, non-identifiable and unforeseeable, in short, wholly other. I would call this a hospitality of *visitation* rather than *invitation*. The visit might actually be very dangerous, and we must not ignore this fact, but would a hospitality without risk, a hospitality based by certain assurances, a hospitality protected by an immune system against the wholly other, be true hospitality? (Derrida 2003: 128–29, emphasis in the original)

Conclusions: Cosmopolitan justice and the rights of strangers

Bringing Levinas's philosophy together with Kant's political writings moves Levinas's ideas from the ethical sphere of moral relationships to the political sphere of justice, and makes them available as principles for cosmopolitan justice. In discussing Benhabib's *The Claims to Culture*, Bohman, referring only to the Kantian 'right to hospitality' says that there is much to commend this principle, and that it has significance for the way that immigration is constructed in right-wing politics in Europe and elsewhere (Bohman 2005). He argues, however, that it fails to capture the sense of political obligations to the whole of humanity that is behind the cosmopolitan impulses in developments in international law. The wider concept of an ethics of hospitality as developed by Derrida and present in the work of Bauman and in Benhabib's later book, can, however, reflect these cosmopolitan aspirations.

Kant's right of everyone to present themselves in the territory of strangers and to be received without violence would, in contemporary terms, be cast as a right to migrate, made realisable because it inscribes a right to immigrate as well as to emigrate. The Levinasian element in Derrida's ethics of hospitality would seem to proscribe classification prior to reception, and would also seem to prescribe the granting to strangers of most of the rights enjoyed by citizens: 'hospitality' ordinarily means sharing facilities, including sociability, with one's visitors, it conveys something beyond mere admittance. Derrida concedes that a fully unconditional hospitality is undesirable and politically unfeasible, but that hospitality can only be withdrawn when visitors are proved to be dangerous, not merely different. Benhabib (2004) also insists that rights can only be denied to immigrants if they prove to be dangerous, and that this danger must be to the fundamental human rights of existing residents – life, integrity of the person, liberty – not to living standards. Basing principles of justice on an ethics of hospitality seems a more secure foundation for the rights of strangers than other constructions, such as Moellendorf's equality of opportunity, Rawls's extension of a Society of well-ordered Peoples, or the various proposals to relax the requirements of citizenship.

Notes

1 Horvath v Secretary of State [2001] 1 AC 489.
2 Macpherson v Secretary of State [2001] EWCA Civ 1955, 19 December 2001.
3 Rehman v Secretary of State [2001] 3 WLR 877, para. 54.
4 Suresh v Canada (Minister of Citizenship and Immigration) [2002] 1 SCR 3, 2002 SCC 1.
5 Amuur v France (1996) 22 EHRR 533.
6 'The Law of Peoples' was first given as an Oxford Amnesty lecture in 1993. A substantially reworked and expanded version was published in 2001 (Rawls 1993, 2001). It is the later version which is drawn upon here.

References

Baubock, R. (1994) *Transnational Citizenship: Membership and Rights in International Migration*. Aldershot: Edward Elgar.
Bauman, Z. (1991) *Modernity and Ambivalence*. Cambridge: Polity Press.
Bauman, Z. (2004) *Wasted Lives: Modernity and its Outcasts*. Cambridge: Polity Press.
Benhabib, S. (2002) *The Claims of Culture: Equality and Diversity in the Global Era*. Princeton, NJ: Princeton University Press.
Benhabib, S. (2004) *The Rights of Others: Aliens, Residents and Citizens*. Cambridge: Cambridge University Press.

Benhabib, S. (2005) 'Beyond Interventionism and Indifference: Culture, Deliberation and Pluralism', *Philosophy and Social Criticism*, 31 (7): 753–72.

Blake, N. and Husain, R. (2003) *Immigration, Asylum and Human Rights*, Oxford: Oxford University Press.

Bohman, J. (2005) 'Rights, Cosmopolitanism and Public Reason: Interactive Universalism', *The Claims of Culture' Philosophy and Social Criticism*, 31 (7): 715–26.

Brock, G. (2005) 'The Difference Principle, Equality of Opportunity and Cosmopolitan Justice', *Journal of Moral Philosophy*, 2 (3): 333–52.

Carens, J. (1987) 'Aliens and Citizens: The Case for Open Borders', *Review of Politics*, 49 (2): 251–73.

Carens, J. (2000) *Culture, Citizenship and Community: A Contextual Exploration of Justice as Evenhandedness*. Oxford: Oxford University Press.

Castles, S. and Miller, M. (1993) *The Age of Migration*. London: Macmillan.

Derrida, J. (1999) *Adieu to Emmanuel Levinas*, trans. P.A. Brault and M. Nass. Stanford, CA: Stanford University Press.

Derrida, J. (2000) *Of Hospitality: Anne Durfourmantelle Invites Jacques Derrida to Respond*, trans. R. Bowlby. Stanford, CA: Stanford University Press.

Derrida, J. (2001) 'Cosmopolitanism', in *On Cosmopolitanism and Forgiveness*, trans. M. Dooley and M. Hughes. London and New York: Routledge.

Derrida, J. (2003) 'Autoimmunity: Real and Symbolic Suicide', in G. Borradori (ed.) *Philosophy in a Time of Terror: Dialogues with Jurgen Habermas and Jacques Derrida*. Chicago: University of Chicago Press.

Dummett, A. and Nicol, A. (1990) *Subjects, Citizens, Aliens and Others: Nationality and Immigration Law*. London: Weidenfeld and Nicolson.

Hudson, B. (2006) 'Beyond White Man's Justice: Race, Gender and Justice in Late Modernity', *Theoretical Criminology*, 10 (1): 29–47.

Juss, S.S. (2004) 'Free Movement and the World Order', *International Journal of Refugee Law*, 16: 289.

Kant, I. (1970) 'Perpetual Peace. A Philosophical Sketch', in H. Reiss (ed.) *Kant's Political Writings*, trans. H.B. Nisbet. Cambridge: Cambridge University Press.

Kostakopoulou, D. (2006) 'Thick, Thin and Thinner Patriotism: Is This All There Is?', *Oxford Journal of Legal Studies*, 26 (1): 73–106.

Melossi, D. (2003) 'In a Peaceful Life: Migration and the Crime of Modernity in Europe/Italy', *Punishment and Society*, 5 (4): 371–97.

Moellendorf, D. (2002) *Cosmopolitan Justice*. Boulder, CO and Oxford: Westview Press.

Nafziger, J.A.R. (1983) 'The General Admission of Aliens Under International Law', *American Journal of International Law*, 77: 804–47.

Obotaka, T. (2005) 'Smuggling of Human Beings from a Human Rights Perspective: Obligations of Non-State and State Actors under International Human Rights Law', *International Journal of Refugee Law*, 2005 (17): 394.

Papastergiadis, N. (2000) *The Turbulence of Migration*. Cambridge: Polity Press.

Peers, S. (2000) *EU Justice and Home Affairs Law*. Harlow: Pearson Education.

Rawls, J. (1971) *A Theory of Justice*. Cambridge, MA: Harvard University Press.

Rawls, J. (1993) The Law of Peoples, in S. Shute and S. Hurley (eds) *On Human Rights: The Oxford Amnesty Lectures 1993*. New York: Basic Books.

Rawls, J. (2001) *The Law of Peoples*. Harvard: Harvard University Press.

Rodier, C. (2006) *Analysis of the External Dimension of the EU's Asylum and Immigration Policies – Summary and Recommendations for the European Parliament*. Brussels: European Parliament.

Statewatch (2006) *Statewatch News Online, 27 July 2006 (18/06)*. See: www. statewatch.org

Unger, R. (2005) *What Should the Left Propose?* London: Verso.

Walzer, M. (1983) *Spheres of Justice: A Defense of Pluralism and Equality*. New York: Basic Books.

Young, J. (2003) 'To These Wet and Windy Shores: Recent Immigration Policy in the UK', *Punishment and Society*, 5 (4): 449–62.

Index